PART 2
1936-1945

VOL. 2
1936-1945
Edited by
MICHAEL ASHLEY

HENRY REGNERY COMPANY · CHICAGO

THE HISTORY OF THE SCIENCE FICTION MAGAZINE
Volume 2:   1936-1945

Introduction and Appendices, © 1975 by Mike Ashley; used by permission of the author and the author's agent, Cosmos Literary Agency.
First published in Great Britain in 1975 by
New English Library, London
First published in the United States in 1976 by
Henry Regnery Company
180 North Michigan Avenue, Chicago, Illinois 60601
Printed in the United States of America
Library of Congress Catalog Card Number: 76-015154
International Standard Book Number: 0-8092-8002-7 (cloth)
                                     0-8092-8000-0 (paper)

Contents

Acknowledgements

While the drafting and compiling of this book has been my own responsibility, including all errors, it would have been a much harder task and a more meagre product had it not been for the assistance of many people, including Walter Gillings, Ejler Jakobssen, Leslie J. Johnson, Robert A. W. Lowndes, Forrest J Ackerman, Frank Parnell, T. Stanhope Sprigg, William F. Temple, John Eggeling and, above all, the herculean aid of Philip Harbottle. To them, and any I have omitted to credit, my sincere thanks.

To Sue
without whom this book may have been finished sooner,
but might not have been started at all.

Preface

Without doubt science fiction is currently enjoying a period of nostalgia, in common with the cinema, television and most other entertainment media. When you consider that their histories run concurrently, then perhaps it is not so surprising.

The film industry, for example, was spawned from experimental dabblings during the 1890s, graduated through the silent era and blossomed into the 'talkies' in 1926. Also, in January 1926, John Logie Baird successfully demonstrated his crude but nevertheless effective form of television. And it was in April 1926 that American publisher Hugo Gernsback issued the pioneer science fiction magazine *Amazing Stories*.

Fifty years later *Amazing Stories* lives on. A different publisher, a different editor, a different format, and most noticeably a very different style and form of science fiction. The magazine has seen science fiction weather two booms, a near fatal Depression, a World War, the birth of the Nuclear Age, manned landings on the Moon – and in its course sf has matured from tales of megalomaniac scientists running amok with their world-shattering inventions, to thoughtful extrapolations of current trends to reveal possible effects on future societies.

And for that half century, the battleground upon which writers have revealed their views about the effects of science upon mankind has, for the most part, been composed of the science fiction magazines themselves. Maligned and denigrated they have been the very background of science fiction, offering the opportunity for writers like Isaac Asimov, Robert Heinlein, Arthur Clarke and John Wyndham to learn their trade.

In this series of five anthologies I am endeavouring to trace the history of the legion of sf magazines that have come and gone during those fifty years, and in so doing reveal the effects the magazines and their editors have had upon the genre. In Volume 1 I showed how the sf magazine was brought into the world and what happened during the first ten years. Now this volume continues with the next ten turbulent years, April 1936 to March 1946. It starts with America recovering from its Depression, and ends with the World recovering from war.

Yet in the field of science fiction it was one of the most fruitful periods, seeing the first appearances of writers of the stature of Asimov, Heinlein, Theodore Sturgeon, A. E. van Vogt, Lester Del Rey, L. Sprague de Camp and many more. To reflect the fiction of those years I have again chosen ten stories, one from every year. In the following pages you will find the famous rubbing shoulders with the neglected. There is an early Eric Frank Russell collaboration 'Seeker of Tomorrow', much heralded as a classic yet never previously reprinted! There is a much overlooked Stanley G. Weinbaum story; a grim lesson from master horror-film scribe, Robert Bloch, plus seven other fascinating reminders of the variety and scope that sf has to offer.

And for those particularly keen to explore yet further into the realms of science fiction history I have supplied a fairly exhaustive appendix of selected authors' fiction, and other details of the period.

For a while let this book be your time machine, powered by your imagination. Back to the days when pulp magazines ruled, and when the sf world suddenly found itself without Hugo Gernsback, but had the halcyon days of John W. Campbell just round the corner.

Happy journey . . .

Mike Ashley
June 1975

Introduction: SF Bandwaggon

1—THE STORY SO FAR . . .

Even the most casual peruser of the bookstalls in 1936 could hardly have been unaware of the proliferation of adventure 'pulp' magazines. Termed pulp because of their cheap-grade paper, these magazines thrust their gaudy covers into the gaze of the unwary citizen wherever he ventured. Whilst they existed in Britain they were, by and large, an American phenomenon, the publishers centred mainly in New York.

The first true pulp magazine was *The Argosy*, published by Frank A. Munsey which had started life in 1882 as a 'slick' juvenile weekly but changed to pulp with the October 1896 number. It carried a range of fiction: western, historical, mystery, thriller and not least scientific. Munsey added other titles to his group, *All-Story*, *Cavalier* and *Munsey's* prominent among them. Gradually, the Munsey magazines began to carry more and more science fiction, the real booster coming with the publication of Edgar Rice Burroughs' *Under the Moons of Mars*, serialised in *All-Story* from February to July 1912. Burroughs followed with more adventures of John Carter and Dejah Thoris, as well as his Tarzan adventures which began in the October 1912 issue. Thereafter sf featured prominently in the periodicals.

The major rivals to Munsey were Street & Smith, the first in the field to issue a specialised magazine: *Detective Story* in 1915. (Hitherto only a regular children's publication, *Frank Reade Library* had specialised in anything, namely 'invention' stories. Often cited as the first sf magazine it was strictly speaking a paperback series.) Street & Smith continued to experiment and had a near-miss sf magazine in the shape of *The Thrill Book*, which saw sixteen issues during 1919. While it carried much sf, it printed a goodly portion of other fiction as well.

Meanwhile the detective magazine field prospered, 1920 seeing the birth of the legendary *Black Mask*, and in 1922 publisher Jacob Henneberger issued *Detective Tales*. He followed this with a companion title, *Weird Tales*, which was first issued in March 1923. The first fantasy magazine was born.

Weird Tales was not a science fiction magazine, but it published more sf than its name implies. Unfortunately it was not an instantaneous success and nearly died after a year. Henneberger had faith in the magazine however, and came to an arrangement with the Popular Fiction Company of Chicago who continued the magazine with Farnsworth Wright as editor. From then on a legend grew.

Although both Germany and Russia can lay prior claim to sf magazines, the first all-sf periodical in the English language finally appeared in April 1926 – *Amazing Stories*. Editor/publisher Hugo Gernsback maintained the ideal that science could be taught through fiction, and *Amazing Stories* was merely an extension of the scientific journals he had published since 1908 and which had regularly featured sf since 1911. The August 1923 *Science & Invention* had been a special 'scientifiction' issue, and he planned to follow this with a magazine of the same name. But the scheme was shelved for nearly three years before *Amazing* hit the stalls. It was an instant success. Initially all reprint, it began to feature more and more new stories and 1928 saw the massing of considerable new talent. Among the new names were David H. Keller, Stanton A. Coblentz, Jack Williamson and E. E. Smith. That same year he issued a companion *Quarterly*, following the success of an *Annual* in 1927.

In 1929 Gernsback found himself manoeuvred into receivership and *Amazing* and the *Quarterly* were continued under new publishers (with Gernsback's Managing Editor, T. O'Conor Sloane, in charge). Gernsback fought back, formed a new company, and brought out *Science Wonder Stories*, *Air Wonder Stories*, *Wonder Stories Quarterly* and *Scientific Detective Monthly*. The last title died after ten issues and the first two merged into *Wonder Stories* during 1930. That same year also saw the appearance of a completely new title, *Astounding Stories*, from the magazine chain of William Clayton.

Neither *Amazing* nor *Wonder* were strictly pulp magazines, though they later became such. They were initially larger in size, $8\frac{1}{2} \times 11$ in as against the standard pulp 7×10 in. The paper was of a heavier stock, slightly better quality and more durable. They had trimmed edges, a real treat since it was often impossible to leaf through a pulp magazine without being covered in a snowfall of pulp confetti. *Astounding Stories*, however, was a straightforward pulp adventure magazine with no such criterion as science taught through fiction. Editor Harry Bates looked for out-and-out adventure and found it. *Astounding Stories* prospered.

In 1933 the United States weathered the worst of the depression years. Many publishers and magazines fell by the wayside, not least in sf. *Astounding Stories* passed away in March only to be reborn in October, now in the hands of Street & Smith who placed F. Orlin Tremaine in charge. An astute editor, Tremaine instituted a policy for startlingly original material – 'thought variants' – which had a large response from a group of authors that included John Russell Fearn, Nathan Shachner, Donald Wandrei, Murray Leinster and Jack Williamson.

Not to be outdone, Charles Hornig, the seventeen-year-old new editor of *Wonder Stories*, advertised his 'new policy' and in poured fine fiction by Edmond Hamilton, Alan Connell, M. M. Kaplan and, notably, Stanley G. Weinbaum. *Astounding* soon cornered Weinbaum's best material, all of which is recalled with fond remembrance, and has been frequently reprinted.

Only *Amazing* lagged in this fight for originality, but such was to be expected from its eighty-two-year-old editor. As issue followed issue, *Amazing* slipped into a moribund state and kept alive only by the loyalty of its readers.

At the start of 1936 Gernsback suddenly announced that he was taking *Wonder Stories* off news-stand distribution. Henceforth it could only be obtained through subscription, and he appealed to his readers to support the scheme. To his great disappointment they did not. Just ten years after Gernsback placed *Amazing* on the stands, what proved to be the last issue of *Wonder Stories* appeared and Gernsback departed from the scene, leaving Tremaine and *Astounding* supreme in the field.

2—THE QUIET BEFORE THE STORM

Follow a science fiction fan in America as he approaches his local bookstall sometime during April 1936. What will he find? Since most magazines appeared the month prior to their cover date, the May 1936 *Astounding Stories* would await him. Costing just twenty cents, its 160 pages included the start of a new serial, *The Cometeers* by Jack Williamson (the eagerly awaited sequel to his epic *The Legion of Space*), and the conclusion of Eando Binder's *Spawn of Eternal Thought*. There was John Russell Fearn with his inspired sequel to 'Mathematica', 'Mathematica Plus'; and 'Elimination' from that brilliant 'new' author Don A. Stuart. Stories by Frank Belknap Long, D. D. Sharp, Raymond Z. Gallun and Clifton B. Kruse rounded out the number. Our hypothetical fan will have snatched up this issue with delight.

What else would catch his eye? Since *Amazing Stories* was now published every other month, the stall would still be carrying the April issue, its tenth anniversary edition. Such was not, however, emblazoned on the cover where Leo Morey depicted a scene from 'Labyrinth', the ninth of the Professor Jameson series by Neil R. Jones. A popular series it would no doubt have attracted buyers even though *Amazing* cost twenty-five cents, five cents more than *Astounding*, yet sported only 144 pages (sixteen less than its rival).

Besides 'Labyrinth', there was the conclusion to Joe Skidmore's intriguing novel, *The Maelstrom of Atlantis*, and Isaac Nathanson's original 'A Modern Comedy of Space'. Otherwise the only author of note was Edmond Hamilton with 'Intelligence Undying'. Hamilton, one of the field's top authors, had been a frequent contributor to *Amazing* since 1928, though he had made his first appearance in *Weird Tales* two years earlier. If Jones did not clinch the sale of this issue, Hamilton would.

But what else? That survey had exhausted the sf magazines on display. However, the May 1936 *Weird Tales* was available, complete with Margaret Brundage's garish cover illustration for Paul Ernst's 'The Devil's Double'. But that should not deter our readers, for just a glance at the contents page would reveal some very familiar names: Edmond Hamilton with 'Child of the Winds', Jack Williamson and the second part of his serial *The Ruler of Fate*, Manly Wade Wellman and 'The Horror Undying'. Wellman had appeared in many issues of the sf magazines and was just as frequent a contributor to *Weird*. A major point in favour of the issue was its reprinting of Donald Wandrei's classic 'The Red Brain' from the October 1927 number, one of *Weird*'s best sf examples. Robert Bloch, August Derleth and Seabury Quinn were also present.

Three issues costing seventy cents would be all our fan was likely to buy, but he might well continue to browse. He would see the latest issues of *Thrilling Mystery, Doc Savage, The Spider, Horror Stories, Terror Tales, Dime Mystery Magazine*, the first issue of *Dr Yen Sin, Operator #5, Spicy Mystery Stories* and *The Shadow* among the plethora of pulp, all with their examples of rather mediocre and low-grade fantasy. Little would urge our sf reader to buy them, so with his three magazines tucked under his arm he would happily wend his way home. We'll come back to him in a few years.

The sf field had never been as low as two titles since 1927, and for that matter never would be again. With so many pulp magazine publishers it was surprising only two of them should experiment in this direction. Teck Publications, which handled *Amazing*, was Chicago based with editorial offices in New York. Street & Smith, who besides *Astounding* handled a score of magazines including *Doc Savage* and *The Spider*, was centred wholly in New York. They were among the city's oldest magazine publishers, having been around since 1855. At the other extreme Standard Magazines were the youngest, founded in 1932 by Ned Pines, who was virtually just out of college. He had commenced a chain of specialised adventure periodicals which became tagged the Thrilling group since all the titles were thus prefixed: *Thrilling Mystery, Thrilling Adventure, Thrilling Detective*. Editor-in-chief of this chain was Leo Margulies who had once been an office boy with Munsey's, thereby becoming acquainted with many big-name authors. New to the field, Pines needed someone of Margulies' stature, and he was to prove invaluable. Now aged thirty-six he commanded the highest salary of his kind.

It was to Pines and Margulies that Gernsback went after his disappointment with the *Wonder Stories*' subscription scheme. The result was that Standard purchased *Wonder* and set it back on the stands as *Thrilling Wonder Stories* in August 1936. In format, little had changed. There were all the same departments: the Science Fiction League, the letter column 'The Reader Speaks', 'Science Questions and Answers' and 'Test Your Science Knowledge'. But as regards fiction, the difference was obvious. Science was now at a minimum and the emphasis was on action.

It had been the policy at Standard for the magazines to be edited by a team of three, but Margulies made an exception with *Wonder*. New to the staff was Mortimer Weisinger who, with Julius Schwartz, had operated the Solar Sales Service, an authors' agency. Weisinger was given a free hand to edit *Wonder*, with the directive that the fiction be aimed at a younger readership since *Astounding* already catered for adult readers.

At fifteen cents the magazine was the cheapest on the market, well within the pocket of a teenage audience. Its first cover depicted a scene from Arthur Leo Zagat's 'The Land Where Time Stood Still', showing a bug-eyed creature helping a human fight off warriors from the past. Incidentally, such covers would later epitomise the magazine. Zagat had appeared in *Wonder* in the early 1930s in collaboration with Nathan Schachner, but he was not a typical *Wonder* writer. Neither was Ray Cummings, whose 'Blood of the Moon' was the lead novelette. And then there were Paul Ernst and Otis Adelbert Kline, names known to sf fans, but not through *Wonder*. In fact the only authors present in that August 1936 issue who had been regular contributors to *Wonder* were Eando Binder and Stanley G. Weinbaum, and they also appeared elsewhere. Eando Binder was the pen-name used to cover the two brothers Earl and Otto Binder. By 1936 Earl was writing less and less, and the name was used by Otto alone, as on 'The Hormone Menace' in this issue. Weinbaum had died tragically of cancer in December 1935, and his sudden departure had made him a legend. His appearance in the issue was a certainty for bringing good sales. Here, too, was Abraham Merritt with 'The Drone Man', a short tale that had previously appeared in the amateur publication, *Fantasy Magazine*, with which Weisinger had been associated.

Perhaps the most surprising feature in the new issue was *Zarnak*, a comic-strip serial set in the year AD 2936. It was the work of Max Plaisted, which turned out to be the pseudonym of Otto Binder, writing with his second brother, artist Jack Binder. Comic strips had been syndicated in newspapers for several years but they were an innovation in a pulp adventure magazine. There is no point in pretending the story line was good; it was not. The first episode revealed how much of the Earth's population was destroyed as a result of germ warfare. The survivors developed a feudal system, with the exception of the descendants of a certain scientist. One such descendant discovered that before the Final War another scientist had succeeded in building a rocket and leaving the Earth. Zarnak thereupon vowed to track him down. The artwork was barely reasonable, which was a surprise considering Jack Binder's usual standard. A common failing with comic strips was the lack of depth. Whereas *Buck Rogers* might be acceptable in a newspaper, *Zarnak* was not acceptable to sf fans. It lasted eight issues and died, incomplete, howled out by the readers.

But, despite its failings, *Thrilling Wonder* was presenting some excellent stories by big names. Since Standard had decided to publish the magazine every other month, the use of serials was jettisoned (although *Amazing*, also published once every two months, did carry them). The next best thing was a story series. These were always popular with author, editor and reader alike. Thereby John Campbell, one of the biggest names in sf since his epic space extravaganzas in the early 1930s and who was currently revolutionising sf in *Astounding* as 'Don A. Stuart', began a series about the space-roving fugitives Penton and Blake. The first, 'Brain Stealers of Mars', appeared in the December 1936 issue. Altogether five stories appeared, ending with 'The Brain Pirates' in October 1938. By then another popular series was well under way, starting with 'Via Etherline' in October 1937. The *Via* series appeared under the byline 'Gordon Giles', all, that is, except the ninth and last, 'Via Jupiter' in the February 1942 issue, which revealed the author as Eando Binder. Again it was the ubiquitous Otto, one of the better and most prolific authors of this period. Otto Oscar Binder was born in Bessemer, Michigan on Saturday 26 August 1911, and finished his education at the University of Chicago. He became a freelance writer in 1932, and first appeared in collaboration with his brother Earl as 'Eando' in *Amazing* for October of that year, with 'The First Martian'. His first solo appearance, still as Eando, was in the April 1935 *Weird Tales* with 'Shadows of Blood'. With his new pen-name of Gordon Giles, Binder created a new popular author. So, for a time, the *two* most popular writers in *Wonder* were, in fact, one man – Binder! As Eando he wrote a separate series in that magazine, about an immortal man, Anton York, which began in 'Conquest of Life' (August 1937).

These were not the only series. Henry Kuttner started his *Hollywood on the Moon* series with the story of the same name in April 1938; and in collaboration with Arthur K. Barnes began the *Pete Manx* series with 'Roman Holiday' (August 1939). Barnes was himself responsible for a very popular series about Gerry Carlisle, who caught alien animals for zoos, starting with 'Green

Hell' in the June 1937 issue. The number for October 1937 saw the return of Tubby, a likeable fellow who had been invented by Ray Cummings for his Munsey stories some fifteen years earlier. A further seven stories appeared up to 1946.

And so on, and so on. These series, combined with the excellent individual stories, soon boosted *Thrilling Wonder*'s circulation and popularity. In effect the magazine became an echo of *Astounding*'s early Tremaine period (1934-35) and, although

tremely entertaining, its future was guaranteed, at least for a while.

Due credit must be given to *Wonder*'s editor, Mort Weisinger, who was only twenty-one when he became editor (making him just one year older than his predecessor, Hornig). Like Hornig, Weisinger had come from the ranks of sf fans, which was unlike Tremaine's situation at Street & Smith. (Tremaine was basically a general fiction editor with a fondness for sf. Besides *Astounding* he was in charge of some six magazines including *Top-Notch*.) Weisinger was also different from Sloane, who was a scientist first and a renowned pessimist, quite sure that man would never accomplish space flight!

Hornig had caught Gernsback's eye through his fanzine (or amateur magazine) the *Fantasy Fan* (despite its obvious lean towards *Weird Tales*). Weisinger had likewise been associated with the editing of amateur journals, and by 1936 there was quite a respectable number in circulation. The leading title was *Fantasy Magazine* – which, since Weisinger had joined Standard, had been left to Julius Schwartz to control single-handed. Schwartz was himself more and more committed to his literary agency, and therefore less inclined to continue *Fantasy Magazine*. So the magazine folded with the January 1937 issue. With its demise the core publication of fandom was gone, and fandom was left to find new directions. The number of amateur publications grew and several of these are worthy of mention for their semi-professional appearance and because they carried science fiction, unlike the critical articles and news contained in most others. Volume 1 of this series mentioned William Crawford's attempts with *Marvel Tales* and *Unusual Stories* in 1934-5. Now it was Donald Wollheim's turn with *Fanciful Tales of Space and Time*, which appeared in the Autumn of 1936 and was edited jointly with Wilson Shepard. Wollheim will be remembered as the voice of the fan group, the International Scientific Association, set up in opposition to the Science

Fiction League of *Wonder Stories.* Many fan storms revolved around the name Wollheim, but there is no denying he kept things active and moving.

Fanciful Tales was a handsomely printed, digest-sized booklet of fifty pages, and boasted, 'The Nameless City' by H. P. Lovecraft, 'The Typewriter' by David Keller, 'The Man from Dark Valley' by August Derleth, and other fiction by Kenneth Pritchard, William Sykora and Wollheim himself, plus 'The Forbidden Room' by jazz pianist Duane Rimel and a poem by Robert E. Howard. This last contribution is particularly pointed as less than four months earlier (11 June 1936), Robert E. Howard had committed suicide.

Wollheim was a highly capable editor. He had toyed with many amateur publications for the previous two years and now, at twenty-two, he might well have made a go of it with *Fanciful.* A second issue was obviously intended, as Wollheim himself tried to promote it in the professional magazines. In *Amazing*'s letter column 'Discussions', in the February 1937 issue, a letter appeared signed 'Braxton Wells'. This was a pseudonym used by Wollheim for occasional fannish articles, but it is doubtful Sloane was aware of that. Commenting on the story 'Hoffman's Widow' by Floyd Oles, Wollheim said:

> I am one of those who thought 'Hoffman's Widow' decidedly out of place. When we want *Amazing Stories* we want them Scientific! Not anything else! There are magazines like *Fanciful Tales* for weird-fantasy and that story probably wouldn't even fit there.[1]

Whatever the intentions, no more issues appeared, and Wollheim went back to *The Phantagraph* and other minor journals.

Fanciful Tales had little, if any, large-scale distribution and today is an extremely rare acquisition. Almost as rare are two other magazines that appeared at the same time, *The Witch's Tales* and *Flash Gordon's Strange Adventure Magazine,* even though these were distributed nationally. A further common link between them is the influence of radio and cinema respectively.

Ever since May 1931 American radio listeners had been treated to the weekly programme *The Witch's Tales,* with stories written by Alonzo Dean Cole. Now, in November 1936, a magazine of the same name was issued, large format, on pulp paper. It featured a lead story by Cole, 'The Madman', plus four other stories and a collection of 'true' experiences. Purportedly edited by Cole, in all likelihood it was the managing editor, Tom Chadburn, who handled most of the work. To the affiçianado of sf the magazine was of but passing interest, unless he looked deeply. After all, none of the names was well known, and what interest did an sf fan have in ghost stories?

If the first issue didn't show it, then the second did. The December 1936 issue carried some seven stories apart from Cole's, and included 'The Monster of Lake La Metrie' by Wardon Allan Curtis. This story dealt with some startling concepts, not least the transplanting of a man's brain into the brain cavity of a prehistoric monster that had somehow survived to the modern day. A correct balance of pathos, excitement and science made this an extremely powerful story and very much science fiction. It turns out that the story was a reprint, appearing first in *Pearson's Magazine* in September 1899. Sf historian Sam Moskowitz has unearthed at least two more reprints in the magazine, and probably the rest of the contents came from *Pearson's Magazine*. Had more readers been aware of this publication they would have found a valuable source for Victorian fantasy, since obviously the editors intended to reprint more, and who knows what masterpieces might have been discovered. But alas, as is common with such attempts, the magazine died after just two issues.

Flash Gordon's Strange Adventure Magazine also appeared in December 1936 and was another pulp publication attempting to cash in on the success of the *Flash Gordon* film serials with Buster Crabbe, and the syndicated comic strip drawn by Alex Raymond. It emanated from Stephen Slesinger, Inc, who also produced two equally juvenile publications, *Dan Dunn Detective* and *Tailspin Tommy*. *Flash Gordon* featured 'The Master of Mars', a long lead story by James Edison Northfield, illustrated in comic-strip style. If Weisinger hadn't pipped this magazine with *Zarnak* it would have been the first to claim comic-strip stories in pulps. It could, however, claim to be the first to use interior colour artwork, and although this never came over well on pulp paper, it was nevertheless impressive at first sight, especially since the package only cost ten cents.

Three other stories filled out this rather thin issue, and what would have struck any sf fan's gaze was the name R. R. Winterbotham. Russell Robert Winterbotham (1904–71) had been a fairly regular contributor to *Astounding* since 'The Star That Would Not Behave' in the August 1935 issue, and appeared to be a promising writer. Now here he was in *Flash Gordon* with one story, 'Saga of the "Smokepot"', and almost certainly another, 'The Last War', under the transparent alias of R. R. Botham. If Winterbotham could appear in this publication then perhaps other sf names would in the future. But there was no future. No further issues of *Flash Gordon's Strange Adventure Magazine* adorned the bookstalls, and in hindsight that was rather a blessing.

By the end of 1936, therefore, ripples were stirring the surface of the sf sea. Throughout 1937 the three sf magazines would appear regularly, although *Amazing* continued to become more and more drab and dull, whilst *Thrilling Wonder* increased in strength and vitality. *Astounding* seemed to have stagnated some-what, though this was hardly surprising considering the size of Tremaine's other editorial duties. Now that *Astounding* was top in its own field Tremaine was content to let it look after itself. That does not mean it was printing dull fiction. Several new authors had made a great impact in the magazine over the last year. Ross Rocklynne, whose 'Man of Iron' in the August 1935 issue had marked an impressive start, was now turning out a series of stories wherein Lieutenant Jack Colbie tried to capture the clever criminal Edward Deverel against all manner of scientific odds. English author Eric Frank Russell had first ap-peared with an amusing Weinbaum imitation, 'The Saga of Pelican West' (February 1937), which tells of the adventure of Pelican West on the satellite Callisto with, amongst other fauna, a reticulated python called Alfred.

In September 1937 L. Sprague de Camp's name was seen for the first time on a story entitled 'The Isolinguals', and coin-cidentally that was the last issue Tremaine edited. He was elevated to Assistant Editorial Director and found it necessary to appoint a new editor to guide *Astounding Stories*. That man was John W. Campbell.

It's difficult to talk about Campbell without launching into ecstatic praise, much of which has been said many times before. Such is the tendency of history to distort. When Campbell stepped into the editorial shoes one is led to believe miracles happened overnight. They did not – but, mind you, they didn't take long.

Campbell's first issue was October 1937, although there is no internal evidence to suggest this. The Statement of Ownership printed in the November issue stated, as at 1 October 1937, that Tremaine was still editor. The only tangible difference in the magazine was that a new legend appeared beneath the title on the contents page: 'This magazine contains new stories only. No reprints used.' Since *Astounding* had never used reprints it was rather an abortive notice. (Campbell only ever broke his no-reprint policy once, in 1948, as the next book in the series will show.) There was no indication as to whether the editorial, 'Into the Future' was by Tremaine or Campbell, though I suspect the latter.

Campbell was serving an apprenticeship under Tremaine and obviously much of the material used had been chosen before Campbell's arrival. Be that as it may, Campbell obviously had plans in mind, and the January 1938 issue proves this. During Tremaine's reign the letter column had been changed to 'Science Discussions'. Campbell now brought back 'Brass Tacks' combined with 'Science Discussions', gradually phasing out the latter. In the same issue he instituted 'In Times to Come', whetting readers' appetites for the next issue. With the March 1938 issue he changed the magazine's name. *Astounding Stories*, a title which in his opinion was too juvenile, became *Astounding Science-Fiction*.

On 1 May Street & Smith changed their policy of retaining editors-in-chief and Tremaine left the outfit. Campbell was left to go it alone, and he needed no prodding. Cover artwork underwent a transformation. Howard V. Brown had been *Astounding*'s mainstay in this area throughout Tremaine's period. Campbell used Brown to draw some special 'mutant' covers, the first for February 1938, portraying the sun as seen from Mercury in astronomically correct fashion. An exceptionally striking cover, it illustrated Raymond Gallun's 'Mercutian Adventure' and would have done more to attract potential buyers than any of Brown's other covers for *Thrilling Wonder*. At the age of sixty, Brown was at last showing what he could really achieve.

Hans Wessolowski, known better as Wesso, who had drawn the covers for the Clayton *Astounding*'s, returned, and the May 1938 issue saw the first cover by Charles Schneeman, hitherto responsible for the better black-and-white interior illustrations. Schneeman's attitude towards cover art is particularly noticeable on the December 1938 issue, illustrating L. Sprague de Camp's 'The Merman'. A simple portrait of reporters anxiously fighting for a photograph of a man in a tank, it carried none of the sensationalism linked with the general pulp magazines. It was hard to class the new *Astounding* as pulp, yet pulp it remained.

And, whilst covers, names and departments changed, what of the content? Nineteen thirty-eight has been called the year that began the Golden Age of *Astounding*. Certainly in that year and the next a tremendous insurge of new talent made *Astounding* a most refreshing publication, with some of the greatest originality in story concept and treatment. This was not just the work of Campbell. Magazine sf was, after all, now twelve years old. Followers who had discovered the early Gernsback magazines in their teens were now in their mid-twenties. They had had time to evaluate the trend of the fiction, to work out new themes for hackneyed plots and to look at sf in a new light. As the 1930s made way for the 1940s many of the big names in sf would fade away and new names take over and, almost without exception, it was in *Astounding* that they made their name.

John Wood Campbell Jr was born in Newark, New Jersey, on Wednesday 8 June 1910. He was nineteen when 'When the Atoms Failed' appeared in the January 1930 *Amazing*. This was, in fact, his second sale to the magazine – Sloane had lost the first. By the end of 1930 he was already being regarded as a major name through the strength of his Arcot, Moray and Wade series. Following in the footsteps of E. E. Smith, whose *Skylark* stories had captured everyone's imagination, Campbell set his stories on vast extra-galactic stages. These culminated in *The Mightiest Machine*, serialised in five parts starting in the December 1934 *Astounding*, concurrent with Smith's *The Skylark of Valeron*. Such was the high spot of these galaxy-spinning yarns. Just one month earlier *Astounding* had carried a short story, 'Twilight', by Don A. Stuart. A 'mood' story, which told of the far distant future Earth and the decline of man, it ironically sounded the death knell for the type of story Campbell himself had popularised. The Stuart name appeared regularly thereafter, and he soon became one of *Astounding*'s top authors; his atmospheric stories setting the standard for the magazine. Few readers at that time realised that Stuart was a pseudonym of Campbell apart from the more knowledgeable fans.

Meanwhile Campbell began to supply *Astounding* with a series of scientific articles: 'A Study of the Solar System', starting with 'Accuracy' in the June 1936 issue. Hitherto, articles had been few and far between in the sf magazines, apart from small fillers, chiefly because Gernsback supplied all such necessary information in his pertinent editorials. Only in the specialised magazines like *Air Wonder* and *Scientific Detective Monthly* had additional articles appeared dealing with related topics. When Tremaine took over *Astounding* he reprinted Charles Fort's collection of the inexplicable, *Lo!*, which ran for eight parts from April to November 1934. Whilst welcomed at first, it began to drag later on. Nevertheless Fort's articles were an influence on many authors, and the books are still available today. Ironically Fort was entirely *un*scientific in his views on the nature of the solar system.

Thus Campbell's series were the first scientific articles to run in a science fiction magazine. There were eighteen in all, and only ceased when Campbell became editor. Even then he continued to supply factual pieces under the pen-name of Arthur McCann. The McCann articles were the prototype of Campbell's editorials, later to become a major feature of the magazine.

Very evidently, therefore, as fiction writer Don A. Stuart and as fact purveyor John Campbell/Arthur McCann, this man did almost as much to improve and set the pattern for *Astounding* before he was editor as he did afterwards. The science fact article has been a regular part of *Astounding* ever since, initially written by people like Harry Parker and Thomas Calvert McClary, and then notably Willy Ley and L. Sprague de Camp.

Such was the development of *Astounding* as a magazine. But of course primarily its content was fiction. A look at some of the events in this sphere during Campbell's first year, October 1937 to September 1938, will show how this was faring.

Robert Moore Williams excelled himself with two particularly enjoyable stories, 'Flight of the Dawn Star' (March 1938) and 'Robot's Return' (September 1938). Williams is much maligned today because of the considerable amount of hack words he turned out later in his career. He had first appeared in the July 1937 *Astounding* as Robert Moore with 'Zero as a Limit', having entered sf rather later than some (he was thirty). 'Flight of the Dawn Star' was his second appearance in *Astounding* and, while he was also building up sales with *Thrilling Wonder* and *Amazing*, it was evident that Campbell was securing his best. The story concerns itself with a ship lost in an unfamiliar region of the Galaxy and how the crew finds the way home. 'Robot's Return' marked the start of the new attitude towards robots in fiction, treating them with sympathy rather than as monsters. A shipful of robots are searching for their creators only to learn that it was that frail non-machine, Man.

April 1938 saw 'The Faithful' and the debut of Lester Del Rey, the more manageable name of Ramon Felipe San Juan

Mario Silvio Enrico Smith Heathcourt-Brace Sierra y Alvarez del Rey y de los Uerdes! Del Rey was twenty-two and showed considerable talent in his emotional portrayal of intelligent dogs and the last human survivor. The story showed the influence of the mood stories of Campbell and Gallun.

That same issue saw the reappearance of L. Sprague de Camp and an example of his humour in 'Hyperpilosity', about a man who starts to grow his own coat of hair. Sprague de Camp was just a few months younger than Robert Moore Williams but had a far different approach to sf. An underlying tone of humour is nearly always present even in the most serious moments, with the result that his stories are far more memorable. Sprague de Camp also had a zestful enthusiasm for learning facts and the July issue presented his article, 'Language for Time Travellers', which thoughtfully set out the problems such travellers would have with future tongues. (A year later Willy Ley supplied a sequel, 'Geography for Time Travellers'.)

May 1938 saw a new serial by Jack Williamson, *The Legion of Time*, and an article by E. E. Smith, 'Catastrophe', which became one of the most talked-about features for many months. June carried Raymond Gallun's poignant 'Seeds of the Dusk', and July saw the return of Clifford Simak after several years with 'Rule 18'. (It has been suggested that Simak would have written no more sf had it not been for Campbell becoming editor. 'Rule 18' was unlike any of Simak's earlier fiction, using time travel to build up an all-time best American football team. At the age of thirty-three Simak now firmly had his sf career on the road again.)

That same issue saw L. Ron Hubbard enter the sf field. The man who was later to become the high priest of Scientology had often been seen in the general pulp magazines like *Argosy*, but 'The Dangerous Dimension', an amusing story about a professor who could think himself anywhere, was his first excursion in to sf. Strictly speaking the story was fantasy, and in future years Hubbard proved what an excellent spinner of fantasy tales he was. Hubbard was twenty-seven.

The August number, besides presenting the first story by Malcolm Jameson, included Don A. Stuart's 'Who Goes There?', the classic story of an alien that takes on the form of the various men and animals in an Antarctic camp.

Campbell's first year at *Astounding* was without doubt an auspicious start, and proved to be an apertif for the future.

Already the two leading magazines of the early 1930s had changed their editors: *Astounding* from Tremaine to Campbell, and *Wonder* from Hornig to Weisinger. Since by 1938 *Amazing*'s O'Conor Sloane was eighty-six it seemed unlikely that he would continue for long. Indeed he did not, but it was not his death that changed matters. Sloane did not die until 7 August 1940, three months before his eighty-ninth birthday. No, Teck Publications could simply no longer support *Amazing*. The circulation was reportedly as low as 27,000 – hardly surprising considering the general dullness of the fiction and presentation. Teck had for several years operated its publishing offices from Chicago, while it was edited in New York. In 1938 *Amazing* was sold to the Chicago firm of Ziff–Davis. Sloane was obviously too old to be expected to move and, in any case, Ziff–Davis would want new blood for their magazine.

Head of the company was William B. Ziff (1898-1953), born and bred in Chicago, and a one-time commercial artist and cartoonist. He established the W. B. Ziff newspaper company in 1920, and in 1935 combined forces with publisher B. G. Davis. By 1938 Ziff–Davis was a fairly profitable company, with such publications as *Popular Photography* and *Popular Aviation*. There was a New York office on Fourth Avenue, but the editorial offices were in Chicago, so naturally it was expected there would be a Chicago editor.

There were several sf writers in and around Chicago. Stanley G. Weinbaum had hailed from Milwaukee, eighty miles to the north, and Ralph Milne Farley, the renowned author of the *Radio Man* series was still living there. Simak and E. E. Smith also lived in Milwaukee. Robert Moore Williams and Ross Rocklynne lived nearby. It was Farley (who had once been a senator, using his real name of Roger Sherman Hoar), so the story goes, who suggested to Davis that a certain Raymond A. Palmer be considered for the editorship of *Amazing*. An interview took place in February 1938 and Palmer was accepted, and with that *Amazing* was set on a new course which would ultimately prove even more eyebrow-raising than anything hitherto.

Palmer was born in Milwaukee on Monday 1 August 1910, making him just seven weeks younger than Campbell. At the age of seven he had been hit by a van which broke his back, and the resultant spinal curvature meant Palmer was only of diminutive stature. What he lost in height he made up for in determination and imagination. His first story, 'The Time Ray of

Jandra', had appeared in the June 1930 *Wonder Stories*, and showed promise.

Palmer was very much an active fan, unlike Campbell, having been involved with the earliest fanzines and won the $100 prize in Gernsback's competition 'What I Have Done to Spread Science Fiction'. In all Palmer sold six sf stories before he became *Amazing*'s editor, one of which, 'Matter Is Conserved' had been bought by Campbell for the April 1938 *Astounding*. Palmer had also sold widely in other fields, western and mystery in particular, and he was a far more competent writer than many people would openly acknowledge. He is often reported as having rewritten a considerable number of the stories submitted to *Amazing*.

The first issue on the stands from Ziff–Davis was dated June 1938. No gap occurred in the publishing schedule of one issue every other month, and all credit should go to Palmer since he is reported to have rejected all but one of the stories left over from Sloane's day. This may well be true, and that story was probably 'Space Pirate' by Eando Binder, a genuine Earl and Otto collaboration which was something Earl had not been involved in for a few years. The other fiction, with two exceptions, came from authors to whom Palmer had easy access: Robert M. Williams, Ross Rocklynne, Charles R. Tanner and Ralph Milne Farley. The two exceptions were both by the English author, John Russell Fearn, one of the figureheads of Tremaine's 'thought variant' period. These stories had been obtained through Fearn's agent, Julius Schwartz, a friend of Palmer's. One, 'The Master of the Golden City', appeared under the pen-name of Polton Cross. The other, 'A Summons from Mars', was voted the most popular story of the issue. Thereby began an association between Fearn and Palmer that would last until 1943 and included a collaboration, 'Mystery of the Martian Pendulum' (*Amazing*, October 1941). Palmer himself had to say about 'A Summons from Mars':

> It seems almost everybody liked it. And it rather tickles us, because we considered it an ideal of our policy. It had good sound science, and a fine human problem, and plenty of the human element. It stayed down to Earth in imagination, and yet was full of interest.[2]

That quotation is worth keeping in mind when looking at the further statements Palmer was to make over the next twenty years.

Phil Harbottle, author of 'The Multi-Man', an admirable study of John Russell Fearn, tells me that 'A Summons from Mars' (originally entitled 'Debt of Honour') had actually been written for Campbell at his request. Beseeched by Palmer for acceptable material, Schwartz was in a dilemma, only resolved when he received Fearn's 'Man of Earth'. Schwartz submitted that story to Campbell who never saw 'Debt of Honour'. Campbell rejected the story, and thereby Fearn failed to join Campbell's coterie. In hindsight Schwartz's action was detrimental to Fearn's career since he also persuaded Fearn to write off *Astounding* as a market and concentrate on easier sales to *Amazing*.

Under Palmer *Amazing* underwent a considerable transformation. No longer the stuffy, greybeard, cerebral publication, it was now lively and rejuvenated. Instead of a lengthy, scientific editorial, Palmer instituted 'The Observatory', where he chatted about anything and everything, very reminiscent of his fan-news sections in the fanzines. Always lively and interesting, it was often full of fascinating facts. A new form of science quiz was introduced, besides 'Questions & Answers', and 'Correspondence Corner' and 'Collector's Corner' were a great asset to fans. A 'Meet the Authors' section was warmly welcomed, and 'Discussions' once again became alive.

As with fiction, Palmer had a rush with artwork. Most of the pulp artists were in New York, so Palmer was forced to use the availability of Ziff–Davis's *Popular Photography* with Frank Lewis, Inc to stage a photographic cover. As a short-term measure it was extremely effective, and was applauded by the majority of readers. The experiment was repeated on the next issue, the issue before Joseph Tillotson, under the alias of Robert Fuqua, became the mainstay cover artist. But Palmer's major innovation was the use of the back cover for artwork. Usually this carried advertisements, but Palmer commissioned Harold McCauley to do a painting for 'This Amazing Universe' around which an article was written. It became standard practice with *Amazing*, and later the veteran artist Frank R. Paul (1880-1963) became the chief talent responsible.

On top of all this the price was reduced to twenty cents. What more could the readership ask for? They did request better interior art, which improved steadily as issues went by, using the work of Jay Jackson. By that time Palmer had acquired fiction from Arthur Tofte, Arlyn Vance, Thorp McClusky, as well as Robert Bloch's first venture into sf, 'Secret of the Observatory', about a camera that could photograph through walls. Bloch had been selling regularly to *Weird Tales* for several years, although he was then only just twenty-one.

The response to *Amazing* was highly favourable, despite much raising of eyebrows. From its October issue it reverted to a monthly schedule for the first time since 1935. Sales rocketed and *Amazing* was firmly here to stay.

Had that just been that, then by Christmas 1938 there would have been three revitalised magazines on the bookstalls, each with their own adoring audience and each prospering. As the sf historian Sam Moskowitz has pointed out, they proved a useful stepping ladder for the fan: *Amazing*'s more sensational adventures for the youngest readers; *Thrilling Wonder*'s more thoughtful fiction for older teenagers; and *Astounding*, with its modern approach, for adult readers. But that was *not* just that, because by Christmas 1938 a fourth publisher had entered the field, and the snowball began to roll. The boom in science fiction was about to begin, and how surprised fans and writers alike were going to be.

3—MEANWHILE, BACK IN BRITAIN

British readers were being fed imported editions of the US magazines and therefore had some knowledge of what was going on. One has only to leaf through the letter columns of all three magazines to find plenty of letters written by British fans. And one should not forget John Russell Fearn, Eric Frank Russell or John Beynon Harris, all three Britons and going strong in America.

But this was not the same as having one's own magazine. Fans still remember the ill-fated *Scoops* that had appeared for twenty weekly issues during the spring of 1934. Slanted towards a juvenile audience, it had started heading in the wrong direction and turned only when it was too late.

By the time *Scoops* dropped into oblivion several British chapters of Gernsback's Science Fiction League existed, and in March 1936 Maurice K. Hanson of the Nuneaton Chapter issued an amateur periodical *Novae Terrae*, which became the backbone of British fandom. Barely missing a monthly issue, its final (twenty-ninth) issue was dated January 1939. By then it had become the official organ of the British Science Fiction Association. After its last issue it metamorphosed into *New Worlds* and Hanson was succeeded by Edward John Carnell.

Only four issues of that title appeared before the call to arms came.

Besides *Novae Terrae*, several other competent British fanzines existed. Leeds fandom issued the *Bulletin of the Leeds Science Fiction League* in January 1938, edited by Harold Gottliffe, but this unwieldy title soon became *The Futurian* from June, and J. Michael Rosenblum took the reins. Leeds fandom also possessed the very active Douglas Mayer who had first organised the chapter. In spring 1937 he issued a smartly produced fanzine *Tomorrow* on a quarterly schedule, together with a companion title *Amateur Science Stories* in October. This latter title is today chiefly remembered because it published some of the first fiction by Arthur C. Clarke. In March 1938 *Tomorrow* had a face-lift. It was now printed instead of mimeographed and was combined with another publication *Scientifiction: The British Fantasy Review*. *Scientifiction* was born in January 1937, its father the Ilford fan, Walter Gillings. It was a sixteen page, digest-size, printed booklet, exceptionally professional in appearance and content and saw six issues before its amalgamation with *Tomorrow*. However, by that time a professional magazine was on the bookstalls, and it was thanks to Gillings that it got there.

Two of Britain's leading publishers were Pearson's (which had issued *Scoops*) and Newnes (the company responsible for the *Strand Magazine* since 1891). Newnes was taken with the idea of an sf magazine as early as 1935 when they had already issued two specialist fiction pulps, *Air Stories* and *War Stories*. They had reached the point of commissioning sf stories from British authors, but finally decided to delay the proposed sf title. With that Gillings approached The World's Work, a subsidiary firm of Heinemann, whose director was Henry Chalmers Roberts.

World's Work (1913) Ltd, as they were known, were publishing pulp magazines from Kingswood in Surrey, having started Britain's first really specialised pulp, *West*, several years earlier. They were now embarking on a *Master Thriller* series which had already included such titles as *Tales of Mystery and Detection* and *Tales of Terror*, with fiction by such notables as Sidney Horler, Oliver Onions, Hector Bolitho and R. Thurston Hopkins. It seemed only natural a science fiction title should be included, and they welcomed the suggestion when approached by Gillings.

Gillings was now a young man of twenty-five. Born in Ilford on Monday 19 February 1912, he had been hooked on sf from an early age, and must surely be numbered among the very earliest of British fans, with his letters to *Amazing* in its formative years. He had a far more mature attitude and approach to sf than some of his American counterparts, as shown in *Scientifiction*, and he brought this experience into action with great delight when compiling what would become the first issue of *Tales of Wonder*. It appeared on the bookstalls in June 1937, priced just one shilling, and was the standard pulp size with 128 pages. Its cover, by John Nicholson, illustrated 'Superhuman' by Geoffrey Armstrong which marked John Russell Fearn's first voyage into the realms of pseudonymity. The name was devised by Gillings because Fearn was also present under his real name with 'Seeds from Space'. Here, too, were all the big names of British sf: John Beynon, a clipped pen-name for John Beynon Harris, the real name of John (*The Day of the Triffids*) Wyndham, penned 'The Perfect Creature', a story that has often been reprinted under alternative titles of 'Una' or 'Female of the Species'. Eric Frank Russell, just beginning to make a name for himself in the States, presented another Weinbaum imitation, 'The Prr-r-eet' (voted the best story in the issue by the readers). Festus Pragnell, one-time policeman, had 'Man of the Future', plus 'Monsters of the Moon' under the alias Francis Parnell, another name invented by Gillings which led to confusion for years afterwards since there was a well-known British fan of the same name!

The issue compared well with its American counterparts and was snatched up by British fans. World's Work were thereby impressed enough to consider a further issue. This is especially admirable when you consider that out of its *Master Thriller* series, only one other title, *Tales of the Uncanny*, saw more than a single issue (three in all). These ephemeral publications have since raised many a problem among collectors and bibliographers, and one particular enigma centres around the shadowy nature of writer Henry Rawle. In 'The Multi-Man', Philip Harbottle had conjectured Rawle was a pseudonym of Fearn, since Fearn was known to have sold stories to later magazines in which the name Rawle appeared. Since then Harbottle has authenticated another by-line in these magazines (published by Gerald G. Swan) as being a pseudonym of Fearn (Alex O. Pearson), so in all probability Rawle was a real name. Fiction he was seen with at this time included 'The Head of Ekillon' and 'Armand's Return' in *Ghosts and Goblins*, and 'Revanoff's Fantasia' in *Tales of Ghosts and Haunted Houses*. Perhaps one day his identity will be clarified and another puzzle laid to rest.

After six months Gillings received the go-ahead to produce *Tales of Wonder* on a quarterly basis. The second issue which appeared in spring 1938 boasted John Beynon's 'Sleepers of Mars', the sequel to his highly popular 'Stowaway to Mars'. William F. Temple made his sf debut with 'Lunar Lilliput'. The issue also included a reprint from *Amazing*, David H. Keller's 'Sternographer's Hands'. Thereafter each issue contained reprints from the States, and these increased as issues went by. By the summer 1938 issue the magazine was featuring science articles with I. O. Evans's 'Can We Conquer Space?' The fifth issue in December saw Arthur C. Clarke's name in print with 'We Can Rocket to the Moon—Now!'

By then *Tales of Wonder* was proving extremely popular. As if that was what Newnes had been waiting for they finally brought out their magazine *Fantasy* in June 1938, long overdue. After nothing at all, Britain suddenly had two sf magazines. Gillings was paying for his fiction out of a lump sum provided by World's Work and, of necessity, his rates were low. But Newnes, with its greater financial backing, was able to afford better rates, and consequently *Fantasy* was going to attract the British writers first. From this you can see that Gillings was getting a rough deal from World's Work. Had Newnes gone ahead with *Fantasy* three years earlier, the British sf scene might have been very different.

The first issue of *Fantasy* had a very professional appearance with the exception of a Frankenstein-like cover by staff artist S. R. Drigin. It illustrated 'Menace of the Metal Men' by A. Prestigiacomo, which had first appeared in the British *Argosy* a few years earlier. We are told that it was written in English at the suggestion of Compton Mackenzie! The plot, a simple case of robots in revolt, was hardly new, but was nevertheless entertaining. As expected, John Beynon, John Russell Fearn and Eric Frank Russell were all present, each contributing fiction well up to his usual standard.

One might feel the issue was biassed towards war stories. 'Menace of the Metal Men' already had the army on the alert, and Beynon's story, 'Beyond the Screen' concerns civilisation's most terrible weapon – 'Judson's Annihilator' (by which title the story later appeared in *Amazing*). This was followed by 'Leashed Lightning' by J. E. Gurdon, an acknowledged expert on aerial warfare. Of especial interest was a science-fact article, 'By Rocket-Ship to the Planets'. It was written by P. E. Cleator, co-founder of the British Interplanetary Society in October

1933 with Leslie J. Johnson. Cleator had sold a story to Hornig's *Wonder Stories*, and had just had an article, 'Spaceward', published in the August 1937 *Thrilling Wonder*. Cleator had all the appearance of becoming an English Willy Ley, had not the War intervened. Ley himself was present with an article in the second issue – an article that had been returned by Gillings for amendment!

Fantasy was the brainchild of, and edited by, T. Stanhope Sprigg, one of a family of Spriggs who had made their names in writing and publishing. Sprigg had been the editor of *Airways* before he joined Newnes in 1934 with the express intention of starting four specialist magazines: *Air Stories*, *War Stories*, *Western Stories* and *Fantasy*. The first three were soon well under way, but it was four years before *Fantasy* received the go ahead. Sprigg had a long-standing interest in science fiction and was certain that not only would such a magazine be a viable commercial publishing proposition but it would also provide a much-needed opening and encouragement to British sf writers.

Sprigg handled his four magazines almost entirely on his own, and their future was thereby fated. Issue 2 of *Fantasy* appeared in March 1939 and a green light was given to a quarterly schedule, issue 3 appearing in June. But that was the last. With war imminent, Sprigg, as a member of the Royal Air Force Reserve, was mobilised, and his magazines, relying entirely on him (with the exception of *Air Stories* which survived for a few more issues), died with his departure.

Tales of Wonder was more fortunate, and World's Work are to be commended for continuing the publication for as long as they did. With wartime restrictions, however, and the inevitable paper shortages, *Tales of Wonder* was bound to suffer. With the ninth issue (December 1939) the page-count dropped to ninety-six, and then to eighty with the twelfth number. By spring 1941 it was down to seventy-two, but at least a regular quarterly schedule was being maintained. The next issue, though, did not appear until the autumn, and then in spring 1942 the sixteenth and final issue appeared. At that point World's Work brought down the axe in favour of *Short Stories*. By this time Gillings had come to rely more and more on American reprint material – hardly surprising with many of Britain's potential writers in the Services. ·

With *Tales of Wonder*'s demise the market for British sf disappeared. Fortunately it was not dormant for too long. Behind the scenes negotiations were showing the determination of British fans for sf magazines although the continuation of this story properly falls within the scope of the next book. British author William Passingham, whose main claim to sf fame had been the serials *Atlantis Returns* and *The World behind the Moon* in *Modern Wonder*, interested The World Says Ltd, a publishing company, in producing an sf magazine in 1939. He approached John Carnell and two meetings were held in October 1939 and January 1940. Financial and production arrangements were settled despite the Second World War, and Carnell was instituted as editor, with a March deadline. The magazine was to be called *New Worlds*. An issue was prepared including fiction by no less a luminary than Robert Heinlein, and then, just a week before the final proceedings, foul play was discovered. Suddenly The World Says Ltd went into voluntary liquidation, and the publisher returned to his native Canada. *New Worlds* was stillborn, and would have to wait until 1946 before Carnell could give it that slap on the bottom to reawaken it and bring it coughing into the world.

However, British fans could still acquire American sf in all its various forms, either in the original imported copy or in one of a rash of reprint editions that began to appear, ironically just as the War put paid to *Fantasy*.

The largest of these reprint companies was the Atlas Publishing & Distributing Company, which had imported most American titles before the War, and then in August 1939 began printing a British edition of *Astounding*. This did not correspond wholly with the concurrent American edition, and as issues continued the disparity grew. Usually Atlas omitted one or two stories, and rearranged the other material. Certain features were left out completely, being replaced with British advertisements. Nevertheless, for those who could not acquire the real thing, it was a healthy substitute.

Another reprint firm was Gerald G. Swan, Ltd, of Marylebone, London. This company was responsible for publishing several comic books, like *Topical Funnies* and *Bitz and Pieces*. In 1942, just as *Tales of Wonder* breathed its last, Swan hit on the idea of producing a series of small magazines called *Yankee Shorts*, starting with *Romance Shorts* and followed by *Mystery Shorts*. The third in the series was *Yankee Science Fiction*, and to give an air of authenticity it was priced at ten cents on the front, and threepence on the back. The issue was standard pulp size and carried just thirty-two pages, with four stories all reprinted from the Summer 1940 *Science Fiction Quarterly*.

The experiment was repeated with numbers eleven and twenty-one in the series, while six, fourteen and nineteen were *Yankee Weird Shorts*. Thereafter Swan began to publish the occasional issue of *Weird Tales*, *Future* or *Science Fiction* throughout the War. A cheap format, and uninspired artwork from their grossly overworked staff artist, hindered the magazines from establishing themselves and they slid into oblivion.

When VE Day came in May 1945 Britain began to struggle back to some form of normality, and high on John Carnell's list of 'things to do' was to get an sf magazine off the ground. His and Walter Gillings's further ventures will be covered in the next book in the series. Now to return to the United States in 1938, where war was still four years away.

4—MULTIPLICATION

Suppose we follow our hypothetical sf fan back to his bookstall in the summer of 1938. He would find the July *Astounding* with its auspicious contents (already covered), and the August *Amazing* (the second under Palmer). The July 1938 *Weird Tales* would catch his eye, its cover sporting Virgil Finlay's illustration of Henry Kuttner's 'Spawn of Dagon', and its contents including Edmond Hamilton's superlative 'He That Hath Wings', to my mind his best story and one of the greatest fantasies ever written. The August *Thrilling Wonder* also presented fiction by Ray Cummings, Henry Kuttner, Gordon A. Giles and even Ray Palmer. These four issues would have cost him eighty cents. Then, with eyes bulging, he would readily pay over another fifteen cents to buy a copy of *Marvel Science Stories*, the first new sf magazine for seven years.

Apart from semi-professional or media-spawned publications, *Marvel* was indeed the first new American sf magazine since *Miracle Science & Fantasy Stories* had made its brief appearance in 1931.

Marvel was a Red Circle Magazine, a common sight on the news-stands including *Real Sports*, *Top-Notch Detective* and *Adventure Trails*. With the obvious popularity of *Astounding* and *Thrilling Wonder* it should have been no surprise to see them enter the sf field. The first issue was dated August 1938, the editor was Robert O. Erisman, and the publishers Western Fiction Publishing Co Inc, whose head office was in the same

building in Chicago from which Teck Publications had issued
Amazing: 4600 Diversey Avenue.

The lead novel was *Survival* by Arthur J. Burks, a particularly
prolific pulp writer in many fields. It was the story of how, in
order to escape from invasion, a band of people venture underground and thereby wrest all their necessities from their surroundings, and one which was soon heralded as one of the year's
best stories. That was some claim considering the competition
from *Astounding*. There were shorter pieces by Stanton Coblentz,
Henry Kuttner and two new names, James Hall and Robert O.
Kenyon. Kenyon wrote for *Marvel*'s companion detective magazines, so it could be supposed he was a detective writer turned
to sf. At the time the illusion was best kept, because the reception of these stories was less than flattering. In fact they
were both pen-names of Henry Kuttner, whose story under his
own name was also criticised.

This was not directly Kuttner's fault. *Marvel*'s publisher,
Martin Goodman, and editor, Erisman, had decided on a new
direction in sf that was to make it more spicy. Such had been
the feature of horror stories ever since Popular Publications'
Dime Mystery Magazine began in 1932. Western published its own
Mystery Tales with a similar emphasis on the sadistic side of
horror, and Kuttner had sold stories there. He was now requested
to include the same kind of scenes in his sf stories 'Dictator
of the Americas', 'The Dark Heritage' and 'The Time Trap'
(the latter appeared in the November issue). By today's standard
the sex content was mild to say the least, but much adverse
criticism was brought to bear, as, for example, in this letter:

> . . . I was just about to write you a letter of complete con-
> gratulations when my eyes fell upon Kuttner's *The Time Trap*.
> All I can say is: 'PLEASE, in the future, dislodge such trash
> from your magazine.'[3]

Such was hardly fair to Kuttner, but it branded his name
among fans for a time thereafter. But the general readers of
Marvel held little against the magazine, and the success of the
first issue was exceeded only by that of the second, in November.
Carrying Arthur Burk's fine sequel to 'Survival', 'Exodus', and
Jack Williamson's 'The Dead Spot', plus a cover by Frank R.
Paul, it was hailed as a great success. Even so the magazine
did not settle down to its intended schedule of one every other
month, since the third issue, carrying Williamson's superb 'After

World's End', did not appear until February 1939. By then *Marvel* had acquired an sf companion *Dynamic Science Stories*, appearing right at the outset of a trend for sister magazines.

Dynamic's intention was to cater for longer fiction, thereby leaving *Marvel* with the shorter pieces. Its first issue (dated February) carried 'The Lord of Tranerica' by Stanton Coblentz which lent itself to a typical cover by Frank Paul. The rest of the issue, apart from a vignette by Nelson Bond (under the alias Hubert Mavity) called 'The Message from the Void', was uninspiring. A second issue, dated April 1939, carried a lead novel by Eando Binder, who, more than most other authors at this time, managed to maintain a prolific ubiquity without too great a sacrifice in quality. After that no more *Dynamic*s appeared; the majority of unused material appearing in *Marvel*. Its passing was certainly not mourned, indeed it went virtually without notice, lost in the sudden upsurge of periodicals.

Marvel had not been the only new magazine in 1938, but it was the most successful. May had seen the sole appearance of *Captain Hazzard* from publisher A. A. Wyn. Its lead novel, *Python Men of Lost City* by Chester Hawks, was an attempt to create a magazine around a central character, much like *Doc Savage*, but it fell by the wayside.

As 1938 made way for the new year, the sf guns began to fire. In 1939 alone nine new magazines appeared. *Nine* – nearly twice as many as already existed. And of that nine, five appeared in the first three months. Furthermore, six of that nine were companion magazines to current titles, and first off the blocks was Standard Magazines with *Startling Stories*.

Thrilling Wonder Stories was having much success, and in the February 1938 issue Weisinger asked for readers' reactions and suggestions regarding a companion sf magazine. Since at that stage *Marvel* was yet to appear it was the first intimation of any new magazine anywhere. Readers were all but unanimous in their approval, many recommending that the new title be published in the old large-size format. Such was not the case, but in January 1939 the first pulp-size, 132-page *Startling Stories* appeared. The policy was to carry a lead novel and a classic 'Hall of Fame' reprint. After all, Standard had bought the rights to *Wonder Stories*, and had all the issues back to June 1929 at its disposal. With many new readers having entered the field during the thirties this was a rich vein to tap.

To lead off the first issue Weisinger had acquired 'The Black Flame' by Stanley G. Weinbaum. When Weinbaum's original version, 'Dawn of Flame' had received several rejections he wrote a sequel (twice the original's length), called 'The Black Flame', but again it was rejected as not having enough action for regular pulp readers, despite being one of Weinbaum's best pieces. 'Dawn of Flame' had hitherto only appeared as the title story in a memorial collection printed in a limited edition of 250 copies by Conrad H. Ruppert, and published by Raymond Palmer. Now, with Weinbaum's posthumous popularity, *Startling* had a real scoop for its first issue.

The initial 'Hall of Fame' reprint was 'The Eternal Man' by D. D. Sharp, which I included in the first book of this series. The uncredited cover illustrated an action-packed scene from Eando Binder's 'Science Island'. Otis Adelbert Kline provided a guest editorial, and Otto Binder a tribute to Weinbaum. Features included a pictorial article by Jack Binder on Albert Einstein, the first in a series *They Changed the World*, and Weisinger himself provided a set of thumb-nail sketches of great scientists for 'Thrills in Science'.

The reception to *Startling* was glowing. Margulies and Weisinger had shown sufficient sense to make the magazine different from *Thrilling Wonder*, which continued to publish an assortment of short stories and novelettes. In *Startling*'s case the lead novels were initially of the 45-60,000 word range, which left little space for much more than the reprint, the features and a few vignettes. The choice of reprint was also wise, two Weinbaum stories, including the legendary 'A Martian Odyssey', being revived in the first year.

But Standard did not stop there. Since *Startling* was appearing alternately with *Wonder*, every other month, they also introduced a new title to run correspondingly with *Thrilling Mystery*. The first issue of *Strange Stories* appeared in February 1939 and sported fiction by all of *Weird Tales*'s favourite authors: Robert Bloch, August Derleth, Mark Schorer, Otis Adelbert Kline, Henry Kuttner and Manly Wade Wellman. In fact Bloch, Derleth and Kuttner made this very much their own magazine and it was rare to find an issue that did not carry at least one of their stories, albeit under a pen-name. It was here that Bloch's second self, Tarleton Fiske was born, as well as Kuttner's alias, Keith Hammond, and Derleth's Tally Mason.

Strange Stories was an obvious imitation of *Weird Tales*. True it was not an sf magazine, but this should not exclude its mention altogether. (As will be seen nearly all publishers who carried an sf magazine also published a companion 'weird' title.)

Strange Stories was outlived by its companion, *Thrilling Mystery*, although that became irregular after November 1939 and finally folded in September 1942. While *Strange* lasted it was very much a rival to *Weird Tales*, which was now heading towards a crucial period in its long history. Since 1924 it had been edited capably (if sometimes erratically) by Farnsworth Wright. In January 1939, however, the magazine was sold to Short Stories Inc, whose editorial offices were in New York. Wright moved with the magazine from Chicago, but already his health was failing and he found it impossible to continue. He left after the March 1940 issue and died shortly thereafter, aged only fifty-two. The choice for editor fell on Miss Dorothy McIlwraith, a middle-aged spinster who had edited *Short Stories*. No matter how ably one might consider she edited *Weird Tales*, it was undeniably the end of an era when Wright departed. Only a few years before, two of its top authors, Robert E. Howard and H. P. Lovecraft had died (the first by his own hand), and another favourite Clark Ashton Smith had virtually ceased writing all together. Other big names were appearing less frequently, too, so the *Weird Tales* that survived with Miss McIlwraith was already a shadow of its greater days. From our point of view, whereas Wright had regularly published a science fiction story, such content now became very rare, and it was chiefly Edmond Hamilton (and later Stanton Coblentz) who kept the sf flag flying.

Now was the ideal time for *Strange Stories* to strike, to succeed to the fantasy throne. But it did not succeed. It only lasted a fateful thirteen issues and in January 1941 passed away. Why? Was there no market for fantasy? Or was the readership too faithful to *Weird Tales*?

The answer really lies in the fact that *Strange Stories* was too much of an imitation of *Weird*, of which there could only be one. Whereas Standard were wise with their choice in *Startling*, they were wrong with *Strange*. (Today its best remembered content was Henry Kuttner's series about Prince Raynor, and that only lasted for two stories.) The man who made the right decision when it came to fantasy was none other than John Campbell. The month after *Strange Stories* appeared, *Astounding*'s companion, *Unknown*, burst upon the scene, a true nova, and with it fantasy grew up.

What *Astounding* had accomplished for sf, *Unknown* was about to do for fantasy. The most obvious difference between *Weird* and *Unknown* fantasy was the approach. In nearly every case

Weird Tales presented gruesome horror fiction. The intent was to frighten and unnerve, with emphasis on the bizarre. Not so *Unknown*, which treated fantasy as an everyday occurrence, and although the occasional scarey story was published it is the note of humour that pervaded *Unknown* that makes it memorable. Here was the type of fiction popularised by Thorne Smith (1893-1934) in his *Topper* series. *Unknown*'s fiction was never complicated, indeed, the opposite, for authors merely suggested a basic premise – What if . . .? – and developed their stories logically from there. The results were more than phenomenal, they were stunning. *Unknown* published without doubt the greatest collection of fantasy stories produced in one magazine. Naturally it proved a boon for anyone capable of mixing humour with fantasy, and consequently many authors proved their true worth in its pages. L. Sprague de Camp, L. Ron Hubbard, Fritz Leiber (whose *Grey Mouser* stories, rejected by *Weird Tales*, here saw the first light of day), Nelson Bond, Henry Kuttner, Theodore Sturgeon, Anthony Boucher, Fredric Brown, H. L. Gold and Malcolm Jameson in particular showed their ability to weave first class gems. Surprises were also in store. Norvell Page, one of the top pulp authors who turned out fiction at a dazzling speed and was responsible for the lead stories in Popular's *The Spider* magazine, appeared with two fine novels based on the legend of Prester John: *Flame Winds* and *Sons of the Bear-God*; and Manly Wade Wellman, hitherto regarded as a fairly good second-rate writer of space heroics, produced a shiveringly memorable story centred around Edgar Allan Poe: 'When It Was Moonlight'.

We British should be justifiably proud that the novel that led the first issue was by Eric Frank Russell. *Sinister Barrier* had been submitted to *Astounding* and was returned for re-writing. Russell apparently succeeded to such an admirable extent that he astonished even Campbell. During this period Campbell had been planning an accompanying fantasy magazine and *Sinister Barrier* seemed more appropriate for that. Russell adapted one of Charles Fort's beliefs, that we are the property of aliens, to produce what has subsequently become regarded as a classic. In the novel Earthmen learn that they are indeed the property of aliens, and thereby begin a desperate battle for freedom.

From its first issue *Unknown* became a must for fans, fantasy and sf alike, since it definitely contained many science fantasy stories, one of the best examples of which is Jack Williamson's

'Darker Than You Think' (December 1940) with its highly scientific approach to lycanthropy.

Hot on the heels of *Unknown*, came *Fantastic Adventures* as a companion to *Amazing*. The first issue being dated May 1939 *Fantastic* arrived too soon after *Unknown* to be looked upon as an imitator, but no doubt the appearance of Campbell's title hastened Ziff–Davis. In his editorial, praising the immense hard work accomplished by the Ziff–Davis team, Palmer states that: 'We have raised fantastic fiction to the level of the quality magazines, and yet retained the lusty appeal of the pulp field.'[4] A strange statement, you will agree, that the pulps and quality do not go hand in hand, for a pulp editor to make.

Be that as it may, *Fantastic Adventures* did have appeal. As a juvenile equivalent to *Unknown* it was satisfactory, and although Palmer never could seem to make up his mind whether to publish science fiction or fantasy, the magazine did contain many good stories. As years went by its quality improved beyond that of *Amazing* and during the 'Shaver-period' (more on this later) in the latter, *Fantastic* proved a haven of retreat.

The first issue was by no means as spectacular as *Unknown*'s. Second-rate fiction by Eando Binder, Harl Vincent, A. Hyatt Verrill, Ross Rocklynne and Frederic A. Kummer amongst others, combined with a comic strip: *Ray Holmes, Scientific Detective* (whose perpetrator sensibly remained anonymous), nevertheless found popularity among *Amazing*'s followers. Without doubt the best facet of the issue was Frank R. Paul's back cover artwork depicting 'The Man from Mars'. The illustration was accompanied by an explanatory article and these again demonstrated Paul's versatility. He was aided here by *Fantastic*'s large-size format which allowed more scope for both cover and interior artwork.

March 1939 saw a new publisher enter the field – Blue Ribbon Magazines of Massachusetts, with editorial offices in Hudson Street, New York. By now the success of *Amazing*, under Palmer, and *Marvel*, was food for thought among pulp publishers and they realised it was about time they jumped onto the bandwaggon. So Blue Ribbon brought out *Science Fiction*, and as editor they employed none other than Charles D. Hornig, now at the seasoned age of twenty-two.

Science Fiction had a favourable launching, despite a mediocre cover by Frank R. Paul, with names like Edmond Hamilton and Amelia Reynolds Long momentarily transporting readers back to the days of *Wonder Stories*. In hindsight it might be felt such memories should have been left to the past, as the stories were of poor quality. The first issue, though, was praised considerably. A young (eighteen) Ray Bradbury said:

> . . . don't let the magazine degenerate to the kindergarten class – let it grow with the minds of the fans. If the other mags want to play up to children, let them forge blindly on – but they won't carve a place for themselves in the hall of science fiction like you certainly will if you keep plugging with the ideas you hold in mind for the future.
>
> [Hornig replied]: I'm trying to give the magazine an appeal to mature minds, and am therefore avoiding illogical fairy tales.[5]

Hornig was obviously deriding Palmer's policy, and possibly also Weisinger. But was this fair when one considers that most of Hornig's material came from Palmer's and Weisinger's mainstay authors? This fact was hidden by the countless pseudonyms used, which also disguised the fact that authors whom Palmer was paying one per cent per word were selling to Hornig at half-a-cent a word. These included John Russell Fearn who had appeared as John Cotton, Ephriam Winiki and Dennis Clive in the first issue, and later as Dom Passante; Edmond Hamilton who appeared as Robert Castle; Henry Kuttner as Paul Edmonds; and Eando Binder (including Earl) as John Coleridge. The device was engineered by the authors' agent Julius Schwartz, the pen-names being mostly concocted by editor Hornig. Where real names were used payment was raised to the standard one cent a word.

Binder appeared under his own recognised name in the second issue with a short novel, *Where Eternity Ends*, a fast-paced, well-written piece for which Binder is still remembered. This story was issued as a booklet by an Australian publisher in the fifties. Binder also supplied a cover article, 'A Vision of Possibility', around which Paul conceived captivating covers – in much the same way as the back cover artwork was proceeding at *Amazing*, while Campbell's special mutant covers were a feature of *Astounding*.

After the first two issues *Science Fiction* began to decline. Obviously with the mushrooming of the field, writers and their agents had far more markets to choose from and aimed for those that paid best. Hornig had been associated with *Wonder Stories* which was notorious for slow payment. When the same thing began to happen with *Science Fiction* the flow of manuscripts from leading authors began to slow down. This meant that authors who were finding it increasingly difficult to keep up with the field – their fiction seemingly now out of date – once again found a market. People like Ed Earl Repp, Harl Vincent, Stanton Coblentz and even Ray Cummings, who seemed in a rut of sub-microscopia. Consequently *Science Fiction* and a bevy of magazines like it seldom had the chance to procure more than second-rate material, and though at times second-rate fiction by good authors (previously rejected by the better markets) was still above the average of other writers, it did mean much mediocre work crept in.

During the summer of 1939 the boom seemed to abate for a while, but as autumn approached the snowballing returned, and with it a spark of originality from the Frank Munsey organisation. Munsey's company had started the whole pulp field over forty years earlier, and that first title, *Argosy*, was still appearing, although sf was forming less and less a part of its content. Often readers would remember the early days of *Argosy* and its companion *All-Story* (now *All-Story Love*, a woman's romance magazine) and affectionately recall the many sf/fantasy tales it had published. Here was a niche to be filled, and in September 1939 Munsey brought out *Famous Fantastic Mysteries*, its intention being to reprint those old classics. Here it did an admirable job under the shrewd editorship of Mary Gnaedinger. She had a vast storehouse of fiction to choose from, and since the most important popular author from the early days had been Abraham Merritt (1884-1943) she picked on his work to lead the revival. Merritt was now fully employed as editor of *American Weekly* so his fiction output was virtually nil, meaning few new fans had had the opportunity to sample his tales. (Gernsback had also picked on Merritt when reprinting novels in *Amazing* twelve years earlier. That choice had proved decidedly influential, and Merritt's second reprinting once again proved a winner.)

The first issue carried 'The Moon Pool' from the 22 June 1918 *All-Story*, and this was followed by a serialisation of the sequel *The Conquest of the Moon Pool*. The second issue also revived 'Almost Immortal' by Austin Hall (*All-Story*, 7 October 1916), and in the third was Edison Marshall's 'Who Is Charles Avison?' (*Argosy*, April 1916) to list just the cream of the reprints.

Famous Fantastic Mysteries (known as *FFM* for convenience) went monthly after its second issue, a status hitherto claimed only by *Astounding* (and *Unknown*) and *Amazing*. Naturally the financial backing of Munsey had much to do with this, but it was also a sign of its popularity. As a consequence, in July 1940, a companion *Fantastic Novels* was issued to carry the full length works, leaving *FFM* the shorter pieces. Here Gnaedinger used a cunning ploy. From the March 1940 issue *FFM* had been serialising *The Blind Spot* by Austin Hall and Homer Eon Flint, a particularly exciting classic from an *Argosy* of 1921. After the third instalment it was suddenly cut short and printed in its entirety in the first *Fantastic Novels*. Those who wished to complete it had no alternative but to buy the new magazine.

As the year drew to a close a companion magazine to *Science Fiction* surprisingly appeared: *Future Fiction*. Charles Hornig was again editor. The title had an interesting genesis. Publisher Silberkleit had begun his business life working with a distributing company connected with Gernsback. When Gernsback was fishing for magazine names for the periodical that saw light as *Amazing Stories*, Silberkleit suggested *Future Fiction*. Thirteen-and-a-half years later that title was eventually born.

Future was initially little more than a carbon copy of *Science Fiction*. A feature of Hornig's editing was his ability to dig up names from the past. The first *Future* included 'The Infinite Eye' by Philip Jacques Bartel, the pen-name of M. M. Kaplan (whose first story 'One Prehistoric Night' was included in Volume I of this series), 'World Reborn' by J. Harvey Haggard and 'The Disappearing Papers' by Miles J. Breuer – all names that had nearly vanished from sight. It is interesting to speculate that Hornig may well have acquired some of the ninety-nine odd manuscripts Palmer rejected when he assumed control of *Amazing* after Sloane; stories which had been written many years earlier.

By Christmas two more magazines had appeared, both quarterlies. The first, dated Winter 1939, was from a new publishing house, Love Romances Inc, of New York, and was called *Planet Stories*. Love Romances published a variety of magazines, the publishing name being extremely misleading. *Northwest Romances*, *Jungle Stories* and *Two Complete Detective Books Magazine* for instance, all went under their general imprint of 'A Fiction House Magazine'. The first *Planet*, edited by Malcolm Reiss, was singularly unimpressive in its fiction, except for the welcome return of the bylines Laurence Manning and Fletcher Pratt. *Planet* maintained a policy of publishing only interplanetary fiction and was unquestionably slanted towards the juvenile market. As issue followed issue the verve of editor Reiss began to take effect and the quality of material improved, even though Reiss would be found apologising for the poor stories as being the best to hand at the time of going to press. In common with many of the new magazines, Reiss also pandered to sf fandom with a fanzine review column, and the magazine soon built up a loyal following.

The other quarterly, *Captain Future*, emanated once again from Standard Magazines. July 1939 had seen the first World Science Fiction Convention, held in New York and attended by fans and professionals alike. Leo Margulies had been present and was apparently impressed by the fans' sincerity. It was at the convention that he and Weisinger dreamed up *Captain Future*. Since this magazine was aimed at the youngest teenage group one wonders just what Margulies's opinion of the fans really was!

Captain Future, first issue dated Winter 1940, was to carry a full novel adventure each quarter telling the saga of Captain Curt Newton and his cohorts. The novels were initially all the work of Edmond Hamilton, starting with *Captain Future and the Space Emperor*. Hamilton was a highly competent author, and fortunately did not make the mistake of writing down to the readership, refraining from *too* juvenilistic adventurings, despite the pulp formula trappings the publisher insisted upon. Rather they were well-done space heroics.

Just as important was that this magazine, like *Startling*, carried reprints, in this case longer stories that could be serialised. The first year saw David H. Keller's *The Human Termites* resurrected from 1929.

Nineteen thirty-nine was certainly a most exceptional year for science fiction, both good and bad. It saw an expansion in the market for writers and artists, but is also brought much low-grade fiction to light. What is remarkable is how much of the material was aimed at a juvenile audience. Whereas Palmer had originally been aiming low, now both *Planet* and *Captain Future* underscored him. In fact *Amazing*'s fiction was often on a par with, if not better than, that in *Science Fiction* and *Future*. On the other hand *Startling* and *Thrilling Wonder* were now far more élite than before, and *FFM* was offering a formidable challenge with its respectable reprints.

But as ever at the top of the tree was *Astounding*, and if 1938 had been a good year, 1939 was even better. This was fortunate for Campbell, because in his strivings for originality he was rejecting a large amount of material. As the sf market grew and the rejected authors found they could readily place their material elsewhere, they no longer wasted their time with Campbell. For that reason Campbell *had* to find his own stable of authors, and without a doubt that's just what he did.

Let us compare his second year (October 1938–September 1939) with his first (and this is excluding *Unknown*). October 1938 presented the first of L. Sprague de Camp's series about Johnny Black, the intelligent bear – 'The Command' – which was voted the most popular story of the issue. December 1938 saw the return of Lester Del Rey with 'Helen O'Loy', a particularly emotional female robot. With that same issue one saw Tremaine's 'thought variants' replaced by Campbell's 'nova' stories, starting with 'A Matter of Form' by H. L. Gold. This was Gold's first appearance under his real name, though he had appeared with several stories in 1934 under the byline of Clyde Crane Campbell.

Clifford Simak's serial *Cosmic Engineers* began in the February 1939 issue, and this was followed in April with Jack Williamson's *One Against the Legion*. With these, *Astounding*'s space opera came to a very mature end, except for those yet to come from E. E. Smith.

John Berryman first appeared in May with 'Special Flight', but of more import was the July issue with 'Black Destroyer', concerning the alien cat-like creature, Coeurl, and its attempts to take over a Terran spaceship. This story marked the first appearance of A. E. van Vogt in sf magazines. The same issue carried 'Trends', Isaac Asimov's first *Astounding* sale, though 'Marooned off Vesta' (*Amazing*, March 1939) had appeared first. 'Trends' was remarkable for its premise that in the future there could well be social resistance to space travel. One month later the August issue gave us Robert Heinlein's first sale, 'Life-Line' (a not too memorable story about a machine that can forecast how long a man will live), and the following month brought us the rascalous adventures of ethereal beings in Theodore Sturgeon's first story, 'Ether Breather'.

In two years Campbell had cornered what would become the biggest names in sf: L. Sprague de Camp, Lester Del Rey, E. E. Smith, Eric Frank Russell, Isaac Asimov, Robert Heinlein, A. E. van Vogt and Theodore Sturgeon, as well as Clifford Simak and Jack Williamson. To get his third year off to a good start E. E. Smith's *Grey Lensman* was serialised in four parts, starting in October.

5—HIGH TIDE

There was hardly any abatement in the spreading of sf pulps at the beginning of 1940, but they were in most cases companion magazines. Charles Hornig found himself with a third magazine, *Science Fiction Quarterly*, a trial issue appearing dated Summer 1940. The emphasis here was on long novels, as with *Startling*, and in this first issue that was a reprint: *The Moon Conquerors* by R. H. Romans from the Winter 1930 *Wonder Stories Quarterly*. Obviously the idea of reprints was catching on fast.

February and March 1940 saw two new magazines, *Astonishing Stories* and its companion *Super Science Stories*. These two titles alternated, and over the next three years proved to be among the most sensible magazines available. The contents page declared the publishers were Fictioneers, Inc, but this was merely a subsidiary of Popular Publications. Popular, surprisingly, had no sf magazines, having made their name from the sex/sadism publications which they more or less had started with *Dime Mystery Magazine* in 1932 and developed in *Horror Stories* and *Terror Tales*. Active sf fan Frederik Pohl had first gone to Red Circle in an attempt to become the editor of *Marvel*. By 1940 that magazine was well on the decline but Erisman put Pohl in touch with Popular's publisher, Henry Steeger. Pohl walked away from that interview as editor of the two new magazines. The date was Wednesday, 25 October 1939. Pohl was one month away from his twentieth birthday, making him the youngest editor in his first job, after Hornig.

However, Pohl was exceedingly mature in his ideas and projects. The two magazines were of the typical companion format, *Astonishing* for shorter pieces, *Super Science* for the full length works. (Indeed for a while it was retitled *Super Science Novels Magazine*.) The first issue of *Astonishing* showed a definite leaning towards interplanetary adventure, leading with J. R. Fearn's 'Chameleon Planet' and Frederic Kummer's 'White Land of Venus'. Isaac Asimov was present with 'Half-Breed', and so, too, were Henry Kuttner and Manly Wade Wellman, although pseudonymously.

Super Science Stories led with 'World Reborn' by Thornton Ayre (Fearn again – who thus scored a unique cover double), and also contained fiction by Raymond Gallun, Frank Belknap Long, Ross Rocklynne and others. It should be remembered particularly for the first appearance of James Blish, a bright eighteen-year-old, with 'Emergency Refuelling'.

Before 1940 was over, these two magazines were to include fiction by L. Sprague de Camp, Robert Heinlein and Clifford Simak, besides Asimov. In most cases these were Campbell rejects, but good fiction nevertheless. Combine this with the fact that *Astonishing* sold for the mere sum of ten cents and it was hardly surprising that it reached a large market. The original reason that Popular had issued Pohl's magazines under a separate house name was because they would only risk a half-cent a word for sf instead of their customary one cent. Yet by the end of 1940 they had raised Pohl's budget which enabled him to pay bonuses on the most popular stories.

Popular Publications now began to expand. In 1935 they had purchased *Adventure* from the Munsey Corporation and with it acquired editor Howard Bloomfield. Now, in 1941, they took over the rest of the magazines. *Argosy* was turned into a 'slick' magazine, and sf phased out. It was this way that Popular came into possession of *FFM* and *Fantastic Novels*, and put their editor, Alden H. Norton, in overall charge of the sf publications.

It was nearly high tide for the magazines: the sf field had reached saturation level. Four more titles were still to appear, though, and the very next heralded the return of F. Orlin Tremaine to the field.

Tremaine (1899-1956) had satisfied himself with a long rest after his stint with Street & Smith and had been content to turn out some fiction, including sf stories such as 'True Confession' (*Thrilling Wonder*, February 1940), a particularly poignant robot story, and fantasy like 'Golden Girl of Kalendar' for *Fantastic Adventures*. Now under the auspices of H-K Publications he became editor of *Comet Stories*, first issue December 1940. By now sf fans were becoming blasé about new publications and, although the name Tremaine was worth more than an inquisitive glance, the contents had to be special to tempt the further fifteen cents from readers' pockets. Tremaine did not produce that extra something, although the second and third issues began to show more promise. *Comet* published fiction by all and sundry in sf, and certainly had no well-defined policy or stable of authors. It was in this magazine that sf's historian Sam Moskowitz first appeared with 'The Way Back' in the January 1941 issue (although he was also present in the Winter 1941 *Planet Stories*).

Unfortunately, just as *Comet* was making its name felt,

Tremaine quit. H-K Publications were not providing the money to pay authors or competition winners, and Tremaine wished to have no part of that. *Comet* was certainly no more than a brief burst of light, and with that Tremaine never returned to sf editing, although he did make a brief reappearance in the late 1940s with a series of articles in *Thrilling Wonder.* He died on Monday, 22 October 1956, leaving behind him *Astounding* as a monument to his achievements.

Money problems reared their ugly heads again with the next few magazines. In the days of *Wonder* and *Amazing* it was not unheard of for authors to wait for payment long after a story was published. Thereby, Street & Smith's *Astounding* became a startling haven with its regular cheque on acceptance. The larger publishers like Standard, Ziff–Davis and Popular were no trouble either. But as sf expanded and the smaller publishers moved in on the sf publishing front, the problems grew.

Things came to a head when Donald Wollheim persuaded Jerry Albert of Albing Publications to issue *Stirring Science Stories* and *Cosmic Stories*, dated February and March 1941 respectively. The trouble was that there was not enough capital to pay for everything at once. Albert instructed Wollheim to obtain stories on the understanding that payment would be forthcoming if the magazines were successful, a gamble that would rapidly lead to the death of the publications. Wollheim was fortunate in that as a member of a New York fan society, the Futurians, he had to hand a ready clan of budding authors who were only too pleased to see their fiction in print, even if the remuneration was next to nothing. As a result most of the issues of both magazines were made up almost entirely from this group, published under a virtual directory of pen-names. It also meant that authors who later became big names were launched on their careers.

The best example is Cyril Kornbluth (1923-58). Kornbluth had first appeared in the April 1940 *Astonishing* in collaboration with Richard Wilson under the pseudonym of Ivar Towers. His first solo appearance was in the May 1940 *Super Science Stories* with 'King Cole of Pluto', under the name S. D. Gottesman. Gottesman was mostly used, however, to mark joint efforts between Kornbluth and Pohl. With the advent of *Stirring*, Kornbluth invented a new pen-name, Cecil Corwin, under which he was to write some of the most original fantasies in print, such as 'Mr Packer Goes to Hell' (*Stirring*, June 1941) and 'The City in the Sofa' (*Cosmic*, July 1941). Kornbluth had four stories in the June 1941 *Stirring*, all solo efforts, as Corwin, W. C. Davies, Kenneth Falconer and S. D. Gottesman.

Damon Knight made his first professional appearance in the February 1941 *Stirring* with 'Resilience'. Knight was only a few months older than Kornbluth, but made nowhere near the same impact at that time. Other members of the group (either wholly or peripherally) who contributed to the Albing venture included James Blish, Robert Lowndes, Walter Kubilius, John B. Michel, Harry Dockweiler, Frederik Pohl and Isaac Asimov.

As was forecast, however, the apparent non-payment for material led to eruptions in the fantasy field and neither Wollheim's or Albert's attempts to smooth things over were to any avail. While the magazines were above average they failed to corner a market and passed away.

Stirring Science Stories is worth recalling for the unique point that it was two magazines in one. The second half, *Stirring Fantasy Fiction*, had its own editorial, contents page and departments. It was the fantasy section that carried the better material, notably Clark Ashton Smith's 'The Coming of the White Worm' (April 1941), and yet it is that name that is forgotten.

And so we reach the summer of 1941, the pinnacle of the sf pulp magazines. In this one period more pulp sf adventure titles were on the news-stands than at any previous time. Just one more American title and a Canadian original magazine were to appear, neither worth more than a passing mention. *Marvel Stories* (by which it was now known) was foundering. A previous companion of the 'weird' variety, *Uncanny Tales* had died in May 1940 after ten issues. (This should not be confused with the Canadian *Uncanny Tales* which survived twenty-one issues between 1940 and 1943. Almost wholly reprinted from US sources, it did carry some new material.) Dated April 1941 a new title, *Uncanny Stories*, materialised. Unimpressive fiction by Ray Cummings, R. De Witt Miller, and F. A. Kummer met with an unenthusiastic response, and only David Keller's 'Speed Will Be My Bride' (reprinted from a 1940 private pamphlet) had any appeal. *Uncanny Stories* disappeared overnight.

The Canadian title was *Eerie Tales*, dated July 1941. Numbered Volume 1, Number 1, there was every intention of it continuing since it began a serial, *The Weird Queen* by prize-fighter Thomas P. Kelley. But it was never concluded because *Eerie* folded. It is worth recalling for a particularly prophetic story, 'The Man Who Killed Mussolini' by Valentine Worth. A timely reminder that Europe was at war.

So, while the United States was enjoying Roosevelt's splendid isolation, its days were numbered. In December 1941 the Pearl Harbour attack occurred, and wartime restrictions were imposed. The resultant paper rationing, ink rationing and metal rationing proved to be the beginning of the end of the pulp magazine. Never again would they hold such sway. So let's send our reader down to his bookstall again in that last peace-time summer, and see just what he would spend on sf magazines currently available, and of US origin only.

There was a total of eighteen current publications, including *Weird Tales* and excluding *Marvel* and *Uncanny*. The general price was fifteen cents, some were ten, others twenty. The total output in one month was as much as $3.15, or about £1.00, a fair outlay in the pre-War days. But the tide was on the turn, and it was time for survival tactics.

6—EBB TIDE

The sudden explosion of sf magazines in 1939 had caught most people by surprise. No one factor led to that mushroom, but several are worth pointing out. Author and scholar, L. Sprague de Camp, in his 1953 book *Science-Fiction Handbook* pointed to the broadcasting of Orson Welles's production of H. G. Wells's *The War of the Worlds*. The radio adaptation by Howard Koch caused many listeners to the Mercury Theatre programme at 8.00 o'clock on the evening of Sunday, 30 October 1938 to really believe a Martian invasion had taken place. When the population in the New York area had recovered, doubtless they had slightly more appreciation for the fantastic and it may well have induced many to test the field.

Marvel and *Amazing* were already enjoying successful sales by this time. *Amazing* had a boost at the 1938 World's Fair held in New York in September. It was decided to bury a Time Capsule, similar to the plethora of miscellania hidden within London's Cleopatra's Needle. The Westinghouse Time Record, as it became known, included a copy of the October 1938 *Amazing* on microfilm. People learning of this may well have investigated the magazine.

However, it is worth remembering that by 1938 a new generation had grown up, introduced to sf by their parents. With two generations reading, it was essential that magazines should cater for young and old alike. Sloane's *Amazing* had become torpid compared with the exciting *Thrilling Wonder* and the literally astounding *Astounding*. Naturally, when Palmer gave *Amazing* a new lease of life, the younger generation flocked to it. *Marvel* came along just at the same time, when the older generation also wanted something refreshing. When both *Amazing*'s and *Marvel*'s sales rocketed, and the other magazines brought out profitable companions, then it was the time for rival publishers to look to their laurels, and they jumped on the bandwaggon.

But most of the later entrants to the field came unstuck. Insufficient capital and lack of originality meant poor sales, and when paper rationing came along the end was inevitable. It was left to the survival of the fittest.

The line-up in December 1941 was already cut back. *Marvel Stories* had folded with its ninth issue in April, although ironically that was one of its best, with two outstanding feature stories, 'Last Secret Weapon' by Polton Cross and 'The Iron God' by Jack Williamson. But too late, *Marvel* had lost much support after its early promise. The publishers were also showing more interest in the growing comic-book field, of which sf comics formed a large part. (I have deliberately avoided this sub-culture except where lines cross, chiefly because several good works have already appeared on the subject such as *The Steranko History of Comics* by James Steranko, published in 1970.)

Wollheim's *Cosmic* had folded, and *Stirring* had but one more issue to run in March 1942, which was surprising since most people thought it had already died. Tremaine's *Comet* had also gone, and *FFM*'s companion *Fantastic Novels* had vanished after five issues (April).

Several editorial changes had taken place, too. Since I have just mentioned the sf comic field, it should come as no surprise to learn that many sf big names were drifting that way, most notably Otto Binder. Nor should it raise eyebrows to discover that Mort Weisinger, who had included the first comic strip in a pulp magazine, should show interest. He had already been associate editor of *College Humour* since 1939, and early in 1941 he received an offer from National Comics to become editor of the various *Superman* comic books, which had begun with *Superman Quarterly* in May 1939. (Incidentally, the *Superman* comics were not the first in the field. *Superman Quarterly* was pipped at the post by *Superworld Comics* illustrated by the stalwart Frank Paul and edited by no less a personage than Hugo

Gernsback.) Weisinger accepted and thereupon left Standard Magazines.

He was replaced by Oscar Jerome Friend, a forty-three-year-old author who wrote in many fields, particularly that of the western. His sf contributions had so far been minor with few exceptions. He was to stay with Standard for three years during which time the infamous 'Sergeant Saturn' editorials grew to immaturity.

Another change was at Blue Ribbon Magazines. Throughout 1940 publisher Silberkleit had grown increasingly dissatisfied with Hornig's handling of the three magazines – which with Blue Ribbon in New York and Hornig in California posed many problems. Silberkleit offered the editorship to Sam Moskowitz, who declined. At that time he received a letter from leading fan Robert Lowndes, who, prompted by Donald Wollheim, had written decrying the current appalling state of sf and proffering his services. After an interview, Lowndes found himself editor of *Future* and *SF Quarterly*. Hornig remained editor of *Science Fiction*, though not for long. With its twelfth issue, and after *Future*'s sixth (Lowndes's second), the two titles were combined under Lowndes' editorship. Hornig departed, and he was soon ensnared by the War. As a pacifist the authorities treated him badly and he vanished entirely from the scene.

One lesser editorial change at this time was at Popular. In November Pohl slipped to the post of assistant editor, with Alden H. Norton in overall charge. However, as previously mentioned, Norton was Popular's chief editor over the sf publications, and in actuality Pohl was still in charge.

Thus, as America entered the War, a total of fourteen magazines from seven publishers were alive and kicking. (To recap, they were: *Amazing* and *Fantastic Adventures* from Ziff–Davis; *Astounding* and *Unknown* from Street & Smith; *Thrilling Wonder*, *Startling* and *Captain Future* from Standard; *Astonishing, Super Science* and *FFM* from Popular; *Future combined with Science Fiction* and *SF Quarterly* from Blue Ribbon/Columbia; *Planet* from Love Romances; and *Weird Tales* from Short Stories.) There was nothing particularly special about any of these in the eyes of the publishers who, after all, had many other titles, several far more popular and lucrative, about which to be concerned. Magazines, therefore, not only had to sell well within the field, but within their own publishing house to stand a chance. With cuts in supplies, publishers had to concentrate on their best-selling titles and fold their weakest, even though the latter may have been viable under normal conditions. Whether a magazine died or survived, it should be borne in mind that no magazine emerged unchanged, and virtually none unscathed from this period. Initially publishers resorted to basic tactics: staggering issues, less pages, smaller type, and with these tactics all the sf magazines weathered the first year of the War. In fact they appeared with remarkable regularity, *FFM* even managing to *increase* its schedule. When the axe fell it came with guillotine-like suddenness and within four months, four titles folded. Simple economics dictated that publishers with more than one sf title in their chain should drop the less successful. In Popular's case this was not so easy. *FFM* probably had the greater following, but more in its favour was that it consisted mostly of reprint material, which was far cheaper to acquire than new fiction. A decision came early in 1943 when Frederik Pohl was called upon to make his contribution to the War effort. Pohl left Popular, and it seemed an appropriate time to wind up his two magazines. Pohl was succeeded in his duties by thirty-one-year-old Finnish editor Ejler Jakobbson, who recalled in a recent letter to me:

Both magazines, however, had already succumbed to wartime paper shortages and my function consisted simply of cleanup. The most memorable incident for me was Fred's handing me a set of partially read proofs on his way out – his last correction consisted of a pencilled circle around a particularly offensive printer's error and a marginal query: 'Printer, what the hell is the meaning of this?!'

The last issues of *Astonishing* and *Super Science* were dated April and May respectively.

April also saw the last issue of *SF Quarterly*. For the same reasons, Columbia closed ranks and preference was given to other publications. *SF Quarterly* was a sad loss nevertheless, since it had carried some excellent long fiction, usually including one sf novel and one fantasy novel in each issue. The magazine had been an outlet for the distinctive writings of artist Hannes Bok (1914-64), publishing his first novel *Starstone World* in the Summer 1942 issue. (Bok's first story had appeared in the February 1942 *Future combined with Science Fiction*, but he had sold many illustrations before this, making a magazine cover first with the December 1939 *Weird Tales* depicting Keller's 'Lords of the Ice'.)

SF Quarterly had also proved a valuable source of reprint material. Silberkleit had bought reprint rights to a number of Ray Cumming's early novels, including *Tarrano the Conqueror* (1925) and *Brigands on the Moon* (1930), which were reprinted in the *Quarterly* and others appeared in *Future*.

The loss of *SF Quarterly* might not have been received so badly had not *Future* also been closed down three months later. It was not even called *Future* by then, although hawkeyes who had followed the volume enumeration would have known it was the same magazine. *Future* changed its name more time than any other magazine with a resultant, only to be expected, confusion, particularly in the 1950s. As previously mentioned Hornig's magazine was combined with Lowndes's from October 1941, as *Future combined with Science Fiction*. One year later it became *Future Fantasy and Science Fiction*. Here Lowndes took up the system used by Wollheim in *Stirring*, of combining sf and fantasy within one issue (although not separating them as Wollheim had). During this time it printed some fine stories like Lowndes's own Lovecraft imitation 'The Leapers', Wollheim's 'Storm Warning' and Damon Knight's 'Devil's Pawn'.

But results proved unsatisfactory and *Future Fantasy* changed its name once again, after just three issues, becoming *Science Fiction Stories* in April 1943. Note the suffix *Stories*. It was not the reappearance of *Science Fiction*, but a continuation of *Future*. However, no casual news-stand browser would know that, and it was hoped sales would perk up. But Columbia had more or less already decided, and before results of the name change could be known, *Science Fiction Stories* folded with the July issue.

The next magazine to go was *Unknown*. The news was a shock to many a fan but it was a fact that had to be faced. Sales were proving disappointing and with paper restrictions it was decided to sacrifice *Unknown* in favour of *Astounding*.

Unknown had undergone several external changes. The first surprise came with the July 1940 issue. Suddenly the magazine was without cover artwork. Fortunately Ed Cartier's wonderfully appropriate drawings continued inside, but for the rest of *Unknown*'s life its cover was merely a contents listing with a tiny drawing alongside each story. Then in December 1940 it went to alternate monthly publishing, and the subheading 'Fantasy Fiction' was brought in. Campbell feared the title *Unknown* was misleading many would-be readers into thinking the magazine was an occult periodical. The subheading proved only temporary, and from the October 1941 issue it became *Unknown Worlds*, and accordingly its size increased to bedsheet size (8½ × 11½ in). Three issues later *Astounding* followed suit, but it was with *Unknown Worlds* that readers had their first taste of a reversion to the old size. Campbell's argument was that it allowed for about 15 per cent more wordage in each issue while at the same time saving paper. But another argument was that, with the legion of pulp magazines on the stalls, a large-size magazine would be displayed separately with the 'slick' titles and thus enjoy better sales. (There was much sense in this. Gernsback had used the same ploy when he first issued *Amazing*, and Palmer followed suit with the first issues of *Fantastic Adventures*. Once that title was established, however, he reverted to pulp.) Unfortunately it did not work out as intended, because the vendors still relegated any sf title to the pulp racks.

Dimensions and title apart, *Unknown*'s fiction was as superb as ever. I must be selective here, but the memorable contents were legion. Suffice it to say that it was here that masterpieces like the *Harold Shea* series by L. Sprague de Camp and Fletcher Pratt were born; L. Ron Hubbard's fascinating 'Fear' and mind-teasing 'Typewriter in the Sky' (wherein a real-life pianist suddenly finds himself ensnared in a story of piracy as it is being written by his friend, and knowing how his friend's stories usually end, tries to outwit the author); and Henry Kuttner's 'The Misguided Halo' and similar short stories. Those disgruntled with Kuttner over the *Marvel* episode were inclined to forgive him after chuckling their way through his *Unknown* contributions. J. Allan Dunn, who appeared in almost every variety of pulp magazine bar science fiction (he was noted for his sea stories), even notched up an *Unknown* tale, two in fact, including a novel *On the Knees of the Gods*. Fans of Fritz Leiber's *Grey Mouser* series found the first five in these pages; and there was a really fine assortment of stories by Lester Del Rey, of which my own favourites are 'The Coppersmith', about the trials and tribulations of an elf in the modern world, and 'Forsaking All Others', wherein a tree dryad sacrifices her immortality for the love of a human.

But all good things come to an end. *Unknown*'s final issue was dated October 1943, and its passing was greatly mourned. There is no denying it left its mark. Thereafter fantasy fiction was never the same.

Just one more magazine succumbed to the war effort, and

it is a miracle it had lasted so long, to May 1944 in fact. By that time, it was almost an anachronism. *Captain Future* saw, in all, a total of seventeen issues for which Edmond Hamilton had written all but two of the lead novels. These two were the work of Dr Joseph Samachson, better known in sf by his pen-name William Morrison, although his *Captain Future* stories were bylined Brett Sterling, as so later were some of Hamilton's. After *Captain Future* folded more adventures appeared in *Startling* up to as late as May 1951, bringing the total to twenty-seven. (Manly Wade Wellman even wrote one.) Curt Newton aside, *Captain Future* did include several shorter new stories, but its best service had been in reprinting longer ones.

In the summer of 1944 eight magazines survived. Having overcome the problems of paper shortages and the loss of authors and artists to the war effort, they should have been ready to master anything. Such was not the case, but at least they were granted a breathing space. It is worth mentioning here, that *Doc Savage* also weathered the War, and had remained monthly. May 1944 saw its 135th issue and it showed no signs of tiring. That was a Street & Smith magazine, yet they sacrificed *Unknown*. Such facts tend to put the sf historian in his place when trying to weigh up the pros and cons of magazines. All the sf magazines that had died had not been true fan magazines but had been evolved by publishers wishing to make a quick dollar, and obviously if a publisher wanted a sf magazine he would have kept it in favour of others. But few publishers were so minded. Economics always came first, and it is a sore fact that sf does not sell as well as say, detective fiction or even general fiction periodicals. Looked at in this way it is surprising that any lived on at all. But, they did.

7—THE SURVIVORS

Eight magazines – eight items of flotsam on the sf sea. Of that eight I have already discussed *Weird Tales* and its declining importance in the field. That five of the other seven survived is not such a surprise, but two were: *Planet Stories* and *Famous Fantastic Mysteries*.

Malcolm Reiss was still in overall charge of *Planet*, but the editorial duties passed to Wilbur S. Peacock from the Fall 1942 issue. Between them they made *Planet* a thoroughly lively magazine, and by then Reiss's efforts were bearing fruit, particularly with fiction. *Planet*, as I have said, was an all-interplanetary magazine, and while this formed but a small part of the range of sf, it nevertheless caused several authors to experiment and create, so that while the usual run-of-the-mill space adventure still appeared, readers could always expect the unexpected.

Planet's major claim to fame is undoubtedly Ray Bradbury, although it did not discover him [Alden H. Norton bought his first sale, 'Pendulum', for *Super Science Stories* (November 1941)], and his best contributions appeared after the period covered by this volume. But it was his *Planet* tales that proved to be his most experimental sf (as were his *Weird Tales* stories in *that* genre). Stories like 'Morgue Ship' and 'Lazarus, Come Forth' were the first steps in the direction that would lead to 'The Million Year Picnic' (Summer 1946), the first of his *Martian Chronicle* stories.

Probably the two most valuable contributors in *Planet*'s early period were Leigh Brackett, the wife of Edmond Hamilton, and the mystery writer, Fredric Brown. Brackett's efforts were among the first in that hybrid sub-genre – interplanetary sword and sorcery which are currently numerous. Robert E. Howard, the creator of the Conan stories, had given the impetus to these with his novel-length *Almuric*, serialised posthumously in *Weird Tales* from May 1939 (one of the last sf serials it was to publish). Leigh Brackett then took up the challenge. Her first appearance in *Planet* (her fourth in all) was with 'The Stellar Legion' (Winter 1940) and thereafter adventure tumbled upon adventure. She even teamed up with Ray Bradbury for a Conan imitation fantasy 'Lorelei of the Red Mist' (again Summer 1946).

The late Fredric Brown was a particularly accomplished mystery writer. He first brought these talents to the sf field with a short piece, 'Not Yet the End' in the Winter 1941 *Captain Future*. Two stories later his masterpiece 'The Star Mouse' appeared in the February 1942 *Planet*, the tale of a German mouse *en route* for the moon. Although an infrequent contributor, his stories were invariably the high spot of an issue.

'The Vizigraph', *Planet*'s letter column, is of particular interest. Here editor and fan mucked in together, and it was no surprise to find one of Peacock's replies far longer than the original letter. As Robert Lowndes recalls:

Reiss was sincere and urbane; Wilbur enjoyed taking off his coat and being one of the crowd. Despite the sharpness of some of his comment, there's no indication that anyone was squelched to the point of not writing again, or not answering back.[6]

Remember that this was in wartime, and such comradeship was a valuable asset to the morale of sf fans called up into the Forces.

Peacock remained editor until the Fall 1945 issue, when his place was taken briefly by Chester Whitehorne. Whitehorne's influence on the magazine was negligible, Reiss still being in command, and his real contribution to sf (albeit minor) was not to come for another eight years.

Famous Fantastic Mysteries had dared to go monthly from June to December 1942, and this proved almost fatal. Nineteen forty-three saw only three issues, one in March, then nothing till September, when it became quarterly, and the third issue appeared in December. It underwent a policy change at the same time. Up until the end of 1942, *FFM* had regularly reprinted from the Munsey pulps, and legendary names like Francis Stevens, J. U. Giesy, and George Allen England had graced its pages. These ceased in 1943. The March issue carried John Hawkins's *Ark of Fire* which had only recently been serialised in *American Weekly* (1938). Thereafter it featured novels that had hitherto usually only appeared in book form, starting with John Taine's 1930 work *The Iron Star* (which shows that the trend in lost race novels was maintained). In this way William Hope Hodgson's *The Ghost Pirates* was revived in the March 1944 issue, followed by his superb *The Boats of the 'Glen Carrig'* (June 1945). Hodgson had been all but forgotten by this time, but thanks to the efforts of fan H. C. Koenig his name was not lost, and since then this twenty-six years dead author began to receive the accolades he deserved. Although, even Koenig would find it hard to believe that *three* different British paperback firms would bring out Hodgson's *Carnacki* simultaneously in 1974.

FFM's particular claim to fame was their use of the brilliant artwork of Virgil Finlay. Finlay (1914-71) had been a discovery of *Weird Tales*, but later was employed by *American Weekly*. When *FFM* began reprinting Merritt's work, Merritt (the editor of *American Weekly*) used his influence to have Finlay illustrate the pieces. Thus began a sensational partnership. Frank R. Paul may be the dean of sf artists, and he may have the edge on Finlay when portraying machinery, but in quality, imagination and superlative execution of art, Finlay had no peer, and his human figures were light years ahead of Paul's. Finlay's fine line and cross-hatch work did as much to attract readers to *FFM* as the fiction. So much so, that in its August 1941 issue *FFM* offered a portfolio of Finlay's drawings from the magazine on individual sheets of high-grade paper selling for sixty cents, or with a year's subscription to the magazine for just one dollar. (A repeat offer was made in 1943, so doubtless Finlay did much to keep *FFM* on the road.) When Finlay joined the army in 1943, *FFM* had to look elsewhere for an artist capable of imitating Finlay, and within their own establishment they found Lawrence Sterne Stevens ('Lawrence'), a pulp veteran who as an old timer had mastered the 'engraving' technique of realism revived by Finlay. He accomplished the feat so well that portfolios of his work were also offered.

FFM might seem the anachronism of the field, but occasional fan polls often voted it the most popular magazine, and it also led in circulation at one time.

Standard Magazines had gallantly kept two sf titles alive, *Thrilling Wonder* and *Startling*. Under Weisinger *Wonder* had achieved a monthly schedule, but under Friend it reverted to every other month, alternating with *Startling*. This was the case throughout 1942, but in 1943 they found themselves on a quarterly schedule (even after *Captain Future* folded), which remained in force until late 1946.

Friend left Standard at the end of 1944, and Samuel Merwin took over. In the sf field Merwin, who was thirty-four, had only been seen in print with two articles about aircraft of the future (in *Thrilling Wonder* during 1943), and one story, 'The Scourge Below', in October 1939. To the sf fan, therefore, he was even more a mystery man than Friend. Merwin was the only son of Samuel Merwin Snr (1874-1936), a noted writer on American history. His literary talents were certainly inherited by his son whose own fiction is highly readable. As for his editing, one immediate change took place. The 'Thrills in Science' feature in *Startling*, begun by Weisinger and kept alive by Friend, was discontinued. Merwin had every capability for continuing it, but this was obviously not his intention. He kept the 'Sergeant Saturn' editorials, but only for as long as was necessary. Merwin had his own ideas and was determined to put them into action, but he had to wait till the War was over, and that must wait for another book.

This leaves three other survivors to be discussed: two sf magazines and one fantasy/sf. I shall leave *Astounding* till last and look first at the phenomenal success of Ray Palmer's magazines.

Much is said of John Campbell in sf histories because in hindsight he did so much to propagate new and original ideas and to point sf into novel directions. No one can deny his title as 'The Father of Modern Science Fiction'. But it is easy to forget that at the time Campbell suffered much criticism for his apparent ruthless sterilisation of *Astounding* of the old ideas and themes. While we have much to thank him for now, readers at the time were not all in favour of the trend. Many thought Campbell would constrict sf rather than let it live freely and follow its own course. That science fiction did not suffocate shows how much readers underestimated the power and imagination of Campbell's stable of authors. And the popularity of *Astounding*'s rival magazines shows just how many readers preferred the old-guard sf. For pure entertainment value, excitement and adventure with little regard for originality, none could surpass *Amazing Stories* and *Fantastic Adventures*. And for sensation seeking there was no one like Raymond A. Palmer.

The instant success of the new look *Amazing* meant that the magazine had been able to resume monthly publication from October 1938, and so it remained till September 1943. *Fantastic* had been published once every two months for its first four issues, then had a run of six monthly issues before a slight irregularity in the winter of 1940-1. But from May 1941 to August 1943 it, too, became monthly, meaning that Palmer was producing twenty-four issues a year, more at that time than any other editor. Concurrently Friend had only sixteen and Campbell eighteen. Only in 1940 had Weisinger exceeded this with twenty-eight issues, but even here it must be remembered that *Startling* and *Captain Future* included reprints, and *Captain Future* was taken up much by Hamilton's novels. If *Amazing* did feature an occasional 'Classic Reprint' it was not in the same proportion. If one also takes total pages into account, Palmer's two titles contained as many as Weisinger's four when spread over a year. Overall Palmer was publishing more sf than any other at this time.

Since Ziff–Davis was the only sf publisher that was Chicago based editorially Palmer was building his own stable of local authors, many of whom were friends from his fan days. While he continued to publish established authors, particularly Robert Moore Williams, Eando Binder (whose *Adam Link* robot series was one of the most popular the magazine ever published) and John Russell Fearn, more and more of the magazine was made up of stories by the local contingent, with one notable exception: Nelson S. Bond.

Palmer's stable took shape immediately. As early as 1939 he had found Don Wilcox and David Vern. Wilcox remained a major contributor for the ensuing decade and was capable of producing very good fiction, but was prone to hack work. His first appearance was with 'The Pit of Death' (*Amazing*, July 1939), but a far better story from these early days is 'The Voyage That Lasted 600 Years' (*Amazing*, October 1940), a memorable generation starship story too often overlooked these days in favour of Robert Heinlein's 'Universe' (*Astounding*, May 1941) which Wilcox anticipated by several months.Vern had no fiction published under his real name, but is remembered for his most prolific pseudonym David V. Reed, which he first appeared under with 'Where Is Roger Davis?' (*Amazing*, May 1939).

J. R. Fearn was not the only British author *Amazing* featured. Another infrequent but successful contributor was William F. Temple, who had decided to try for the greater financial awards of the American market, a step he was frequently exhorted to take by Fearn. His first sale to Palmer was 'Mr Craddock's Amazing Experience', an intriguing short story of a man who regresses to childhood but retains his adult awareness. His polished style was a strong contrast against many of Palmer's regulars. Temple's next effort, 'The 4-Sided Triangle' was immediately recognised as a winner. It was given the cover spot of the November 1939 issue and won the fifty dollars bonus for being placed first by readers' votes. Fearn, who had also just won the bonus for his story 'The Man from Hell' in the concurrent issue of *Fantastic Adventures* wrote jubilantly to Temple saying: 'It takes we British guys to put it over, huh?' With the intervention of the War, however, Temple temporarily dropped out of sight.

Over the next few years more new names appeared: David Wright O'Brien, William P. McGivern, Berkeley Livingston, Chester S. Geier, William Hamling and Leroy Yerxa. These formed the bulk of Palmer's early coterie, and were all astonishingly prolific, particularly O'Brien, who besides appearing regularly under his own name, maintained a healthy number of sales under the alter-egos John York Cabot and Duncan Farnsworth, amongst others. As an example, in the twenty months from January 1941 to August 1942 he had fifty-seven stories in the two magazines including four in the June 1942 *Fantastic* alone. We have the War to blame for cutting short O'Brien's career and life, and although several stories appeared posthumously it is ironic to think that probably the last story he would have seen in print was 'I'll See You Again'.

One peculiarity of the Ziff–Davis chain was the use of housenames. These are pseudonyms used by more than one author. (This practice was not restricted to Ziff–Davis. Standard had Will Garth for instance, and the Futurians used a vast menagerie of house-names for their various publications. But the variety of proliferation was not so profound as with Ziff– Davis.) In the sf magazines it was instigated by Palmer, mostly as his own personal pen-names at first, and then turned over to other authors. Names like Henry Gade, G. H. Irwin and Morris J. Steele. But the most ubiquitous names were Alexander Blade, Gerald Vance and P. F. Costello, names used on both fiction and features. Alexander Blade was introduced in the May 1941 *Amazing* with 'The Strange Adventure of Victor MacLeigh', a story probably the work of David Vern. The next appearance though, in September, 'Dr Loudon's Armageddon', was by Louis H. Sampliner. Thereafter nearly all of Palmer's coterie used the pen-name for a variety of fathomable and unfathomable reasons. We may never know to our satisfaction just who was responsible for some of these stories, and perhaps, after all is said and done, that might not be such a bad thing, since seldom did an author's best work appear under one of these ghost names. But they are an early example of Palmer's secret delight in confusing and tantalising. For instance he would enjoy giving substance to pen-names by including biographies of them in the 'Meet the Author' slot, sometimes even including a 'gag' photo. This he did with his own alias A. R. Steber (see *Amazing*, March 1945), to Robert Bloch's Tarleton Fiske (*Fantastic*, August 1943) and to David Vern's Peter Horn (*Amazing*, March 1940). One learned early never to quite know when to believe Palmer or not.

To Palmer's credit though, whenever he received a good story from outside of his coterie he had the sense to publish it, and thus odd gems would often crop up, such as John Beynon Harris's 'Phoney Meteor' (*Amazing*, March 1941) and Eric Frank Russell's 'Mr Wisel's Secret' (*Amazing*, February 1942).

After about a year *Fantastic Adventures* began to find its stride. Its early issues were a mishmash of fantasy heroics and sf blunderings, but Palmer, seeing the success of rival *Unknown* with its humorous fantasies, decided to go out of his way to include such funnies in *Fantastic*. As an example he utilised the work of Nelson Bond, probably the most underrated and yet most influential of fantasy authors.

Nelson Slade Bond, born in Scranton, Pennsylvania on Monday 23 November 1908, had been employed in the public relations field when he began to make fiction sales. Today he is better known as a philatelist and a skilled bridge player, a strange twist of destiny for one who from his earliest sales showed he possessed an exceptionally vivid imagination combined with a wicked sense of humour. He was first noticed in the sf field with 'Down the Dimensions' in the April 1937 *Astounding*, having sold several stories to Street & Smith for companion magazines. But he scored premature fame in November that year with the appearance of a whimsical fantasy 'Mr Mergenthwirker's Lobblies', in the slick magazine *Scribner's*. Instantly acclaimed it has since been produced for radio and television on various occasions and appeared in many anthologies and reprints.

While Bond continued to write science fiction, it was evident that fantasy was his real forte. Often his sf would verge on the fanciful, and few of his serious sf efforts are remembered. One particular exception is his series about Meg, who becomes the priestess of her clan in a future set after the fall of civilisation, but fails in her duties through her discovery of love. The first story, 'The Priestess Who Rebelled' (*Amazing*, October 1939), was an excellent piece of writing and was followed by a provocative sequel, 'The Judging of the Priestess' (*Fantastic Adventures*, April 1940). The superiority of this series was proved when the third story, 'Magic City' was purchased by Campbell and appeared in *Astounding*!

But as a general rule much of Bond's sf was written on the same witty plane as his fantasy, and this was what Palmer wanted. He set about acquiring Bond's manuscripts, and it was his second story that Palmer published that showed the way for subsequent authors. With 'The Amazing Invention of Wilberforce Weems' Bond established a trend for giving stories ridiculous titles, showing also that he could write the Thorne Smith-style fiction Campbell was emulating in *Unknown*. In this tale Weems gives a child he is baby-sitting a foul concoction of medicines in an endeavour to keep it quiet. The resultant potion, however, has the property of endowing its taker with instant knowledge from any book just by applying the book to the head. With the next *Fantastic* (November 1939), Bond introduced his memorable character Lancelot Biggs, a rather cracked space adventurer with a knack for involvement in crazy situations. Soon this style was not to be kept exclusively for Palmer and we find 'The Unusual Romance of Ferdinand Pratt' in no less a publication than *Weird Tales* (where later Biggs adventures would also appear), and 'Cartwright's Camera' in *Unknown*. Bond would not restrict himself though, and often *Unknown* would carry his serious fantasies such as 'Take My Drum to England' (August 1941).

The popularity of Bond's stories could only mean one thing – imitations. Palmer's stable were always willing to oblige, and hence the *Fantastic Adventures*' school of slightly 'nutty' fiction was born. David Wright O'Brien was perhaps the earliest to succeed with 'The Strange Voyage of Hector Squinch' in the August 1940 issue. He then introduced the trend to *Amazing* with 'Skidmore's Strange Experiment' (January 1941). O'Brien had also collaborated with William P. McGivern, who is today rated a worthy thriller writer, and McGivern went out of his way to imitate Bond. Thus in 1941 we find McGivern's byline on stories like 'The Masterful Mind of Mortimer Meek', 'The Quandary of Quantus Quaggle', 'Sidney, the Screwloose Robot' and 'Rewbarb's Remarkable Radio', as well as a series of stories which began with 'Tink Takes a Hand'. Thereby Robert Bloch, renowned for his irrepressible sense of humour, who had also sold to *Unknown*, began his own series of stories about layabout Lefty Feep with 'Time Wounds All Heels' (*Fantastic Adventures*, April 1942). Bloch's Feep stories typify this style of fiction, and show every evidence of being influenced by Bond, but Bloch's own clever and original embellishments stand out. He brought back his pen-name, Tarleton Fiske, to confuse readers by writing both serious and strong sf like 'Almost Human', side by side with zany tales like 'The Mystery of the Creeping Underwear'. Thereafter imitation Feep stories often appeared, such as Leroy Yerxa's *Freddie Funk* yarns, and throughout the early 1940s *Fantastic Adventures* provided considerable light relief, particularly in the War period. The fiction might not have been as sophisticated as *Unknown*'s, but it was still enjoyable.

Fantastic also published serious fantasy, of which O'Brien and Yerxa were the best exponents. It was a great blow to the field that by 1946 both these authors would be dead.

The effect of the War on sf was manifold. It stimulated plots to which Palmer seemed particularly receptive. Thus his magazines contain stories entitled: 'Nazi, Are You Resting Well?' by Leroy Yerxa (*Fantastic Adventures*, July 1943), 'Hitler's Right Eye' by Lee Francis (*Fantastic Adventures*, June 1944), 'The Ghost That Haunted Hitler' by William P. McGivern (*Fantastic Adventures*, December 1942) and 'They Forgot to Remember Pearl Harbour' by P. F. Costello (*Amazing*, June 1942).

There is a school of thought that the pulp magazines are a valuable source of social commentary, and those who subscribe to the idea might find the September 1943 *Amazing* of particular interest. Almost all of the pulp periodicals for that month carried covers built around 'women in war work', emphasised with a hand-held torch emblem captioned 'Women War Workers'. Robert Gibson Jones's cover showed a blonde in overall and peaked cap observing a saboteur in an aircraft factory which illustrated 'War Worker 17' by Frank Patton (Palmer himself).

To boost the morale of troops Palmer also produced a remarkable issue of *Amazing* composed of stories written entirely by authors in the forces with letters from the troops. This special issue appeared in September 1944. Actually Palmer took some liberties, attributing ranks to pseudonyms, and even including his own alias amongst the group. Nevertheless it gives an idea of the range of contributors, and for the record the fiction line-up was as follows:

Star Base X	Private Robert Moore Williams
The Thinking Cap	Sergeant William P. McGivern
Private Prune Speaking	Corporal David Wright O'Brien
Professor Thorndyke's Mistake	Sergeant P. F. Costello
Dolls of Death	Private E. K. Jarvis
Weapon for a Wac	Sergeant Morris J. Steele
Double Cross on Mars	Sergeant Gerald Vance
Warburton's Invention	Private Russell Storm
Overlord of Venus	Lieutenant W. Lawrence Hamling
Matches and Kings	Corporal John York Cabot
I'll See You Again	Corporal Duncan Farnsworth

You may well be thinking that this appears to be a long list, especially at a time when paper shortages were reducing issues. But as was typical with Palmer, he would never conform to standards. When everyone else was reducing the number of pages, Palmer increased them. Ordinarily the two titles ran at

148 pulp-size pages each. From April 1942 *Fantastic* increased
to 244 pages, and *Amazing* followed suit in August. This remained so until May 1943 when they dropped to 212 pages,
and later to 180 pages. This was apparently achieved by sacri-
ficing certain of Ziff–Davis's titles in favour of Palmer's. Such a
rare occurrence in the sf world emphasises the faith that William
Ziff had in Palmer as a money-spinner. Neither would it be the
first time it was to happen, as will be shown in 1947.

Palmer's ability to seek out sensation never seemed to leave
him. It was this that made his magazines so lively, and despite
all that was happening in Campbell's titles, Palmer's magazines
were invariably circulation leaders. For instance in the special
anniversary issue of *Thrilling Wonder* (June 1939) Weisinger
had acquired some fiction by the two sons of Tarzan's creator,
Edgar Rice Burroughs: John Coleman and Hulbert. Palmer went
one better. The January 1941 *Amazing* carried a new novel, *John
Carter and the Giant of Mars*, by Edgar Rice Burroughs himself.
The March issue contained 'The City of Mummies' and then
Fantastic carried 'Slaves of the Fish Men'. In all, the two
magazines published thirteen 'ERB' stories up to and including
'Skeleton Men of Jupiter' in the February 1943 *Amazing*. A
fourteenth story written at the time, 'Savage Pellucidar', was
apparently lost and was finally published in the November
1963 *Amazing*.

Some doubt has been cast on Palmer's actually securing work
from Burroughs Senior, and fans knowing Palmer's whims for
practical jokes suspected that many of these stories were the
work of Burroughs's two sons. The allegations, however, have
never been substantially proved as far as I know.

Fiction aside, Palmer's magazines carried several interesting
features worth at least a mention. For instance from its July
1939 issue, *Fantastic Adventures* carried a pictorial feature
'Romance of the Elements', giving historical and scientific facts
on every element from actinium to tungsten. 'Scientific Mysteries' was the name of a small informative department in
Amazing, started by Joseph J. Millard in the October 1940 issue
with 'The Fate of the Mammoth'. From June 1942 though the
series was taken over entirely by L. Taylor Hansen. The practice
grew in both magazines to print a vast number of small 'filler'
items all painstakingly credited in the table of contents.

In 1945, Palmer really went to town. The March 1945
Amazing carried 'I Remember Lemuria!' by Richard S. Shaver
and with that the Shaver Mystery began, marking the start of

Palmer's move away from sf towards the occult. However, since the shaver 'scandal' came to a head in 1947, I shall leave the details until the next volume. Suffice it to say that unlike any editor before or since, Palmer really knew how to get the most sensation and fanaticism out of a subject, but never quite knew when to stop. And with Shaver those floodgates really opened.

In the wake of Palmer's headline activities, Campbell's methodical editorship seems almost tame. The Campbell/Palmer relationship is reminiscent of Aesop's fable about the race between the hare and the tortoise and how the tortoise eventually won. Palmer jumped hectically from one scoop to the next, only finally to burn up his energies and veer off into obscure directions. Campbell, by his determination and dogged persistence, proved to be the winner. As I mentioned with *Unknown*, *Astounding* also tried a large-size format in 1942, but reverted to pulp in May 1943. With 160 pages this was by then more than either *Amazing* or *Fantastic*, as well as having twelve regular issues a year.

And then the unprededented happened. With the November 1943 issue *Astounding* went digest size, and fans, hitherto sceptical that it would prove a disaster, were satisfied that they were not being cheated. There were a growing number of pocket-sized magazines on the book-stands, the majority of them were considered to be of a high standard. It was hoped that *Astounding* might also reach a new audience by going digest.

The term 'digest' had been applied to these magazines ever since the appearance of *Reader's Digest* in 1922. Its original meaning was that the magazine reprinted fiction and features from other periodicals in an abbreviated and more *digestable* form. Other publications, such as *Science Digest* and *Writer's Digest*, followed suit, but there were few all-fiction magazines. The pulp magazine remained the norm during the 1930s and into the 1940s. Only a few semi-professional magazines had dabbled in that format, such as Crawford's *Marvel Tales*, so *Astounding* was the first professional magazine to make the change. When the blight settled on the pulp industry in the early 1950s and it was digest or die, Campbell could rightly have sat back and smugly rubbed his hands in pleasure at his foresight – but he was not that kind of man.

The magazines suffered in no way by going pocket-size. All its sections and features remained, plus the regular article, book reviews and as much fiction as possible. During its bedsheet days *Astounding* had even acquired an assistant editor in the shape of Catherine Tarrant, but she disappeared after the first digest issue, only to reappear in March 1949. Indeed, she stayed with *Astounding* until February 1972.

Those who were familiar with the late P. Schuyler Miller's regular book review column, 'The Reference Library', which was part of the very backbone of *Astounding*, would find it conspicuous by its absence in the 1940s. It did not start until 1951. Until then irregular book reviews appeared by a multitude of reviewers including Campbell himself, Anthony Boucher, L. Sprague de Camp, Robert Heinlein, Willy Ley and Milton Rothman.

Astounding was still publishing the best fiction. With the entry of the USA into the Second World War, Campbell found himself in trouble. His regular contributors were all called up – Asimov, Heinlein, Sturgeon, even Williamson – just when they were turning out their best. Heinlein, of course, was perhaps the biggest name just before the War with stories like 'If This Goes On –' and 'Methusaleh's Children'. Van Vogt was a close second as a result of his powerful novel, *Slan*. But with these temporarily out of action Campbell had again to find capable authors. *Astounding* was virtually boycotted by the regular pulp writers, but Campbell knew where to look.

Henry Kuttner had produced several brilliant stories for *Unknown*, but as an sf writer he was still considered a hack. Campbell therefore disguised Kuttner and his wife Catherine Moore under the pen-name of Lewis Padgett, and another chapter of sf history was opened. The Kuttners approached sf in the *Unknown* style and began a series of humorous stories, initially about robots ('Deadlock', 'The Twonky' and 'Piggy Bank') and then moved into other themes. As they found their stride the humour became more grim, the stories more effective, and February 1943 saw 'Mimsy Were the Borogoves', an exceptionally startling story about toys from the future in the hands of children from the present.

Besides the Padgett stories, the Kuttners were also writing for *Astounding* as Lawrence O'Donnell with more classics like 'Clash by Night' and its sequel 'Fury', extremely vivid tales of Venusian adventure.

When it was eventually discovered that both O'Donnell and Padgett were the Kuttners, fans forgave Henry all his past indiscretions (as if it was necessary), and he was thereafter accorded the just praise he deserved.

Since *Astounding* was the top-paying market in the sf field, Campbell never had any trouble recruiting new writers, but in order to assist his stable and extract the best from them he would very often suggest ideas to them. Probably the most famous example is that of Isaac Asimov's 'Nightfall', inspired by Campbell from lines by a poem by Ralph Waldo Emerson. That story of a planet with near eternal day and the catastrophic results when nightfall does come, appeared in the September 1941 issue, and today, over thirty years later, is still reckoned as among Asimov's best stories and nearly always heads the list of all-time sf greats. Another method of recruiting fiction was to commission an artist to paint a striking scene to be used on a cover and then send that to an author to write a story around. There was nothing new in this. It was a system adopted unerringly by Mort Weisinger for *Thrilling Wonder*, and had resulted in such coups as Henry Kuttner's 'Beauty and the Beast' (April 1940). Weisinger, however, was content to let the author jump in at the deep end, whereas Campbell would give unfailing aid. His continuous striving for originality, although at first it made him unpopular, ultimately reaped rich rewards.

During the War Campbell was fortunate in that the occasional story by Asimov, Heinlein, Russell and de Camp still trickled through to him, but he did discover other new names in this period. The October 1942 issue gave birth to George O. Smith, a thirty-one-year-old radio engineer, who employed his knowledge on a series of stories about a radio-relay station starting with 'QRM – Interplanetary'. Raymond F. Jones had first been seen in the September 1941 issue with 'Test of the Gods', wherein three men who crash-land on Venus pass themselves off as gods to their native rescuers. All goes well until the natives expect them to pass the test of the gods; and he produced other such pearls as 'Fifty Million Monkeys' (October 1943) and 'Pacer' (May 1943).

In 1942 Campbell welcomed Murray Leinster back to science fiction. A real doyen of sf, Leinster was a successful writer of westerns and other fiction under his real name of Will F. Jenkins. Starting in the October 1942 *Astounding*, he began to turn out a fresh stream of new and original sf, totally removed from his previous efforts, which included 'First Contact', 'The Power' and 'A Logic Named Joe' (the latter concerns a robot that goes to the ultimate extreme in helping people), all of which proved Jenkins's adaptability.

Simak was also proving a boon to Campbell. His award-winning *City* series, which plots the future progress of the Earth as humans leave and only intelligent dogs and robots remain, commenced in the May 1944 issue. And then there was Fritz Leiber whose *Gather, Darkness!* was serialised in the May, June and July 1943 issues. A classic post-atomic culture story, with all the trappings of sf and all the style of fantasy, it showed Leiber's adeptness at working in both elements.

During the period 1943 to 1947 *Astounding* was the only magazine to regularly publish serials, which must be some sign as to its stability. *Amazing* carried two serials in 1943 but then nothing appeared till 1948. The serials, once a major part of magazines, had all but been replaced by major lead novels, such as those regularly featured in *Startling*, although many of those, especially Kuttner's, were science fantasy. *Astounding*'s serials were hard-core sf and provided a wealth of idea and adventure. Eleven in all appeared between January 1943 and March 1946 (plus George O. Smith's *Pattern for Conquest* which began in the March issue). They were: *Opposites – React* by Will Stewart; *The Weapon Makers* by A. E. van Vogt; *Gather, Darkness!* by Leiber; *Judgement Night* by C. L. Moore; *The Winged Man* by Edna Mayne Hull (Mrs van Vogt); *Renaissance* by Raymond F. Jones; *Nomad* by George O. Smith (as Wesley Long); *Destiny Times Three* by Leiber; *World of Ā* by van Vogt; *The Mule* by Asimov (part of the *Foundation* series); and *The Fairy Chessman* by Padgett. Had any other magazine carried just one of these it could have felt satisfied, but to scoop them all was an honourable achievement.

The story has often been told of how Campbell ran into trouble with the authorities during the War. He had been requested to soft-pedal stories about atomic warfare in the cause of security. To Campbell this was nonsense, and it came to a head with the publication of 'Deadline' by the late Cleve Cartmill in the March 1944 issue. Not a particularly exceptional story as sf went, 'Deadline' dealt with an agent's attempts to stop an atomic bomb's detonation. Military Intelligence descended on Campbell and Cartmill, charging them with a violation of security. Cartmill proved that all his facts were culled from public libraries, and eventually the scare was over. Thereafter, *Astounding*'s readers were justifiably proud that a science fiction story had caused such a stir, and it definitely moved sf one more rung up the ladder of respectability.

March 1946 and what do we have? Eight sf magazines of varying degrees of maturity and quality. A respectable *Astounding*, with its stable of stimulating authors. A Shaver-mad *Amazing* plus its more pacific companion, *Fantastic Adventures*. An aspiring *Thrilling Wonder* with a more juvenile *Startling*, both striving for maturity but currently dogged by the stigma of their Earle K. Bergey covers which had fostered the description 'bug-eyed monsters'. *Famous Fantastic Mysteries*, home of the scientific romance, and *Planet Stories*, the haven of space travel. And the senescent, and somewhat dour, *Weird Tales*.

Eight survivors, four of whom had been around before the boom, and four who gained their impetus as a result of it. Had the War continued many more titles would have disappeared. With great relief, however, it was over. The publishing industry could breathe again, and as paper restrictions were relieved it would be seen that the period after 1943 was only a temporary hiatus in the science fiction boom. By 1947 the snowball would start to roll again towards an Everest in 1953-54, against which 1939 was but a Matterhorn.

By 1945 the science fiction magazine had set its own patterns and trends. It was no longer the Gernsbackian purveyor of 'science taught through fiction'. Instead it was essentially the scientific adventure, ranging from the juvenilistic adventures of *Planet Stories* and *Amazing* to the scientific and political prognostications of *Astounding*. Yet, in the eyes of the general public, the standard of respectability that Campbell waved cast a meagre shadow indeed compared to the aura of juvenility suggested by the gaudy covers and luscious titles of the other publications. Indeed, *Astounding* aside, the fiction in *Thrilling Wonder*, and to a point even *Planet Stories*, was becoming more sensible. Primarily this was as a result of Campbell's special team of authors expanding to other markets, but one cannot forget that the cataclysmic finale to the Second World War had revealed just what horrors science could achieve. The public were suddenly made aware that there just might be something in science fiction, and the authors were quick to respond. Immediate postwar magazines would see a flood of 'post-atomic' warning stories, which were far removed from the prewar adventure romance. In hindsight it would appear that Campbell had loaded the gun of respectability, but the Second World War had fired it.

If the 1939 boom had done anything it had sorted out the men from the boys, and it had forced magazines to be individual. Frederik Pohl's magazines were of a far better quality than, say,

Amazing, but Palmer was miles ahead in gimmickry and sensationalism. By 1945, thanks to the efforts of John Campbell and his team, both sf and fantasy had matured. It was still growing, and still looking for new directions. If one boom could do this much for sf, what would the next do? But that question needs another book for the answer. For the moment just recall these years when men, fighting for their country and their lives, could look forward to their few days rest and escape into their private world of science fiction.

8—INTERNATIONAL GROWTH

The course of sf runs so much in the United States, with Britain a poor second, that it is difficult to fit other countries into the scheme of things, but I am determined not to neglect them even if my coverage will be but brief.

It is strange to imagine that the USA's nearest neighbour, Canada, had placed a ban on the importation of pulp magazines, and consequently a hash of Canadian reprint editions appeared. These were all styled on the American issues, with the same names, and only a few like *Eerie Tales* and *Uncanny Tales* carried any new fiction, mostly donated by good-hearted Americans. The consequence of all this is that collectors must be careful when hunting editions of American magazines to ensure that they do not mistake a Canadian reprint for the real thing.

One notable exception was the Canadian *Science Fiction* which saw six issues between October 1941 and June 1942. The magazine was a rather attractive large-size production, with sixty-four pages, selling for twenty-five Canadian cents. The covers were the work of Canadian artists, but the editor's (William Brown-Forbes's) claim that the magazine contained Canadian authors and artists only was rather false as it reprinted from Columbia's *Science Fiction* and *Future Fiction*, also using some of the illustrations. However, some of the original artwork was dropped and replaced with new drawings, presumably by Canadian artists. Covers often illustrated a story that had not been so honoured in the original US magazine, such as 'Science from Syracuse' by Polton Cross.

More important for fans in foreign countries, who could not understand English, was the appearance of three foreign language magazines, in Argentina, Sweden and France. The Argentine's

Narraciones Terrorificas, virtually all reprint, was born in 1939 and lasted until 1950. It attempted to keep to a monthly schedule and achieved this goal remarkably often considering the circumstances.

But most surprising of all was the regular *weekly* publication from Sweden: *Jules Verne Magasinet*, with the first issue dated 16 October 1940. This magazine was all reprint, but this was fine for the Swedes who kept the magazine going for 331 issues, until 1947. The stories came mainly from the Fictioneers, Standard and Ziff–Davis magazines, John Russell Fearn and Edmond Hamilton (especially with *Captain Future*) being the two authors appearing most frequently, along with Robert Bloch, Malcolm Jameson, Jack Williamson, William McGivern and Robert Moore Williams. The covers were colourful and usually fair copies of Ziff–Davis originals by Fuqua and Krupa, with those artists being credited inside. Occasional original covers by Swedish artist Eugen Semitjov were used, chiefly for Thornton Ayre stories. The magazine had 64 pages and was originally digest-size but grew to pulp's $6\frac{1}{2} \times 9\frac{1}{4}$ in. Although very attractive, the occasional additional interior illustrations of very poor standard marred the production, contrasting oddly with the American artwork. Another strange juxtaposition was the inclusion of non-fiction articles on boxing and athletics, plus a whole clutch of American comic strips such as *Superman*, which ran consistently on the inside covers in full colour, *Batman* and Alex Raymond's *Jungle Jim* on the back cover. No doubt this news will set the comic fans and dealers clamouring for copies but they are likely to be unlucky since copies are extremely scarce. Only three complete sets are known to exist in Sweden, and I am indebted to Fearn completist, Phil Harbottle, for much of the detail of content. As time went by it featured more westerns and detective yarns (again of US origin) and the title was supplanted by *Veckans Aventyr* (*Adventures of the Week*) in July 1941.

Perhaps the most ambitious and astonishing achievement was the appearance of *Conquetes* from France. Edited by George H. Gallet, the first issue of this proposed weekly periodical was dated 24 August 1939. Gallet had recently been on a visit to England where he met several fans and authors, and Walter Gillings, editor of *Tales of Wonder*. An arrangement was made whereby Gillings acted as agent for the translation rights to material which had appeared in *Tales of Wonder*, as well as other material by the same authors. Two issues appeared before

Hitler's policies put an end to it. Festus Pragnell's *Green Men of Graypec* was serialised and other material had been scheduled. John Russell Fearn went so far as to arrange to have his new stories simultaneously translated into French, and it seems likely that with the addition of original French material Gallet's magazine might well have brought about a healthy development of sf in France. Gallet did succeed in launching sf in France after the War with the novel series *Le Rayon Fantastique*.

In the next volume it will be seen how more and more countries began their own sf publications and how the spark of originality began to flare. One must remember that few foreign fans were able to obtain English language magazines, and they were reliant on translations for their share of the cake. It is odd how in France particularly, the home of Verne and the Boëx brothers, sf had not had a greater boost. The day would come . . . but that's yet another story.

Mike Ashley
June 1975

SOURCES OF QUOTATIONS

Quotations have been extracted from private correspondence unless enumerated, in which case their origin was as follows:

[1] *Amazing Stories*, February 1937, published by Teck Publications Inc, Springfield, Massachusetts. From a letter by 'Braxton Wells' in the 'Discussions' letter column, page 144.

[2] *Amazing Stories*, August 1938, published by Ziff–Davis Publishing Co, Chicago, Illinois. From 'The Observatory' editorial column by Raymond A. Palmer, page 4.

[3] *Marvel Science Stories*, February 1939, published by Western Fiction Publishing Co, Chicago, Illinois. From a letter by W. Lawrence Hamling in the 'Under the Lens' letter column, page 128.

[4] *Fantastic Adventures*, May 1939, published by Ziff–Davis Publishing Co. From 'The Editor's Notebook' editorial column by Raymond A. Palmer, page 4.

[5] *Science Fiction*, June 1939, published by Blue Ribbon Magazines, Inc, New York. From a letter by Ray Bradbury and comment by Charles Hornig in 'The Telepath' letter column, page 126.

[6] *The Original Science Fiction Stories*, July 1958, published by Columbia Publications Inc, New York. From Robert A. W. Lowndes's editorial 'Those Letter Columns', page 122.

The Circle of Zero

BY STANLEY G. WEINBAUM

from *Thrilling Wonder Stories*, August 1936

Science fiction, like all other forms of literature, has its share of tragedy, and perhaps the most telling was that of Stanley G. Weinbaum, whose career was cut short, after his meteoric rise to fame, on Saturday, 14 December 1935, as a result of throat cancer. Weinbaum was thirty-three.

Nineteen thirty-five had been Weinbaum's year. His first sale, 'A Martian Odyssey', had been to Charles Hornig and had made the July 1934 issue of *Wonder Stories*. It became instantly one of the most talked about sf tales of that decade. Weinbaum had created totally alien aliens, and yet treated them humanly. His Mars was inhabited by a catalogue-defying range of fauna whose sheer existence was beyond human ken, and yet one understood them. Such was the skill of Weinbaum. A sequel, 'Valley of Dreams', appeared in the November *Wonder*, and then *Astounding* was after him.

Ten stories appeared in 1935, seven of them in *Astounding*, and every one of those seven is of a superlative brilliance. The first, 'Flight on Titan', was an Odyssey-type adventure, apparently rejected by Hornig because it did not contain a 'new idea'. But thereafter tales like 'The Lotus Eaters', 'The Planet of Doubt' and 'The Red Peri', provided evidence of Weinbaum's brilliant ability to conceive both plot and character.

When death curtailed this flow of ingenuity, Weinbaum instantly passed into legend. Magazine editors did their utmost to acquire whatever unpublished stories remained, of which there seemed a surprising amount. Since Mortimer Weisinger had been in partnership with Julius Schwartz acting as Weinbaum's agent, he was in an ideal position, and when he became editor of the new *Thrilling Wonder Stories* he took advantage of that fact and procured 'The Circle of Zero'. It was written early in Weinbaum's career, so forms a perfect link between the first volume in this series covering the Gernsback era, and this current book.

Forty years have now passed since his death, and his fiction has been constantly reprinted, remaining fresh and enjoyable to each new generation. The April 1936 *Astounding*'s 'Brass Tacks' published an open letter to Weinbaum written by 'Doc' E. E. Smith before he knew of his death. It said in part: '. . . I want to thank you for that "indefinable something" you have brought into science fiction – a something it has never had before and of which it was badly in need.'

You'll find that something in the story you are about to read.

CHAPTER 1

Try for Eternity

If there were a mountain a thousand miles high and every thousand years a bird flew over it, just brushing the peak with the tip of its wing, in the course of inconceivable eons the mountain would be worn away. Yet all those ages would not be one second to the length of eternity.

I don't know what philosophical mind penned the foregoing, but the words keep recurring to me since last I saw old Aurore de Neant, erstwhile professor of psychology at Tulane. When, back in '24, I took that course in Morbid Psychology from him, I think the only reason for taking it at all was that I needed an eleven o'clock on Tuesdays and Thursdays to round out a lazy program.

I was gay Jack Anders, twenty-two years old, and the reason seemed sufficient. At least, I'm sure that dark and lovely Yvonne de Neant had nothing to do with it. She was but a slim child of sixteen.

Old de Neant liked me, Lord knows why, for I was a poor enough student. Perhaps it was because I never, to his knowledge, punned on his name. Aurore de Neant translates to Dawn of Nothingness, you see; you can imagine what students did to such a name. 'Rising Zero' – 'Empty Morning' – those were two of the milder soubriquets.

That was in '24. Five years later I was a bond salesman in New York and Professor Aurore de Neant was fired. I learned about it when he called me up. I had drifted quite out of touch with University days.

He was a thrifty sort. He had saved a comfortable sum, and had moved to New York and that's when I started seeing Yvonne again, now darkly beautiful as a Tanagra figurine. I was doing pretty well and was piling up a surplus against the day when Yvonne and I . . .

At least that was the situation in August, 1929. In October of the same year I was as clean as a gnawed bone and old de Neant had but little more meat. I was young and could afford to laugh – he was old and he turned bitter. Indeed, Yvonne and I did little enough laughing when we thought of our own future – but we didn't brood like the professor.

I remember the evening he broached the subject of the Circle of Zero. It was a rainy, blustering fall night and his beard waggled in the dim lamplight like a wisp of grey mist. Yvonne and I had been staying in evenings of late. Shows cost money and I felt that she appreciated my talking to her father, and – after all – he retired early.

She was sitting on the davenport at his side when he suddenly stabbed a gnarled finger at me and snapped, 'Happiness depends on money!'

I was startled. 'Well, it helps,' I agreed.

His pale blue eyes glittered. 'We must recover ours!' he rasped.

'How?'

'I know how. Yes, I know how,' he grinned thinly. 'They think I'm mad. *You* think I'm mad. Even Yvonne thinks so.'

The girl said softly, reproachfully, 'Father!'

'But I'm not,' he continued. 'You and Yvonne and all the fools holding chairs at universities – yes! But not I.'

'I will be all right, if conditions don't get better soon,' I murmured. I was used to the old man's outbursts.

'They will be better for us,' he said, calming. 'Money! We will do anything for money, won't we, Anders?'

'Anything honest.'

'Yes, anything honest. Time is honest, isn't it? An honest cheat, because it takes everything human and turns it into dust.' He peered at my puzzled face. 'I will explain,' he said, 'how we can cheat time.'

'Cheat –'

'Yes. Listen, Jack. Have you ever stood in a strange place and felt a sense of having been there before? Have you ever taken a trip and sensed that sometime, somehow, you had done exactly the same thing – when you know you hadn't?'

'Of course. Everyone has. A memory of the present, Bergson calls it.'

Bergson is a fool! Philosophy without science. Listen to me.' He leaned forward. 'Did you ever hear of the Law of Chance?'

I laughed. 'My business is stocks and bonds. I *ought* to know of it.'

'Ah,' he said, 'but not enough of it. Suppose I have a barrel with a million trillion white grains of sand in it and one black grain. You stand and draw single grains, one after the other, look at each one and throw it back into the barrel. What are the odds against drawing the black grain?'

'A million trillion to one, on each draw.'

'And if you draw half of the million trillion grains?'

'Then the odds are even.'

'So!' he said. 'In other words, if you draw long enough, even though you return each grain to the barrel and draw again, some day you will draw the black one – *if you try long enough!*'

'Yes,' I said.

He half smiled.

'Suppose now you tried for eternity?'

'Eh?'

'Don't you see, Jack? In eternity the Law of Chance functions perfectly. In eternity, sooner or later, every possible combination of things and events must happen. *Must* happen, *if* it's a possible combination. I say, therefore, that in eternity, *whatever can happen, will happen!*' His blue eyes blazed in pale fire.

I was a trifle dazed. 'I guess you're right,' I muttered.

'Right! Of course I'm right. Mathematics is infallible. Now do you see the conclusion?'

'Why – that sooner or later everything will happen.'

'Bah! It is true that there is eternity in the future; we cannot imagine time ending. But Flammarion, before he died, pointed out that there is also an eternity in the past. Since in eternity everything possible must happen, it follows that everything *must already have happened!*'

I gasped. 'Wait a minute! I don't see –'

'Stupidity!' he hissed. 'It is but to say with Einstein that

not only space is curved, but time. To say that, after untold
eons of millennia, the same things repeat themselves because
they must! The Law of Chance says they must, given time
enough. The past and the future are the same thing, because
everything that will happen must already have happened. Can't
you follow so simple a chain of logic?'

'Why – yes. But where does it lead?'

'To our money! To our money!'

'What?'

'Listen. Do not interrupt. In the past all possible combinations
of atoms and circumstances must have occurred.' He paused
then stabbed that bony finger of his at me. 'Jack Anders, *you*
are a possible combination of atoms and circumstances! Possible
because you exist at this moment!'

'You mean – that *I* have happened before?'

'How apt you are! Yes, you have happened before and will
again.'

'Transmigration!' I gulped. 'That's unscientific.'

'Indeed?' He frowned as if in effort to gather his thoughts.
'The poet Robert Burns was buried under an apple tree. When,
years after his death, he was to be removed to rest among the
great men of Westminster Abbey, do you know what they found?
Do you know?'

'I'm sorry, but I don't.'

'They found a root! A root with a bulge for a head, branch
roots for arms and legs and little rootlets for fingers and toes.
The apple tree had eaten Bobby Burns – but who had eaten
the apples?'

'Who – what?'

'Exactly. Who and what? The substance that had been Burns
was in the bodies of Scotch countrymen and children, in the
bodies of caterpillars who had eaten the leaves and become
butterflies and been eaten by birds, in the wood of the tree.
Where is Bobby Burns? Transmigration, I tell you! Isn't that
transmigration?'

'Yes – but not what you meant about me. His body may be
living, but in a thousand different forms.'

'Ah! And when some day, eons and eternities in the future,
the Laws of Chance form another nebula that will cool to
another sun and another earth, is there not the same chance
that those scattered atoms may reassemble another Bobby
Burns?'

'But what a chance! Trillions and trillions to one!'

'But eternity, Jack! In eternity that one chance out of all those trillions must happen – *must* happen!'

I was floored. I stared at Yvonne's pale and lovely features, then at the glistening old eyes of Aurore de Neant.

'You win,' I said with a long sigh. 'But what of it? This is still nineteen twenty-nine, and our money's still sunk in a very sick securities market.'

'*Money!*' he groaned. 'Don't you see? That memory we started from – that sense of having done a thing before – that's a memory out of the infinitely remote future. If only – if only one could remember clearly! But I have a way.' His voice rose suddenly to a shrill scream. 'Yes, I have a way!'

Wild eyes glared at me. I said, 'A way to remember our former incarnations?' One had to humour the old professor. 'To remember – the future?'

'Yes! Reincarnation!' His voice crackled wildly. '*Re-in-carnatione*, which is Latin for "by the thing in the carnation", but it wasn't a carnation – it was an apple tree. The carnation is *dianthus carophyllus*, which proved that the Hottentots plant carnations on the graves of their ancestors, whence the expression "nipped in the bud". If carnations grow on apple trees –'

'Father!' cut in Yvonne sharply. 'You're tired!' Her voice softened. 'Come. You're going to bed.'

'Yes,' he cackled. 'To a bed of carnations.'

CHAPTER II

Memory of Things Past

Some evenings later Aurore de Neant reverted to the same topic. He was clear enough as to where he had left off.

'So in this millennially dead past,' he began suddenly, 'there was a year nineteen twenty-nine and two fools named Anders and de Neant, who invested their money in what are sarcastically called securities. There was a clown's panic, and their money vanished.' He leered fantastically at me.

'Wouldn't it be nice if they could remember what happened in, say, the months from December, nineteen twenty-nine, to June, nineteen thirty – next year?' His voice was suddenly whining. 'They could get their money back then!'

I humoured him. 'If they could remember.'

'They can!' he blazed. 'They can!'

'How?'

His voice dropped to a confidential softness. 'Hypnotism! You studied Morbid Psychology under me, didn't you, Jack? Yes – I remember.'

'But, hypnotism!' I objected. 'Every psychiatrist uses that in his treatments and no one has remembered a previous incarnation or anything like it.'

'No. They're fools, these doctors and psychiatrists. Listen – do you remember the three stages of the hypnotic state as you learned them?'

'Yes. Somnambulism, lethargy, catalepsy.'

'Right. In the first the subject speaks, answers questions. In the second he sleeps deeply. In the third, catalepsy, he is rigid, stiff, so that he can be laid across two chairs, sat on – all that nonsense.'

'I remember. What of it?'

He grinned bleakly. 'In the first stage the subject remembers everything that ever happened during his life. His subconscious mind is dominant and that never forgets. Correct?'

'So we were taught.'

He leaned tensely forward. 'In the second stage, lethargy, my theory is that he remembers everything that happened in his other lives! He remembers the future!'

'Huh? Why doesn't someone do it, then?'

'He remembers while he sleeps. He forgets when he wakes. That's why. But I believe that with proper training he can learn to remember.'

'And you're going to try?'

'Not I. I know too little of finance. I wouldn't know how to interpret my memories.'

'Who, then?'

'You!' He jabbed that long finger against me.

I was thoroughly startled. 'Me? Oh, no! Not a chance of it!'

'Jack,' he said querulously, 'didn't you study hypnotism in my course? Didn't you learn how harmless it is? You know what tommy-rot the idea is of one mind dominating another. You know the subject really hypnotizes himself, that no one can hypnotize an unwilling person. Then what are you afraid of?'

'I – well,' I didn't know what to answer.

'I'm not afraid,' I said grimly. 'I just don't like it.'

'You're afraid!'

'I'm not!'

'You are!' He was growing excited.

It was at that moment that Yvonne's footsteps sounded in the hall. His eyes glittered. He looked at me with a sinister hint of cunning.

'I dislike cowards,' he whispered. His voice rose. 'So does Yvonne!'

The girl entered, perceiving his excitement. 'Oh!' she frowned. 'Why do you have to take these theories so to heart, father?'

'Theories?' he screeched. 'Yes! I have a theory that when you walk you stand still and the sidewalk moves back. No – then the sidewalk moves back. No – then the sidewalk would split if two people walked towards each other – or maybe it's elastic. Of course it's elastic! That's why the last mile is the longest. It's been stretched!'

Yvonne got him to bed.

Well, he talked me into it. I don't know how much was due to my own credulity and how much to Yvonne's solemn dark eyes. I half-believed the professor by the time he'd spent another evening in argument but I think the clincher was his veiled threat to forbid Yvonne my company. She'd have obeyed him if it killed her. She was from New Orleans too, you see, and of Creole blood.

I won't describe that troublesome course of training. One has to develop the hypnotic habit. It's like any other habit, and must be formed slowly. Contrary to the popular opinion morons and people of low intelligence can't ever do it. It takes real concentration – the whole knack of it is the ability to concentrate one's attention – and I don't mean the hypnotist, either.

I mean the subject. The hypnotist hasn't a thing to do with it except to furnish the necessary suggestion by murmuring, 'Sleep – sleep – sleep – sleep . . .' And even that isn't necessary once you learn the trick of it.

I spent half-an-hour or more nearly every evening, learning that trick. It was tedious and a dozen times I became thoroughly disgusted and swore to have no more to do with the farce. But always, after the half-hour's humouring of de Neant, there was Yvonne, and boredom vanished. As a sort of reward, I suppose, the old man took to leaving us alone. And we used our time, I'll wager, to better purpose than he used his.

But I began to learn, little by little. Came a time, after three weeks of tedium, when I was able to cast myself into a light somnambulistic state. I remember how the glitter of the cheap stone in Professor de Neant's ring grew until it filled the world and how his voice, mechanically dull, murmured like the waves in my ears. I remember everything that transpired during those minutes, even his query, 'Are you sleeping?' and my automatic reply, 'Yes.'

By the end of November we had mastered the second state of lethargy and then – I don't know why, but a sort of enthusiasm for the madness took hold of me. Business was at a standstill. I grew tired of facing customers to whom I had sold bonds at a par that were now worth fifty or less and trying to explain why. After a while I began to drop in on the professor during the afternoon and we went through the insane routine again and again.

Yvonne comprehended only a part of the bizarre scheme. She was never in the room during our half-hour trials and knew only vaguely that we were involved in some sort of experiment which was to restore our lost money. I don't suppose she had much faith in it but she always indulged her father.

It was early in December that I began to remember things. Dim and formless things at first – sensations that utterly eluded the rigities of words. I tried to express them to de Neant but it was hopeless.

'A circular feeling,' I'd say. 'No – not exactly – a sense of spiral – not that, either. Roundness – I can't recall it now. It slips away.'

He was jubilant. 'It comes!' he whispered, grey beard awaggle and pale eyes glittering. 'You begin to remember!'

'But what good is a memory like that?'

'Wait! It will come clearer. Of course not all your memories will be of the sort we can use. They will be scattered. Through all the multifold eternities of the past-future circle you can't have been always Jack Anders, securities salesman.

'There will be fragmentary memories, recollections of times when your personality was partially existent, when the Laws of Chance had assembled a being who was not quite Jack Anders, in some period of the infinite worlds that must have risen and died in the span of eternities.

"But somewhere, too, the same atoms, the same conditions, must have made *you*. You're the black grain among the trillions of white grains and, with all eternity to draw in from, you must have been drawn before – many, many times.'

'Do you suppose,' I asked suddenly, 'that anyone exists twice on the same earth? Reincarnation in the sense of the Hindus?'

He laughed scornfully. 'The age of the earth is somewhere between a thousand million and three thousand million years. What proportion of eternity is that?'

'Why – no proportion at all. Zero.'

'Exactly. And zero represents the chance of the same atoms combining to form the same person twice in one cycle of a planet. But I have shown that trillions, or trillions of trillions of years ago, there *must* have been another earth, another Jack Anders, and' – his voice took on that whining note – 'another crash that ruined Jack Anders and old de Neant. That is the time you must remember out of lethargy.'

'Catalepsy!' I said. 'What would one remember in that?'

'God knows.'

'What a mad scheme!' I said suddenly. 'What a crazy pair of fools we are!' The adjectives were a mistake.

'Mad? Crazy?' His voice became a screech. 'Old de Neant is mad, eh? Old Dawn of Nothingness is crazy! You think time doesn't go in a circle, don't you? Do you know what a circle represents? I'll tell you!

'A circle is the mathematical symbol for zero! Time is zero – time is a circle. I have a theory that the hands of a clock are really the noses, because they're on the clock's face, and since time is a circle they go round and round and round . . .'

Yvonne slipped quietly into the room and patted her father's furrowed forehead. She must have been listening.

CHAPTER III

Nightmare or Truth?

'Look here,' I said at a later time to de Neant. 'If the past and future are the same thing, then the future's as unchangeable as the past. How, then, can we expect to change it by re-covering our money?'

'Change it?' he snorted. 'How do you know we're changing it? How do you know that this same thing wasn't done by that Jack Anders and de Neant back on the other side of eternity? I say it *was*!'

I subsided, and the weird business went on. My memories – if they were memories – were becoming clearer now. Often and often I saw things out of my own immediate past of twenty-seven years, though of course de Neant assured me that these were visions from the past of that other self on the far side of time.

I saw other things too, incidents that I couldn't place in my experience, though I couldn't be quite sure they didn't belong there. I might have forgotten, you see, since they were of no particular importance. I recounted everything dutifully to the old man immediately upon awakening and sometimes that was difficult – like trying to find words for a half-remembered dream.

There were other memories as well – bizarre, outlandish dreams that had little parallel in human history. These were always vague and sometimes very horrible and only their inchoate and formless character kept them from being utterly nerve-racking and terrifying.

At one time, I recall, I was gazing through a little crystalline window into a red fog through which moved indescribable faces – not human, not even associable with anything I had ever seen. On another occasion I was wandering, clad in furs, across a cold grey desert and at my side was a woman who was not quite Yvonne.

I remember calling her Pyroniva, and knowing that the name meant 'Snowy-fire'. And here and there in the air about us floated fungoid things, bobbing around like potatoes in a water-bucket. And once we stood very quiet while a menacing form that was only remotely like the small fungi droned purposefully far overhead, toward some unknown objective.

At still another time I was peering, fascinated, into a spinning pool of mercury, watching an image therein of two wild winged figures playing in a roseate glade – not at all human in form but transcendently beautiful, bright and iridescent.

I felt a strange kinship between these two creatures and myself and Yvonne but I had no inkling of what they were, nor upon what world, nor at what time in eternity, nor even of what nature was the room that held the spinning pool that pictured them.

Old Aurore de Neant listened carefully to the wild word-pictures I drew.

'Fascinating!' he muttered. 'Glimpses of an infinitely distant future caught from a ten-fold infinitely remote past. These things you describe are not earthly; it means that somewhere, some-time, men are actually to burst the prison of space and visit other worlds. Some day . . .'

'If these glimpses aren't simply nightmares,' I said.

'They're not nightmares,' he snapped, 'but they might as well be for all the value they are to us.' I could see him struggle to calm himself. 'Our money is still gone. We must try, keep trying for years, for centuries, until we get the black grain of sand, because black sand is a sign of gold-bearing ore . . .' He paused. 'What am I talking about?' he said querously.

Well, we kept trying. Interspersed with the wild, all but indescribable visions came others almost rational. The thing became a fascinating game. I was neglecting my business – though that was small loss – to chase dreams with old Professor Aurore de Neant.

I spent evenings, afternoons and finally mornings, too, living in the slumber of the lethargic state or telling the old man what fantastic things I had dreamed – or, as he said, remembered. Reality became dim to me. I was living in an outlandish world of fancy and only the dark, tragic eyes of Yvonne tugged at me, pulled me back into the daylight world of sanity.

I have mentioned more nearly rational visions. I recall one – a city – but what a city! Sky-piercing, white and beautiful and the people of it were grave with the wisdom of gods, pale and lovely people, but solemn, wistful, sad. There was the aura of brilliance and wickedness that hovers about all great cities, that was born, I suppose, in Babylon and will remain until great cities are no more.

But that was something else, something intangible. I don't know exactly what to call it but perhaps the word decadence is as close as any word we have. As I stood at the base of a colossal structure there was the whir of quiet machinery but it seemed to me, nevertheless, that the city was dying.

It might have been the moss that grew green on the north walls of the buildings. It might have been the grass that pierced here and there through the cracks of the marble pavements. Or it might have been only the grave and sad demeanor of the pale inhabitants. There was something that hinted of a doomed city and a dying race.

A strange thing happened when I tried to describe this particular memory to old de Neant. I stumbled over the details, of course – these visions from the unplumbed depths of eternity were curiously hard to fix between the rigid walls of words. They tended to grow vague, to elude the waking memory. Thus, in this description I had forgotten the name of the city.

'It was called,' I said hesitatingly, 'Termis or Termoplia, or . . .'

'Termopolis!' cried de Neant impatiently. 'City of the End!'

I stared amazed. 'That's it! But how did you know?' In the sleep of lethargy, I was sure, one never speaks.

A queer, cunning look flashed in his pale eyes. 'I knew,' he muttered. 'I knew.' He would say no more.

But I think I saw that city once again. It was when I wandered over a brown and treeless plain, not like that cold grey desert but apparently an arid and barren region of the earth. Dim on the western horizon was the circle of a great cool reddish sun. It had always been there, I remembered, and knew with some other part of my mind that the vast brake of the tides had at last slowed the earth's rotation to a stop, that day and night no longer chased each other around the planet.

The air was biting cold and my companions and I – there were half a dozen of us – moved in a huddled group as if to lend each other warmth from our half-naked bodies. We were all of us thin-legged, skinny creatures with oddly deep chests and enormous, luminous eyes, and the one nearest me was again a woman who had something of Yvonne in her but very little. And I was not quite Jack Anders, either. But some remote fragment of me survived in that barbaric brain.

Beyond a hill was the surge of an oily sea. We crept circling about the mound and suddenly I perceived that sometime in the infinite past that hill had been a city. A few Gargantuan blocks of stone lay crumbling on it and one lonely fragment of a ruined wall rose gauntly to four or five times a man's height. It was at this spectral remnant that the leader of our miserable crew gestured then spoke in sombre tones – not English words but I understood.

'The Gods,' he said – 'the Gods who piled stones upon stones are dead and harm us not who pass the place of their dwelling.'

I knew what that was meant to be. It was an incantation, a ritual – to protect us from the spirits that lurked among the ruins – the ruins, I believe, of a city built by our own ancestors thousands of generations before.

As we passed the wall I looked back at a flicker of movement and saw something hideously like a black rubber doormat flop itself around the angle of the wall. I drew closer to the woman beside me and we crept on down to the sea for water – yes, water, for with the cessation of the planet's rotation rainfall had vanished also, and all life huddled near the edge of the undying sea and learned to drink its bitter brine.

I didn't glance again at the hill which had been Termopolis, the City of the End. But I knew that some chance-born fragment of Jack Anders had been – or will be (what difference, if time is a circle?) – witness of an age close to the day of humanity's doom.

It was early in December that I had the first memory of something that might have been suggestive of success. It was a simple and very sweet memory, just Yvonne and I in a garden that I knew was the inner grounds on one of the New Orleans' old homes – one of those built in the Continental fashion about a court.

We sat on a stone bench beneath the oleanders and I slipped my arm very tenderly about her and murmured, 'Are you happy, Yvonne?'

She looked at me with those tragic eyes of hers and smiled, and then answered, 'As happy as I have ever been.'

And I kissed her.

That was all, but it was important. It was vastly important because it was definitely not a memory out of my own personal past. You see, I had never sat beside Yvonne in a garden sweet with oleanders in the Old Town of New Orleans and I had never kissed her until we met in New York.

Aurore de Neant was elated when I described this vision.

'You see!' he gloated. 'There is evidence. You have remembered the future! Not your own future, of course, but that of another ghostly Jack Anders, who died trillions and quadrillions of years ago.'

'But it doesn't help us, does it?' I asked.

'Oh, it will come now! You wait. The thing we want will come.'

And it did, within a week. This memory was curiously bright and clear, and familiar in every detail. I remember the day. It was the eighth of December, 1929, and I had wandered aimlessly about in search of business during the morning. In the grip of that fascination I mentioned I drifted to de Neant's apartment after lunch. Yvonne left us to ourselves, as was her custom, and we began.

This was, as I said, a sharply outlined memory – or dream. I was leaning over my desk in the company's office, that too-seldom visited office. One of the other salesmen – Summers was his name – was leaning over my shoulder.

We were engaged in the quite customary pastime of scanning the final market reports in the evening paper. The print stood out, clear as reality itself. I glanced without surprise at the date-line. It was Thursday, April 27th, 1930 – almost five months in the future!

Not that I realised that during the vision, of course. The day was merely the present to me. I was simply looking over the list of the day's trading. Figures – familiar names. Telephone $210\frac{3}{4}$ – US Steel – 161; Paramount, $68\frac{1}{2}$.

I jabbed a finger at Steel. 'I bought that at 72,' I said over my shoulder to Summers. 'I sold out everything today. Every stock I own. I'm getting out before there's a secondary crash.'

'Lucky stiff!' he murmured. 'Buy at the December lows and sell out now! Wish I'd had money to do it.' He paused, 'What you gonna do? Stay with the company?'

'No, I've enough to live on. I'm going to stick it in Governments and paid-up insurance and live on the income. I've had enough of gambling.'

'You lucky stiff!' he said again. 'I'm sick of the Street too. Staying in New York?'

'For a while. Just till I get my stuff invested properly; Yvonne and I are going to New Orleans for the winter.' I paused. 'She's had a tough time of it. I'm glad we're where we are.'

'Who wouldn't be?' asked Summers, and then again, 'You lucky stiff!'

De Neant was frantically excited when I described this to him. 'That's it!' he screamed. 'We buy! We buy tomorrow! We sell on the twenty-seventh of May and then – New Orleans!'

Of course I was nearly equally enthusiastic. 'By heaven!' I said. 'It's worth the risk! We'll do it!' And then a sudden hopeless thought. 'Do it? Do it with what? I have less than a hundred dollars to my name. And you . . .'

The old man groaned. 'I have nothing,' he said in abrupt gloom. 'Only the annuity we live on. One can't borrow on that.'

Again a gleam of hope. 'The banks. We'll borrow from them!'

I had to laugh, although it was a bitter laugh. 'What bank would lend us money on a story like this? They wouldn't lend Rockefeller himself money to play this sick market, not without security. We're sunk, that's all.'

I looked at his pale, worried eyes. 'Sunk,' he echoed dully. Then again that wild gleam. '*Not* sunk!' he yelled. 'How can we be? We *did* do it! You remembered our doing it! We must have found the way!'

I gazed speechless. Suddenly a queer, mad thought flashed over me. This other Jack Anders, this ghost of quadrillions of centuries past – or future – he too must be watching, or had watched, or yet would watch, me – the Jack Anders of this cycle of eternity.

He must be watching as anxiously as I to discover the means. Each of us watching the other – neither of us knowing the answer. The blind leading the blind! I laughed at the irony.

But old de Neant was not laughing. The strangest expression I have ever seen in a man's eyes was in his as he repeated very softly, 'We must have found the way because it *was* done. At least you and Yvonne found the way.

'Then all of us must,' I answered sourly.

'Yes. Oh, yes. Listen to me, Jack. I am an old man, old Aurore de Neant. I am old Dawn of Nothingness and my mind is cracking. Don't shake your head!' he snapped. 'I am not mad. I am simply misunderstood. None of you understand.

'Why, I have a theory that trees, grass and people do not grow taller at all. They grow by pushing the earth away from them, which is why you keep hearing that the earth is getting smaller every day. But you don't understand – Yvonne doesn't understand.'

The girl must have been listening. Without my seeing her, she had slipped into the room and put her arms gently about her father's shoulders, while she gazed across at me with anxious eyes.

CHAPTER IV

The Bitter Fruit

There was one more vision, irrelevant in a way, yet vitally important in another way. It was the next evening. An early December snowfall was dropping its silent white beyond the windows and the ill-heated apartment of the de Neants was draughty and chill.

I saw Yvonne shiver as she greeted me and again as she left the room. I noticed that old de Neant followed her to the door with his thin arms about her and that he returned with very worried eyes.

'She is New Orleans born,' he murmured. 'This dreadful Arctic climate will destroy her. We must find a way at once.'

That vision was a sombre one. I stood on a cold, wet, snowy ground – just myself and Yvonne and one who stood beside an open grave. Behind us stretched rows of crosses and white tomb stones, but in our corner the place was ragged, untended, unconsecrated. The priest was saying, 'And these are things that only God understands.'

I slipped a comforting arm about Yvonne. She raised her dark, tragic eyes and whispered, 'It was yesterday, Jack – just yesterday – that he said to me, "Next winter you shall spend in New Orleans, Yvonne." Just yesterday!'

I tried a wretched smile, but I could only stare mournfully at her forlorn face, watching a tear that rolled slowly down her right cheek, hung glistening there a moment, then was joined by another to splash unregarded on the black bosom of her dress.

That was all but how could I describe that vision to old de Neant? I tried to evade. He kept insisting.

'There wasn't any hint of the way,' I told him. Useless – at last I had to tell anyway.

He was very silent for a full minute. 'Jack,' he said finally, 'do you know when I said that to her about New Orleans? This morning when we watched the snow. This morning!'

I didn't know what to do. Suddenly this whole concept of remembering the future seemed mad, insane. In all my memories there had been not a single spark of real proof, not a single hint of prophecy.

So I did nothing at all but simply gazed silently as old Aurore de Neant walked out of the room. And when, two hours later, while Yvonne and I talked, he finished writing a certain letter and then shot himself through the heart – why, that proved nothing either.

It was the following day that Yvonne and I, his only mourners, followed old Dawn of Nothingness to his suicide's grave. I stood beside her and tried as best I could to console her, and roused myself from a dark reverie to hear her words.

'It was yesterday, Jack – just yesterday – that he said to me, "Next winter you shall spend in New Orleans, Yvonne". Just yesterday!'

I watched the tear that rolled slowly down her right cheek hung glistening there a moment, then was joined by another to splash on the black bosom of her dress.

But it was later, during the evening, that the most ironic revelation of all occurred. I was gloomily blaming myself for the weakness of indulging old de Neant in the mad experiment that had led, in a way, to his death.

It was as if Yvonne read my thoughts, for she said suddenly:

'He was breaking, Jack. His mind was going. I heard all those strange things he kept murmuring to you.'

'What?'

'I listened, of course, behind the door there. I never left him alone. I heard him whisper the queerest things – faces in a red fog, words about a cold grey desert, the name Pyronive, the word Termopolis. He leaned over you as you sat with closed eyes and he whispered, whispered all the time.'

Irony of ironies! It was old de Neant's mad mind that had

suggested the visions! He had described them to me as I sat in the sleep of lethargy!

Later we found the letter he had written and again I was deeply moved. The old man had carried a little insurance. Just a week before he had borrowed on one of the policies to pay the premiums on it and the others. But the letter – well, he had made *me* beneficiary of half the amount! And the instructions were –

'You, Jack Anders, will take both your money and Yvonne's and carry out the plan as you know I wish.'

Lunacy! De Neant had found the way to provide the money but – I couldn't gamble Yvonne's last dollar on the scheme of a disordered mind.

'What will we do?' I asked her. 'Of course the money's all yours. I won't touch it.'

'Mine?' she echoed. 'Why, no. We'll do as he wished. Do you think I'd not respect his last request?'

Well, we did. I took those miserable few thousands and spread them around in that sick December market. You remember what happened, how during the spring the prices skyrocketed as if they were heading back toward 1929, when actually the depression was just gathering breath.

I rode that market like a circus performer. I took profits and pyramided them back and, on April 27th, with our money multiplied fifty times, I sold out and watched the market slide back.

Coincidence? Very likely. After all, Aurore de Neant's mind was clear enough most of the time. Other economists predicted that spring rise. Perhaps he foresaw it too. Perhaps he staged this whole affair just to trick us into the gamble, one which we'd never have dared risk otherwise. And then when he saw we were going to fail from lack of money he took the only means he had of providing it.

Perhaps. That's the rational explanation, and yet – that vision of ruined Termopolis keeps haunting me. I see again the grey cold desert of the floating fungi. I wonder often about the immutable Law of Chance and about a ghostly Jack Anders somewhere beyond eternity.

For perhaps he does – did – will exist. Otherwise, how to explain that final vision? What of Yvonne's words beside her father's grave? Could he have foreseen those words and whispered them to me? Possibly. But what, then, of those two tears that hung glistening, merged and dropped from her cheeks?

What of them?

Seeker of Tomorrow

BY ERIC FRANK RUSSELL AND LESLIE J. JOHNSON

from *Astounding Stories*, July 1937

There can be no denying the influence the works of H. G. Wells had upon later science fiction writers, and it was Wells's 'The Time Machine' that was the direct genesis of 'Seeker of Tomorrow'.

The immediate brains behind the story, however, belong to Leslie Joseph Johnson who was born in the Seaforth area of North Liverpool on Monday 18 May 1914. He had discovered sf magazines in the traditional way for Britons, 'remainders' sold cheaply in Woolworth's. In the March 1931 *Amazing* he came across a letter by John Russell Fearn whom he wrote to and subsequently visited in nearby Blackpool. Both admirers of Wells, they set about to outdo the Master and wrote their own version of 'The Time Machine', called 'Amen', and later rewritten as 'Through Time's Infinity'.

The story went no further than that at the time. Fearn, of course, went on to notch up his excellent 'thought variant' sales with Tremaine. Johnson on the other hand became the driving force behind the British Interplanetary Society, co-founded with Philip Cleator in October 1933. Johnson, as secretary of the Society, did much to promote its activities and a letter written by him published in *Amazing Stories* attracted the attention of a certain commercial traveller, by name Eric Frank Russell. Russell then lived in nearby Bootle and in the late summer of 1934 he paid a visit to Johnson that was to be the start of a fruitful acquaintance.

Russell was nine years older than Johnson, having been born at Sandhurst in Surrey on Friday 6 January 1905. Upon his contact with Johnson he showed him a series he had been writing for the private publication, *The Ida and Victoria Magazine*, called 'Interplanetary Communication'. Johnson was impressed with Russell, the man and the writer, and urged him to tackle science fiction. Johnson supplied an idea and Russell wrote the story of 'Eternal Rediffusion'. Submitted to Tremaine it was rejected and barely saved by Johnson from destruction by Russell. The story was then scheduled for Johnson's own magazine *Outlands* in 1946, but the magazine died after one issue and the story again failed to see print. Only recently has it appeared, but in both cases in small circulation publications: in Britain in Philip Harbottle's privately printed *Fantasy Booklet* (1973), and in America in the Fall 1973 issue of Sam Moskowitz's revived *Weird Tales*. Russell was to make his first sale, however, with 'The Saga of Pelican West', a story showing the influence of Stanley G. Weinbaum and published in the February 1937 *Astounding Stories*.

By then Johnson had shown Russell 'Through Time's Infinity'. Russell rewrote the story as 'Seeker of Tomorrow', and submitted it to Newnes where T. Stanhope Sprigg was requesting stories for his proposed magazine. Initially accepted, it was returned when Newnes temporarily shelved the title. Submitted then to Tremaine, it was accepted and appeared in the July 1937 *Astounding Stories*, inspiring a cover by Howard Browne, later voted the most popular cover of the year, and has ever since been proclaimed an excellent and memorable tale. Yet it has never been reprinted.

Russell, of course, went from strength to strength. Before the War, as an aspiring writer searching for plots, he had the invaluable early assistance of Johnson, combined with his own interpretation of Weinbaum-style fiction. During and after the War Russell developed a style of his own and became self-reliant. He adopted a very 'Americanese' way of writing which has on many occasions caused readers to believe him to be an American. His *Jay Score* series in *Astounding* proved to be exceptionally popular, and in the early 1950s he went on to produce gems like 'Dear Devil', 'Legwork', 'Diabologic', and won the Hugo award for his short story 'Allamagoosa'.

Johnson, on the other hand, devoted his time more to fandom and the British Interplanetary Society rather than fiction, although his solo effort 'Satellites of Death' was bought by Walter Gillings and published in *Tales of Wonder*'s third issue in Summer 1938.

In the next volume in this series, Johnson reappears with his own magazine *Outlands*, and it is impossible to avoid Russell in any decade of sf magazine history. But for the moment here is a chance to read that first successful collaboration for which we have to thank H. G. Wells, Leslie J. Johnson, John Russell Fearn and, above all, Eric Frank Russell.

The Venusian city of Kar shimmered beneath an inverted bowl of blue glory. It was a perfect day for a civic demonstration such as the welcoming home of the first expedition to Earth in many centuries. Citizens appreciated the cooperation of the weather; Liberty Square was packed with a murmuring, multi-coloured concourse that swirled in kaleidoscope patterns. Something shrieked in the vault of space; the kaleidoscope turned uniformly pink, as five hundred thousand faces lifted to the sky.

High in the stratosphere appeared a pair of metallic pencils, their rear ends vomiting crimson flames. Sound waves from the rocket tubes fleeted downwards, bounced from the eardrums of the expectant crowd. The pencils swelled; the crimson spread along their under-surfaces as the retarding rockets belched with maximum power. In a short time the objects had resolved themselves into long, streamlined space ships.

With startling suddenness they loomed hugely to the view, sinking behind the mighty mass of university building. They seemed to pause for a moment, while the great, circular ports in their sides stared over the edge of the roof at the mob beneath. Then they were gone. Came one tremendous, reverberating crash succeeded by a moment's perfect silence. The great audience found tongues, broke into a babble of sound, as, with one accord, it stretched itself into a stream of individuals rushing along University Avenue toward the Kar Airport.

The landing field of Kar Airport presented a scene of utmost confusion. To one side lay the space ships surrounded by a shouting, struggling mob. The uproar was loudest at a point where the overwhelmed City Guards had reformed themselves into a wedge and were desperately battling their way through the barrier of bodies.

Babbling and bawling arose into a crescendo, when it was perceived that the nearer space ship was opening its bow door. Steadily, the circular piece of metal revolved along its worm, retreating more and more into the shadow. A final half revolution and it was drawn into the interior of the ship, while the form of a man appeared in the gap thus left.

The crowd bellowed itself red in the face: 'Urnas Karin! Urnas Karin!'

Karin acknowledged the shouts and raised his hand for silence. Half the crowd hissed for silence, while the other half continued to bawl. The hissers reproved the bawlers and the bawlers answered back. Somebody pushed somebody and somebody else resented it. A woman fainted, collapsed, and a little man ten yards away was struck on the cranium by way of retaliation. In a flash, fifty different individuals assumed fifty different versions of what they regarded as a menacing pose. A hidden dog yelped, as somebody trod on it, and from the back of the crowd a piercing voice shrilled, 'Woopsey! Woopsey!'

Immediately, the crowd laughed; an ugly situation passed away and silence fell.

Karin jumped to the ground, followed by twenty of his companions from inside the ship. A small platform, about twice man-height, stood near. Karin mounted and let his sharp eyes pass over the waiting audience. A uniformed guard placed before him a small ebony box mounted on a tripod. He waved away the guard, stood before the box and spoke.

'My friends,' he said, his voice pleasantly magnified by the disseminator he was using, 'your marvellous welcome is a reward in itself. I thank you; and again, on behalf of my colleagues, I thank you! Now, I am sure that you are all fairly bursting to know whether this expedition has made any startling discoveries upon our Mother Planet.' He paused and smiled, as the crowd signified with a roar that it *was* fairly bursting.

'Well, I am afraid that our story is far too long to narrate in detail. Let it suffice if I tell you that we did not find a trace of the civilisation of those who were our ancestors. The great cities, the mighty machines that once were theirs have crumbled into the dust and have been obliterated completely by the foot of Time. Old Mother Earth is airless, waterless and lifeless, thoroughly and completely.

'But we did make one most remarkable discovery.' He hesitated for a tantalizing minute. 'We found the body of a prehistoric man! It was truly an amazing discovery. There, upon a world so ancient that every artificial mark had been smoothed away, atmosphere had leaked off into space, and even axial rotation had ceased, lay the body of this man.

'Examination of the corpse disclosed the seemingly impossible fact that life had departed from it not more than fifty hours previously. Fortunately, we had with us, as part of our standard first-aid equipment, a normality chamber. We placed the corpse therein, warmed it, liquefied the blood and have succeeded in bringing it safely home in a condition that gives us good cause to hope that the experts in our Institute of Medicine and Surgery will be able to resuscitate it.

'The body of this man is in perfect condition. The cause of death, literally, was lack of breath. He appears to belong to a period placed several thousands of years before our ancestors departed from the dying Earth and settled here on Venus, a period so far back in time that our history reels do not talk of it. Why, his head is covered with hair and he even has hairs upon his chest and legs!

'The ability of scientists, in this our most progressive time, to revive the dead in cases where death is not due to old age and is not accompanied by serious injury is a marvel too well-known to need emphasis by me. Possibly there are some people here who would not be with us but for the miracles performed by our most able men and women.' He was interrupted by several cries of assent.

'I feel that there is a most excellent chance of the institute bringing this man back to life and permitting him to tell us his story with his own lips. If my hopes prove to be justified, I intend to make an official request to Orca Sanla, chairman of the stereo-vision committee, that this lone inhabitant of a long-dead planet be allowed to stand before the screen at Kar Stereo Station and give to our world an explanation of circumstances which, to be quite candid with you, we regard as absolutely inexplicable.' Karin turned and gestured toward a burly individual standing in the front rank of his scores of followers.

'In any case, you will receive entertainment to-night. Olaf Morga, aided by his brother Reca, who is on our companion ship, has made a complete pictorial record of our venture from the time we departed from Kar to the time we left Earth. The record is being dispatched to the K. S. Station and will be radiated from sunset this evening.'

Karin started to descend, as a storm of cheering broke out. A woman in the centre of the crowd screamed 'Belt!'

The word was caught up by a thousand others; ere Karin had placed his foot upon the topmost step the whole mob was roaring, 'The belt! We want the belt!'

Morga and Karin exchanged smiles. The latter returned to the centre of the platform, slowly and deliberately unbuckling the flexible metal belt encircling his middle. He held it loosely by one end, while the crowd danced with excitement.

Suddenly, he whirled it above his head, flung it upward and out. It snaked through the air toward where the throng clustered thickest. Half a hundred men leaped for it as it fell. Then it vanished beneath a mass of human beings all fighting madly for the prized souvenir.

Quick to profit by the diversion, the city guards cleared a path from the rocket ships to the control tower. Karin and his crew, together with the crew of the sister ship, sped along the path, entered the tower. The crowd swarmed out of the airport field, poured in a colourful torrent down University Avenue and put a test load on the moving roadways to the suburbs.

Dusk fell over Venus. The stars set in a Moonless sky penetrated the thick veil of atmosphere just sufficiently to paint faint glimmers of steely brightness upon the sides of two voyagers of interplanetary space. Side by side, in a littered field, the rocket ships slept.

II

Two months later, Bern Hedan, the man who got the buckle of the belt, fiddled with the controls of his stereo set and cursed. The brand-new pan-selenite screen of the set displayed, in natural colours and with stereoscopic effect, the final stage of transformation of a sample of Venusian pond life. A hidden announcer betrayed the fact that Sanla's myrmidons regarded a dirge played upon an asthmatic oboe as fit accompaniment to the tri-monthly acrobatics of a frog-faced fish.

'By the death of Terra!' he ejaculated, using the most fearful oath his imagination could conceive at the moment. 'I pay fifty-five yogs down and twelve more every high tide to be the owner of the set. I pay exorbitant bills for power to operate it; I produce eighteen yogs per annum for the right to make use of that which I have purchased – or am purchasing.' He gestured to nothing in particular and talked aloud. He was very fond of talking to himself.

Common-sense views appealed to him. 'And what do we get for this outrageous expenditure? What do we get, I say? Pictorial demonstrations of the domestic habits of red-hammed Venusian baboons accompanied by the noise of wailing catgut. Or the amatory adventures of a deep-sea worm who pays court to somebody's symphony for ten harmonics. Bah!'

He wound savagely at the coordinating handle protruding from the front of the stereo cabinet. The screen dimmed, clouded over, then cleared and depicted a new scene. It was an interior view of the Hall of Debate in the city of Newlondon. Two men were seated upon chairs placed on a semicircular stage, facing a great auditorium packed with people from floor to ceiling. A third individual stood upon the stage facing a stereo screen. Bern Hedan noticed that a mirror suspended on the wall at the rear of this stage was responsible for the peculiar effect of showing the transmission screen in his own screen, giving him a double image of the three people on the stage.

The stereo announcer was saying: 'This evening you have heard and seen an extremely interesting and most instructive debate upon the subject of another Great Migration. You all know the reasons why the human race was compelled to make use of its discovery of the means of travelling through cosmic space by indulging in a wholesale move to our present abode – Venus. The symptoms of planetary senile decay, such as loss of atmosphere, loss of orbital velocity and speed of axial rotation, became so alarming that eventually it was obvious that Earth's characteristics were altering faster than humanity could accommodate itself to the change. Earth's days were numbered – from the human viewpoint, at least. Venus was a suitable habitat for our forefathers, ourselves and our children's children, and the means to get to Venus were at hand.

'The question that has been discussed to-night has been, to put it briefly: 'Will history repeat itself?' In the course of time, somewhere in the distant future, our planet's fate will duplicate that of Earth. We may not like to think of it, but it is a fact, a perfectly natural fact, an inevitable one. Will Venusians die with Venus, or shall there be another Great Migration?' He signed with his hand to the man seated on his right-hand side.

'The pessimist thinks we are doomed for the reasons he has given you, the most unanswerable of which is that the next foothold in space is the planet Mercury – and Mercury is quite uninhabitable by human beings.' He signed to the opposite side. 'The optimist believes that humanity shall never disappear from creation, mainly because of our steady scientific advancement which, he has said, will enable us to perfect the art of space travel to such a degree that we shall have the choice of a dozen worlds long before our present one has grown uncomfortable.

'This concludes the debate between Leet Horis of Kar and Reca Morga of the Newlondon Debating Society.' He stood staring into the transmission screen while the auditorium thundered with applause.

'Now we come to the event to which all Venus has been looking forward with the keenest anticipation. Since the Kar Institute successfully resuscitated the prehistoric man two months ago, the entire world has been waiting to hear his story. There has been some comment about this delay of two months, which I am now to tell you was due to the fact that the revival of this man was not, in itself, enough to justify his immediate appearance. He needed a period of convalescence, during which he has learned how to speak our language. You will find that he can speak with fair fluency, the reason for this being that his own language proved to be the root of ours.'

Bern Hedan adjusted the clarity knob of his set, making the screen depict the stage more sharply. He moved an easy-chair before the stereo, sat in it and switched on the automatic head-scratcher. Soothed by the restfulness of the cushions and the gentle rubs and tickles of the scratcher, he prepared to listen with tolerance.

Seen in the screen, the pair of debaters left the stage. The announcer walked to the rear, opened a door and, with a dramatic air, ushered in the prehistoric man. The man stood directly in front of the screen and studied twelve thousand Venusians. Two hundred million Venusians studied the man.

The Venusians felt slightly disappointed. The object of their examination did not look as though he lived in trees and ate nuts. His head was covered with disgusting hair, but otherwise he looked quite normal. He stood six feet in height; his eyes were dark, alert, his face intellectual even by Venusian standards of judgment. A woven *silvoid karossa* hung from his shoulders; the inevitable Venusian belt encircled his middle. He seemed to be quite at ease; it was evident that he did not agree with his audience in giving his own personality a purely antiquarian value.

'It is my privilege,' said the announcer, 'to introduce to you Glyn Weston, the man from AD 2007 – a date placed approximately seventy thousand years before the Great Migration, about one hundred and fifty thousand years from to-day.' Murmurs of surprise rippled around the serried rows of seats.

'Glyn Weston has told his story to the university board at

Kar; he has made a most valuable contribution to the pages of ancient history. I shall now request him to repeat his narrative, and I think that after you have heard what he has to say you will agree that this voice from the past has recounted the most amazing tale ever to be projected over the stereo. *Glyn Weston!*'

III

'My friends,' began Weston, speaking in a pleasantly modulated voice, 'there is one thing I must say before I tell you my story. God's greatest gift to man is life. I cannot say that you have given me life, but to the remarkable abilities of your wonderful civilization I owe the restoration of that which was snatched from me – *life!* The poor and faulty power of speech is quite inadequate to convey to you the gratitude I feel. I want every one of you to know how deeply I appreciate what has been done for me by Venusian science.

(A roar of applause shook the auditorium. The audience decided that it was to listen to a man and not to a savage.)

'As you have been informed, my name is Glyn Weston. My age I do not know; the reason will become apparent later in my story. In the period that is called mine, if any particular period can be so called, I was a physicist.

'My work commenced at the age of twenty-eight, when I was fortunate enough to inherit a very large sum of money. I was then assistant to the famous Professor Vanderveen, astrophysicist at the Glasgow Observatory. For many years my hobby had been the study of the work of McAndrew, popularly called "The Death-ray Man".

'McAndrew was a scientist of the previous decade. His life's work had advanced that of certain mathematicians and physicists of the twentieth century, most particularly Einstein, Graham, Forrest and Schweil. He was the world's most authoritative exponent of the space-time concept and, like many other geniuses, he died discredited by his contemporaries because he had asserted that it would be found possible to travel in time, to move through time into the future.

'Schweil, with whom McAndrew had been coworker, had shown that time was not an independent concept but an aspect of motion. There could be no time without motion – no motion without time.

'This may seem rather obscure to some of you, but **it really** is quite simple. Try to imagine time without motion; consider the means whereby you estimate time. The two cannot be separated, for they are merely different aspects of the same thing. McAndrew's life was dedicated to discovering the true relationship between these aspects and, if I may put it so, to defining the "difference".

'His work was crowned with success two years before his death. Working upon the theory that the velocity of motion and the rate of time invariably maintained a constant parallel, he evolved a ray with which he made a number of objects vanish. It was his claim that the ray speeded up the velocity of electronic motion, causing the atoms to experience time at a faster rate and thus forcing the objects into the future. Of course, he was laughed at.

'His discovery was described in the absurdest terms, such as "the automatic disintegrator" and "the death ray". McAndrew left his data in the safe-keeping of the only scientist who believed in him. That scientist was Vanderveen, my superior.

'Vanderveen was in the late fifties when he caught the torch cast by the fallen McAndrew. During my association with him he gave me constant, almost fatherly, encouragement. My interest in McAndrew pleased him immensely. When I received my inheritance I told him that it was my desire to use it in carrying on from where McAndrew had left off.

'"Weston," he said, placing a hand upon my shoulder, "I have prayed that this should be your ambition. McAndrew, alas! found in me a dog too old to learn new tricks. But as for you – you are young."

'Thus the seed was sown. But Vanderveen did not live to see the crop. Twenty-two years later I became the human subject of a time-travel experiment. I had set up my laboratory in the wilds of the Peak District of Derbyshire, in England, where work could be carried on with the minimum of interference. From this laboratory I had dispatched into the unknown, presumably the future, a multitude of objects, including several live creatures such as rats, mice, pigeons and domestic fowl. In no case could I bring back anything I had made to vanish. Once gone, the subject was gone forever. There was no way of discovering exactly where it had gone. There was nothing but to take a risk and go myself.

'To this end I designed an air-tight time-travel room and had it fabricated immediately. The room was capable of holding the much perfected Schweil–McAndrew ray projector, myself and a quantity of material I considered necessary to take with me. The projector fitting was designed so that the entire room, with all its contents, would vanish immediately the ray was turned on. I knew, of course, that if this room actually transported me into the future it was imperative that I take into account the possible alteration of ground contours over the period of time I covered. It would be foolhardy to experiment at a point where the ground might rise and leave me embedded yards below Earth's surface. So I hired a field upon a hilltop nine miles northwest of Bakewell – a very lonely spot; and equipped the roof beams with a parachute of my own design, to thwart an opposite possibility.

'Upon the fourteenth of April, AD 1998, all was prepared for the great test. My financial affairs had been settled with an eye to the future in more ways than one. The time-travel room, lavishly set with windows and looking like a very large telephone kiosk, stood waiting in the middle of Farmer Wright's field. As I walked toward it, not knowing what Fate held in store for me, I thought what an incongruous object it looked standing amid the furrows. Without the slightest hesitation, I unlocked the door, stepped inside and relocked it, started the air-purifying apparatus, took one last look at Earth, fresh with the aura of spring, and closed the projector switch.

IV

'The sensation of being under the influence of the rays was weird in the extreme. My mind seemed to be emptied of all thoughts, retaining only alternating impressions of roughness and smoothness, stickiness and gloss, for all the world as if the very nature of my brain material was swaying between a pseudo-fibrousness like that of pulled toffee and a satisfying softness like that of a newly rolled ball of putty. A veil of mist came between myself and the world I strained my eyes to see. The mist was elusive, intangible. Some temporary optical fault intervened to defeat all my efforts to decide whether this mist lay over the windows of the room or was coating my own eyeballs.

'A sudden panic assailed me, and I pressed down the switch handle to which my right hand was still clinging. A sensation of immense strain racked my body from hair to toes, my blood vessels fizzed as if their contents had been replaced with soda water. The fugitive mist was whisked away like the gauzy veil of an oriental dancer. I felt as sick as a dog.

'My key clicked in the lock of the door. I stepped outside and looked around. Everything looked exactly as I had left it. The field was still furrowed; a few trees and bushes were displaying their awareness of spring; the sky was still cloudy, the air as stimulating as before. My experiment had failed.

'It was a miserable man who wended his way along the lonely lanes to his laboratory. I remember that birds were singing, but I did not hear them – at the moment; early flowers were adding their sweet beauty to this ugly world of mine and I did not see them – just then.

'Mentally cursing my lack of foresight in not parking my car in the hired field, I turned a bend in the road and began to climb a hill lying between the field and the laboratory. A farm labourer emerged from a lane to my left and trudged along behind me. He increased his pace, caught up to me and requested the time. He was an old man of the garrulous type and, to my mind, his question was merely an excuse for a conversation. Nevertheless, I lugged at my gold chain and glanced at the cheap timepiece hooked upon its end.

' "I'm sorry," I said, "my watch has stopped."

' "So has mine," he responded. "Guess I'll have to get it on the wireless when I land home." He lighted a cigarette and climbed up the hill in silence for a little while. "What d'you think of the great rocket flight?" he asked suddenly.

'I had some difficulty in gathering my wits, and had to make a definite mental effort before I could reply. Somehow, I managed to recall the sensational flight across the Channel of Robert Clair. This had been hailed as the first really successful experiment with a man-carrying rocket. If I remembered rightly, the event had taken place at least a month before. The science of rocketry held the interest of only a very small number of people; it was strange that this old man should still betray an interest in such an event placed a month earlier. Courtesy demanded a reply.

' "Merely another step in the inevitable march of progress," I answered.

' "D'you think they'll ever get to the Moon?"

' "Who can tell," I said evasively.

' "Well, they're talking about it; they're talking about it," he persisted. "I was reading in the papers only the other day that some professor had worked out how long it would take to get to Venus, how a suitable rocket could be built and how much it would cost. Always thought Venus was a naked woman, not a planet. Shows how knowledge has advanced since my younger days."

' "Ah! It is the fate of all of us to be considered ignorant by later standards," I soothed.

' "What's the world coming to?" he demanded, puffing furiously at his cigarette. "What with steam engines, then motor cars, airplanes and them auto-whatyamacallits that look like windmills and have got no wings, stratosphere planes – and now rockets! I remember when I was a kid there was a furore in the papers because Ginger Leacock circum – circum – went right round the world without a stop, in one of them crazy old stratosphere planes. They've gone round six times since them and aren't satisfied with that! So they've started meddling with rockets.

' " First of all some maniac hops over a house and breaks his neck. They called him 'a martyr to science'. Then another idiot who wants to be a martyr rockets across the Channel and breaks both his legs. Not to be outdone, another fool starts out from Dublin and plunges clean through a skycraper in New York, smearing himself all –"

' "Here!" I interrupted. "What the devil are you talking about?"

' "Rockets," he replied, startled. "And now when they can get from here to New Zealand in twenty-four hours, including stops, or eighteen hours without, what *I* say is –"

' "Will you listen to me," I shouted, grabbing him by the shoulders. "What, in Heaven's name, are you talking about?"

' "No offence, guv'nor, no offence!" he said nervously, trying to draw back. "I didn't mean anything, really I didn't!"

' "Of course there's no offence," I roared. Then, realising that my behaviour was making the man nervous, I calmed myself and continued in quieter tone, "You must pardon me. This subject you have been talking about is one that interests me very considerably and, for certain reasons, I have been out of touch with the news concerning it. My foolish excitement was caused by your mention of a rocket flight to New York. Will you tell me when that flight took place?"

' "Now let me see!" Apparently reassured, he stood and contemplated the skies while he exercised his memory. "As near as I can guess it was in the late summer of 2004."

' "What year?"

' "2004," he repeated.

' "And when was this great rocket flight to which you alluded in the beginning?" I asked, making a tremendous effort to control myself.

' "Yesterday."

' "You will think this a strange question," I told him, "but there is nothing seriously wrong with me. I am suffering from a slight trouble with my memory. Now tell me, what day was yesterday?"

'He looked sympathetic, pulled a folded newspaper from his left pocket, opened it with deliberation and handed it to me. A two-inch streamer was spread across the top of the front page. It said: NEW ROCKET RECORD. Beneath appeared: TO N.Z. IN EIGHTEEN HOURS – Lampson Crashes In Hawkes Bay. I took little notice of this news, red-hot though it was. My eyes searched eagerly along the top. There it stood in plain, indisputable print: DAILY VOICE – May 22, 2007.

'Before the startled native had time to move I had seized him and kissed him. I flung his paper into the air and caught it with a mighty kick as it came down. I whoope-e-ed at the top of my voice and danced a fandango in the roadway. My hat fell off and rolled without hindrance into a ditch; my watch jumped out of my pocket and danced in sympathy at the end of its chain. My time-travel experiment had *succeeded*! For a space of five minutes I went stark, staring mad, while my erstwhile companion, forgetting the dignity of age and his rheumatism, galloped up the hill like a hunted deer and vanished over the crest.

V

'The remarkable feat of making a short trip through time had an effect upon me totally different to what I would have prophesied a few years before. I did not rush, flushed with triumph, to place the new before an astounded world. On the contrary, I became as suspicious and as secretive as any village miser. My desire for fame and the respect of the scientific world faded away, being replaced by a curiosity so insatiable that each today became a mere period of speculation about tomorrow. The future had grasped me like a vicious drug.

'Formerly, I was secretive because I was determined not to permit my work to fall into unworthy hands. Now, the motive was fear of being deprived of the means to satisfy my desire to explore the future as thoroughly as possible.

'From every point of view it seemed highly desirable that my next venture be undertaken at once. My personal fortune became a matter of little moment; my money was cached securely – but not securely enough to withstand the onslaught of time. I came to the conclusion that I could afford to ignore the fate of my wordly possessions; it was not likely that I could claim them at a distant date.

'In the quiet atmosphere of the dust-covered laboratory, I thought it over. The time-travel room must be removed as soon as possible. Heaven alone knew what weird story had been told by my late companion upon his return home, what curious eyes and prying fingers would explore the object in Wright's field. Come to that, I did not know whether the field still belonged to Farmer Wright. The owner, whoever he might be, could arbitrarily uproot the trespasser upon his property. My next move must be made that night.

'It was an hour after sunset when I entered the time-travel room and locked the door preparatory to my second adventure. My stomach was empty; the laboratory had been devoid of food and nothing had passed my lips for several hours. I consoled myself with a nine-year-old cigarette – still fresh! Faint streamers of light still permeated the sky in the direction of Staffordshire; a crescent moon hung low and stars twinkled clearly. The cigarette, surrendered its last fragrant puff. I stamped on it and said, "Good-bye, 2007!"

'With my hand on the switch, I hesitated. On the last occasion the switch had been closed between six and ten seconds, as near as I could estimate, and I had covered nine years. Was the distance travelled in direct proportion to the time the switch was closed? Would I drop dead when the rays carried me to the very day that Nature intended to be the day of my death, or, whether it seemed logical or not, could one travel past what should be one's day of death? Silence answered my unspoken questions. There was nothing for it but to find out. It was a straight issue of success or suicide. I rammed home the switch with exaggerated determination. The die was cast!

I shall not weary you with another description of the sickness that I have called time nausea. The rays operated for a period about ten times longer than the last occasion – about one minute. Then the switch was opened; my body was subjected to a powerful but momentary strain and I had arrived. The key clicked in the door lock; the door swung inward. With my eyes raised to the distant hills, I stepped out. Something snatched at my unwary feet and I fell upon my face. Regaining my feet, I discovered that the time-travel room was sunk into the soil to a depth of six inches, I had been tripped by the step of earth outside the door. It was fortunate that I had not fitted the time-travel room with an outward-opening door and thus imprisoned myself.

'Looking around me, the first thing I noticed was that the field was uncultivated. A few miserable trees and bushes displaced their last tattered rags of brownish foliage. The sky was grey, angry and overcast; I concluded that it was late autumn or early winter. There was not a soul in sight as I paced across the field toward the lane.

'Reaching a stone wall, about four feet in height, I mounted it and surveyed the distant horizon and the intervening terrain. There was not a sign of life or human habitation. My eyes roamed eagerly around, caught a glimpse of an inexplicable shape in the mid-distance, about four miles away. I took out my spectacles, polished them and adjusted them carefully on my nose. The object was a huge hemisphere of drab colour.

'The edifice, if such it was, bulged from the top of a tor like a wart upon an Earthly nose. It lay in the opposite direction from where my laboratory stood, or had once stood. I felt very hungry; my stomach suggested that this, the only artificiality on the landscape, held promise of food. I jumped down from the wall and trudged in the general direction of the distant tor.

'Maintaining a rapid pace for best part of an hour brought me to within a few hundred yards of the object which had resolved itself into a great, smooth hump of concrete about one thousand feet in diameter by five hundred feet in height. There seemed to be a large hole in its top. I did not get a chance to pause and examine it before proceeding nearer; I hesitated in my stride and a voice materialised out of the air behind me. It spoke in accents curiously clipped, somewhat as the Scottish speak, briefly and to the point. It said, "Keep it up!"

'I whirled around. Facing me was a man in dark-brown clothes cut in the manner of a compromise between an engineer's dungarees and a soldier's uniform. A helmet, nothing more than a dull metal skullcap, rested on his head; his hands grasped and pointed at me an object bearing only the faintest re-semblance to a rifle. His attire was quite devoid of decoration; it made him look like something between an infantryman and a plumber.

' "Where did you come from?" I exclaimed.

' "Under a gooseberry bush," said he, grinning broadly. "Where did you?"

' "From the year 2007."

' "Indeed! Then the past is rising up against us!" A tinge of sarcasm suffused his voice, but he appeared to be an intelligent fellow.

' "You must believe me," I argued. "My tale is very long, but when you have heard it you will find it –"

' "Very plausible!" he interrupted. "If you're a better liar than most of us, you must be good. Now, get going. You can tell us all about how you saved the world in 2300 when you get inside."

' "2300! Did you say 2300?" I tried to clutch his arm.

'He placed the muzzle of his weapon against my middle. "Of course I said 2300. Move those feet of yours a little more and your tongue a little less. And, just in case you want to keep up the play, Methuselah, may I anticipate a question by informing you that this is the year of disgrace 2486?"

' "Good heavens!" I cried, turning and moving up the hill. "I've jumped nearly four centuries!"

' "Right out of the frying pan into the fire," my companion remarked.

' "Why, what d'you mean?"

' "Exactly what I said," he answered, his face taking on a sardonic expression. "You may be a good jumper, but you're a darned poor picker. Why didn't you jump a little less or a good bit more? The jumper who picks on this year is crazy. Hell, I knew you were crazy, anyway!"

' "Yes, but –"

' "Walk on, jumper, walk on!" he commanded. "I don't want to use my economy gun on a white man, even if he is cracked."

' "Why d'you call your weapon an 'economy gun'?" I asked him.

'He heaved a sigh. "Well, if you must talk, and if you must pretend ignorance of commonplace things, it's because it uses poisoned darts propelled by compressed air and thus saves expenditure of explosives that are sorely needed elsewhere."

'I was about to ask him where the explosives were needed, and for what purpose, when I found that we had arrived at the foot of the concrete mound and were facing a metal door set in its side.

'My companion touched the door and slid aside a small trap set in its centre, revealing a fluorescent screen behind. He faced the screen and spoke. "Number KH.32851B4, with a gentleman from the year 2007."

VI

'The door opened silently. We entered. Facing us was a long passage indirectly illuminated from slots set in the sides. With synchronised step, which aggravated me and which I vainly tried to break, we marched down the passage, turned to the right at the bottom, *clump-clump-clump*ed along a concrete corridor and entered a large room.

'A leather-skinned, mustached individual looked up from his desk. "What do you want?" he snapped.

' "Food," I answered, briefly.

' "Bring him food," he said, addressing my guardian. Turning to me, he said, "Sit."

'A high cube of red rubber squatted on the floor behind me. I seated myself on it gingerly. It was an air cushion and it felt luxurious. The man behind the desk leaned forward, switched on an instrument bearing a vague resemblance to the old-time voice recorders. He stroked his mustache and looked me over.

' "Name?" he demanded.

' "Professor Glyn Weston."

' "Professor eh? Of what seat of learning?"

' "Originally of Glasgow Observatory; since then I have been working in my own laboratory, about nine miles from here."

' "There is no laboratory within a dozen miles of here," he said, acidly.

' "My laboratory was within nine miles of here in the year 2007," I replied, doggedly.

' "In 2007! How old are you then?"

' "From one point of view I am a little over fifty, from another I am nearly five hundred."

' "Absurd!" he exclaimed. "Obviously absurd!"

' "There is an explanation for this seeming absurdity. In the year 2007 I was the first man to have made a trip in time – that is to say, into the future. I had travelled to that year from 1998. The experiment has been repeated. This is the result – I am here!"

' "Hah!" He rubbed one side of his nose with a forefinger and regarded me queerly. "The popularity of science fiction has made the subject of time travel quite familiar to us. But time travel is impossible."

' "Why?" I asked.

' "It is illogical."

' "Life is illogical; earthquakes are illogical."

' "True," he agreed. "From some aspects that is profoundly true. But can you reconcile yourself with the idea of shaking hands with your ancestors a few centuries before you are born?"

' "No – that would be really illogical. My experiments have shown me that time can be travelled in one direction only – and that is forward, into the future. There can be no returning, no motion into the past by as much as a fraction of one second."

'He stood up, moved away from his desk toward a corner bookcase, searched along the serried volumes and pulled out a large, black tome. He ruffled its pages. Turning to me, with the book open in his hand, he questioned me. "What was the population of Bakewell in 2007?"

' "I cannot tell you," I replied. "I spent very little time in that year. But in 1998 it was about 4500."

' "Hm-m-m! Who was the Premier of Great Britain?"

' "Richard Grierson."

' "Correct! Clair flew the Channel that year. Who designed his rocket?"

' "The German astronautical experimenter, Fritz Loeb."

' "Again correct!"

' "Listen to me," I begged. "If that's some sort of ancient encyclopedia you've got there, please turn up the time concept and see who wrote books about it."

'He wet a finger, searched through the pages of his book. Placing it on the desk, he grabbed another and searched through that also. Four books were explored before he found what was wanted.

' "Here we are. By the way, my name is Captain Henshaw," he added, as an afterthought. "Let me see, Schweil, Herman, philos. Dutch 'Der something-or-other'; Schweil again, with another book; McAndrew, Fergus, 'Space-Time Coordinates'; McAndrew again, 'Time-Motion Relationship'; Weston, Glyn – well I'm a yellow man! – Weston, Glyn, 'Atomic Acceleration In The Time Stream'; again: Weston, Glyn, 'Schweil–McAndrew Theories Simplified'. Another and another; one, two, three, four, five, six! Glyn Weston – that's *you*!"

' "And I can prove it," I said, feeling supremely satisfied that my work had been recorded over five centuries.

' "How?" asked Captain Henshaw.

' "My time-travel room stands awaiting your inspection at a place that I can describe to you only as Farmer Wright's field. It is an hour's walk from here."

'A door to my left-hand side opened suddenly. A uniformed man appeared wheeling a dinner wagon constructed of bright metal tubes and mounted upon doughnut-tired castors. He twisted the wagon dexterously, turning it before my seat, listed a well-loaded tray from the top and, with the casual air of an expert conjurer, drew four telescopic legs from its underside. Adjusting the contraption to a nicety, he stepped backward, flourished a cloth and bowed with an impudent grin.

' "You must be hungry after five hundred years of abstention!" he said. Throwing another grin at Henshaw he marched from the room.

' "To be perfectly candid with you," said Henshaw, as I commenced the welcome meal, "your story is too utterly ridiculous to believe, despite the evidence you have to offer. Now don't think that I am about to call you a liar, for I am not. All that I can say is that I intend to keep an open mind about the matter until I've had the opportunity to examine this magic kiosk of yours, and I am going to take a look at it immediately my spell of duty ends, in about two hours' time."

' "You are welcome," I mumbled with full mouth, waving a fork in the air.

' "After I've taken a look at your gadget, I'll make a report to Manchester. My superiors can then decide how to treat you."

' "Sounds threatening," I remarked, chewing rapidly.

' "And, just in case your story happens to be true in every respect, is there anything you would like to know?"

' "Yes!" I speared a potato. "Where am I?"

' "You are inside No. 37 Interceptor Fortress." He moved from his desk and began to pace the room.

' "No. 37 what?" I asked with sudden energy.

' "Interceptor Fortress," he repeated. "There is a war on."

' "A war!" I echoed, feebly.

' "The biggest and most ferocious war the world has known. It has been on for the last five years and looks like lasting for the next five. One tenth of Earth's population has been wiped out, obliterated. The Metropolis, which was called 'London' in your time, no longer exists except as a great area of shattered bricks, slates and concrete, which harbour the bones of those they harboured in life. If you can travel in time, as you say you can, you will live to curse the invention that plunged you into the present day." Henshaw's face grew bitter, his voice hoarse.

' "With whom is Britain fighting?" I asked, my dinner almost forgotten.

' "There is no Britain," Henshaw answered. "The name was given up two centuries ago. There is no British Empire, either. You are now living in England, which is a self-ruling state and part of the White World, just as Scotland, Ireland, Australia, Germany, Russia and all the others are part of the White World. The Earth of today has only three divisions: the White World, the Yellow World and the Brown World."

' "The Brown World is the smallest and most insignificant of the three. It includes the so-called black races and is neutral – up to the moment. The White and Yellow Worlds are decimating each other to assert their right to breed regardless of the room available. But I am disturbing your meal; please finish it and I will take you to the telescan room. There I can show you something of the war."

'My mind, pestered by a dozen vagrant thoughts, I ate in silence, while Henshaw fidgeted before the bookcase, taking out volumes and putting them back again. Eventually, the meal came to an end. I drank the last drop of liquid, munched the last fragment of biscuit and arose.

'Henshaw signed towards the door through which I had entered. We passed through it, moved down a long corridor, through another door, up a corkscrew staircase into another corridor, reached its end and found ourselves in a long, rectangular room set under the roof of the fortress.

' "This is the telescan room," said Henshaw.

VII

'The walls and floor of the room were littered with a mass of instruments and equipment. Four men were moving about in the jumble, occupying themselves with various jobs, while, at the distant end, two more were seated at what I deduced to be control boards of some description. The most prominent object was a great glass disk secured in a metal frame in the centre of the floor. The disk was tilted slightly out of the horizontal, had a mirror surface and bore a strong resemblance to the astronomical reflectors of my own day.

'Henshaw produced a chair from somewhere. Placing it near the mirror, he bade me be seated, moved to the men at the control boards and held a brief conversation with them. He returned and stood by my chair.

' "This telescan was the result of permitting amateur short-wave experimenters to play with television. It is much too complicated to explain to you here but, to put it briefly, a beam is directed into the sky, passes through the Heaviside and Appleton Layers and rebounds from the Grocott Layer, which lies at an altitude of about eight hundred miles. The beam then returns to Earth and catches the scene at its striking place.

' "It bounces right round the Earth, registering the scene wherever it happens to strike; the first impression is the strongest, and when we pick up the beam again we have no great difficulty in tuning out the confusion of underlying scenes, leaving the first clear and sharp. The operators are now trying to angle the beam to give us a view of the Metropolis. We should get results any second."

'Even as he spoke, the mirrored disk came to life with startling suddenness. There was no preliminary clouding or blur. One moment the surface was devoid of all but glitter; the next moment it depicted a scene with astonishing clarity. I leaned forward and looked at it.

'A ruined road, pitted with ragged craters, passed through an area filled with hummocks of crushed building material. Carefully though I searched, I could not perceive one place where two bricks still clung together, neither could I find a single unbroken brick. The scene maintained a harrowing uniformity from the foreground to the background, a square mile of pathetic evidence.

'Nothing stirred in that dismal scene; no step was taken where once ten million pairs of feet had trod; no voice was raised where the voices of children once were raised in play. A hump came in my throat, as I realised that the Metropolis – dear old London – was no more. It lay like a great, grey scar upon what I still imagined as the sweet green face of Mother Earth; it lay like a scar upon the soul of humanity.

'The Mirror altered its focus as the men at the end of the room manipulated their controls. The nearest end of the road seemed to rise toward me and show itself in greater detail. I saw bones protruding from a mound of dirt fifty yards from a large crater; near the legs lay the flattened skeleton of a dog.

Henshaw bent his head forward, rubbed his chin with a harsh, scratching sound and spoke.

' "Before you lies one of the most heart-rending incidents of the war. The dog refused to leave its stricken master. It stayed there until it starved to death. Thousands of people watched its long, drawn-out act of devotion, watched it through the telescan with curses and tears born of helplessness. Flight Lieutenant O'Rourke, disobeying orders, made a mad attempt to rescue the dog about the time its belly disappeared into its ribs. He was brought down by a Yellow squadron. His rocket plane is mixed with the dust of the Marble Arch. God rest a gallant gentleman!"

' "Are the Yellows winning?" I asked, feeling sick at heart.

' "No, I would not say that. Warfare has now reached the stage of perfection where nobody wins and everybody loses. The Metropolis, or what is left of it, is in no worse condition than Kobe and Tokyo. The campaign consists of a series of destructive assaults, followed by equally destructive retaliation; there have been no prolonged battles such as featured the past, just a delivering of rapid blows by one side or the other. The end of this great city was the result of such a blow; the end of Tokyo was our reply. Come, we'll take a look at your time-travel room."

'With that I arose. We departed from the telescan room, retraced our steps through the corridors and came to the metal door. It opened silently as we reached it, revealing a small, streamlined vehicle standing on the path outside. Henshaw struggled to get his long legs beneath the steering wheel, while I took a seat by his side. Slamming the off-side door, Henshaw pressed a button protruding from the wheel boss. A smooth whir came from beneath the bonnet and we were off.

' "Don't take the telescan picture too much to heart," said Henshaw, juggling with the wheel, "We received warning of that raid from our very excellent espionage service and managed to evacuate nine tenths of the population in time. The remaining tenth was wiped out, but the death toll was not as large as the picture suggests."

' "What caused the damage," I asked.

' "Bombs – high-explosive bombs dropped from the strato-sphere airplanes and also from rocket ships flying at tremendous heights. The next raid will be upon Manchester or Sheffield, for these are now the southernmost towns of any importance, also centres of the armaments industry. Our fortress is one of a chain strung across the Derbyshire hills to protect Manchester. We cannot prevent a raid, but we can administer severe punishment with our rocket shells and our aerial torpedoes, which can ascend to very great heights, the latter by means of power picked up from the North Radiation Station."

' "The Continent must have dropped in for it!" I offered.

' "Not so much as you would think," he replied. "The opposing forces have vented their spite on what they consider to be the nerve centres of the enemy; thus England and Japan are the favourite targets. Neither side keeps its air fleet for purposes of defence but for retaliation. That is why these fortresses are very important – they are one of the few defence concessions wrung from the powers that be who worship the policy of attack, attack and again attack." He jerked at the steering wheel, avoided the curve of a stone wall and continued in a voice that grew more bitter.

' "I am not looking forward to the next raid with eager anticipation. Information has reached us, from certain sources, telling that the Yellows have perfected a disintegrator bomb, the result of some nosey scientist occupying himself with the problem of how solar radiation is maintained. I understand that the bomb drops, bursts, upsets the stability of surrounding matter and causes it to burn itself away.

' "The process does not continue indefinitely, but lasts as long as the original energy in the bomb lasts; the bigger the bomb the greater the area of matter affected. The process was described to me as 'readjustment of electronic balance,' and I believe that it takes place at a rate that will trap all but champion sprinters."

'The car went over the crest of a hill. A field came into view. Simultaneously, we saw the time-travel room. We shot down a slight slope towards it, took an equally slight rise and came to rest beside the wall from which I had viewed the distant fortress. Henshaw squirmed from his seat, took out a watch and glanced at its dial.

' "Four minutes – not so bad considering the state of the road."

' "You've averaged about sixty miles per hour," I told him. "What sort of motor is this?" I asked, gesturing to the car.

' "Electric. Runs on Freimeyer high-capacity batteries employing silvertantalum alloy plates." He vaulted the wall, stared at the object in mid-field. "So that's the magic box, eh? Let's go and put a penny in."

'I climbed the wall. We started for the room together. Henshaw stroked at his mustache, an expression of keen interest in his face. The turf was damp and slippery beneath our feet. We had covered half the distance to the room when a hoarse whistle ran over the hills and echoed in the valley. Henshaw stopped abruptly. The whistle ended, then was succeeded by six short toots.

'Henshaw whirled around, grabbed me by the arm, pulled me towards the car. "By the Mandarin's Button," he roared, his face red with excitement, "*a raid!* Did you hear the siren? It's a raid warning from the fortress. We must return at once! Put a move on, for Heaven's sake! There's not a second to lose."

'We ran towards the wall. Twenty yards from it I slid, staggered with wildly waving arms, slid again and fell upon the flat of my back with force that knocked the breath from my body. Henshaw, half a dozen jumps ahead, skidded in a circle, returned and grasped my hands, preparatory to helping me up.

' "Look!" I gasped weakly, my eyes bulging at the sky. "*Look!*"

'About a mile away, coming in our direction at a fast pace, was a golden-coloured air machine shaped like a bullet, small, stubby wings protruding from its sides, a long tail of fire streaming from its rear. It looked sinister, threatening; my heart turned to ice.

' "By Hades! a fighting scout of the Yellows," shouted Henshaw. He's got us spotted and intends to have a little amusement. Run like the very devil. We're as good as dead men already."

'So saying, he gave a tremendous heave that swung me to my feet. I clutched his shoulders. We swayed about like a pair of adagio dancers, slipped and went down together. Somebody rattled a piece of rock in a monster can; a roar swept overboard; a flood of hot air washed our recumbent bodies. We regained our feet. The scout had passed us by a mile and was nosing upward in a great loop. The car was a smoking ruin.

' "He's coming back for us," Henshaw screamed. "We're done. There's nowhere we can hide!"

' "Heaven help –" I commenced, paused as a thought struck me. "The time-travel room! Come on. We can make it with luck. We'll be safe there."

VIII

'I turned, made for the centre of the field, arms working like pistons, my pace hampered by fear of falls. Henshaw raced beside me, his chest labouring, his face livid.

'Despite the telling pace, he found breath enough to ask a question as he ran. "What good will it do to get into that thing? He'll simply blow it sky high!"

' "Wait and see!" I grunted.

'A noise grew loud behind us, filling us with fear that added to our speed. With surprising suddenness, the scout roared overhead followed by its wake of heated air. A terrific blast came somewhere in the rear. Henshaw looked over his shoulder.

' "A disintegrator bomb!" he shouted. "It's eating towards us like greased lightning. Run! Run as you've never run before!"

'My protesting feet increased their speed. The total distance from the wall to the room was a bare five hundred yards. I would not have believed that such a distance could be so punishing. Thirty yards separated us from the time-travel room, it seemed like thirty miles. The distance already covered told in this final stage; we did not run it; we reeled it.

'Henshaw, ahead of me, reached the room and tugged madly at the door, as a sensation of heat penetrated to the back of my legs. He danced with excitement as he pulled in vain. I sobbed out to him *"Push! Push!"* and he fell headlong inside. A fraction of a second later I staggered through the open door, turned and saw the earth literally melting and boiling within a yard of the step. We were barely in time.

'Without further ado, I slammed the door and closed the switch of the ray apparatus. Red flames jumped upward and peered at us through the windows; a film of mist blotted them out. My body tingled with the old, familiar sensation and, as I breathed a prayer of thankfulness, the whole room fell over on its side. My head struck a projection on the wall. Frantically, I tightened my grip upon the switch as I slipped into unconsciousness.

'The period of stupour did not last long – or it did not seem to. I came to my senses, jerked out a hand in search of the switch, found it and pulled it.

'Somebody said, "Ouch!"

'I sat up hastily. I was in bed!

'My astonishment can well be imagined. I was in bed, there was not the slightest doubt about that. I stroked and felt the clothes, studied the weave of them and pinched myself. There was nothing else for it: definitely, beyond all dispute, I was sitting up in bed clad in a crimson nightgown.

'A half-seen movement to one side drew my attention that

way. I rubbed my eyes and looked again. Standing beside the bed, his face expressive of kindly solicitude, was a bald-headed man garbed in rompers of brilliant hue. His forehead was high, his eyes large, liquid and brown, his mouth and chin small, almost womanly. Suspended from a chain encircling his neck was a plated instrument which, I guessed, had taken the tug that brought forth the "Ouch!"

'I stared at him. He contemplated me with quiet serenity.

'"Where am I?" I asked weakly, making use of the conventional phrase under such circumstances.

'" You are within my house situated in the city of Leamore," he answered in a pleasantly modulated voice, "and the year is 772 by the new reckoning, or 34656 by the old. You have leaped a chasm of time representing about thirty-two thousand years!"

'"How did you know that I am a time traveller?" I demanded.

'"Because your time-travelling device materialised out of thin air before the eyes of half a hundred citizens. You chose the centre of a busy road as your arriving point. Dozens of people witnessed the phenomenon which, in the far past, undoubtedly would have been given a supernatural explanation. Our solution was that you had travelled through time: a simple solution seeing that your feat is the second within the last five centuries. Finally, your companion confirmed our –"

'"Henshaw!" I interrupted, realising that I had company on my time trip. "Henshaw – Where is he?"

'"He is having his hair plucked," was the amazing response.

'"Hair plucked! *Hair!* Why? What?" My mind relapsed into confusion at this nonsensical twist in the conversation. For the second time I pinched myself to make sure I was not asleep. The man in the blue rompers smiled as he noted the effect of his words. Seating himself on the edge of the bed, he hugged a knee and continued.

'"Your friend appears to be a person accustomed to making quick decisions. It is scarcely thirty minutes since your time-conquering device staged its dramatic appearance, yet already he has discovered that, according to present-day conventions, hair is regarded as not nice. Apparently he is determined to look nice at all costs, so he is having his hair removed by a painless method of extraction. We are depriving him of his mustache and head covering. The bristles on his face will have to grow longer before we can deal with them."

'"Well, I'm damned!" I exploded. "Henshaw – the blessed goat!

I boost him through a multitude of centuries and what happens? He rushes into a beauty parlour leaving me to expire in bed." Indignation brought me out of the bed and to my feet. "In a crimson nightgown!" I added.

'My companion laughed aloud. "No fear of you expiring just yet," he assured me. "You received a nasty bump from which you will recover soon. As for the nightgown, as you call it, we put you into it after giving you a much-needed bath, while we looked around for some suitable clothes."

' "What's wrong with my own clothes?" I demanded.

' "They have been burned; your friend's have been burned, also. The contents of your pockets have been fumigated; so has your time-travel room. This is a hygienic world you've stepped into. We don't mind you coming here, but we object, in the strongest possible manner, to you importing large quantities of germs of types that we have gone to considerable pains to eliminate. We like you; we like your friend; we *don't* like your passengers."

' "Sorry!" I said, humbly.

' "It's quite all right," he answered, releasing his knee and standing up. "Perhaps I have been too blunt. The apology should be mine." He walked across the room, pressed a button. A panel in the wall slid silently downward. Behind lay a recessed wardrobe. He reached inside, produced a complete outfit of clothing made of some material resembling silk, tossed them on to the bed.

'Removing the crimson wrap with secret relief, I commenced to put on the apparel. The soft, almost dainty material enveloped my bathed, refreshed body pleasantly. There was not a button in the outfit. Everything fastened with a sort of glorified zipper. I pulled on one strangely cut garment after another, zipped them tight and, in the end, stood before a mirror regarding myself attired in emerald-green rompers, green socks and sandals to match, a green tricorn hat cocked rakishly on my head. I stared into the mirror, thinking it depicted the biggest fool alive.

' "How do you like it?" questioned the onlooker.

' "Not so bad. All I want now is the cat."

' "The cat?" he repeated, mystified.

' "Yes, the cat. I look like the principal boy in Dick Whittington."

' "Dick Whittington?" he muttered.

' "You wouldn't know about that – let it pass!" I tried the tricorn at a different angle; the result was an abomination. Finally,

I gave it up. If all of them dressed like this, an extra idiot wouldn't be noticed.

' "Well, I'm ready, Mr – Mr –"

' "Ken Melsona is my name," he responded.

' "And Glyn Weston is mine." We shook hands. Melsona opened a door, led the way down a passage to another door, which sank at the pressure of a button. Outside lay the street. Conscious of my unfamiliar garb, I hesitated; Melsona, dressed like Little Boy Blue, stepped boldly out. I followed.

IX

'Before me stretched a scene so unexpected I stopped and gasped. Between the pavement curbs ran a moving roadway, smooth, soft-surfaced, flowing evenly from west to east. It was divided into three sections, all travelling in the same direction, the outer sections at about five miles per hour, the middle section at about ten. Hundreds of people clothed in gaudy colours stood and chatted on the road or stepped from one section to another, all carried along steadily like an array of targets in a gipsy shooting gallery. The total width of the roadway was about one hundred feet; fixed, mosaic-patterned pavements bordered it.

'Picturesque villas set in lavish, well-cultivated gardens lined the roadway on both sides. Ornamental trees of every size and colour, drilled and trimmed into every conceivable shape, sprouted from the pavements at intervals of thirty yards. It was a beautiful sight indeed, the most beautiful I had ever seen. The road deserved the name of Boulevard of Heaven.

'Melsona made for the nearest-moving section of roadway, warning me to step on it while facing the direction of motion. We passed over to the middle section, stood upon it, side by side, and glided to the east. I felt as pleased as a kid at a fair.

' "Let us call at one or two shops," suggested my guide. "Then we can pick up your companion – er – Henshaw you said his name was, didn't you?"

'I mumbled an affirmative, my eyes roaming busily over the scenery and the accompanying crowd of road-riders, my mind inveigled by the novelty of it all.

'We swept along for the best part of a mile, before Melsona nudged me into attention, dexterously transferred himself to the right-hand slow track, crossed it and gained the pavement. With me tagging behind, he made a bee-line for a section of half a dozen shops, entering one displaying a mass of goods I had not time to examine. A man and a woman, both brightly clad and equally bald, advanced at our entrance.

'"Pray serve this gentleman," said Melsona, making a patronising wave in my direction.

'"Ah, certainly, it is a pleasure," purred the male assistant, washing his hands with invisible soap. "What is the gentleman's need?"

'"Money," I said, succinctly.

'"Money!" he parroted. "Money! What a strange request! It is obtainable, of course, but you will have to apply to a collector."

'"Then how the devil can I –"

'"It's quite all right," Melsona interrupted. "All you have got to do is to ask for whatever you require. If this shop has it, you will get it; if it hasn't, then some other shop may stock it."

'"Ask and it shall be given unto you," I quoted. The idea sounded crazy to me, but who was I to question the economics of this age? "Cigarettes," I said, hopefully.

'The words were no sooner out of my mouth than the lady assistant darted to a shelf, beating her confrere by a foot, grabbed a dozen packages of assorted size and shape and placed them on the counter. My eyes stared in astonishment and delight. They were packets of cigarettes. I took one of the biggest. The lady wanted to know whether she could provide me with anything else. I asked her for a cigarette case and got it. I asked her for an automatic lighter. She provided me with a replica of the instrument dangling from Melsona's neck, which I had mistaken for the switch. I spent thirty minutes in that shop, emerging convinced that I had stepped into Utopia.

'We stood on the pavement outside. I opened my cigarette packet, placed a welcome tube between my lips, and Melsona showed me how to use the lighter. It was shaped like an elongated fir cone, made of metal and affixed to the conventional neck chain. One merely squeezed it. A small lid in the wide end popped open, revealing a glowing filament underneath. I lighted it, inhaling the fragrant smoke with indescribable satisfaction.

'"How long will this last?" I asked, studying the glowing end of the lighter curiously.

'"For the whole of your lifetime," answered Melsona. "It's –"
He looked upward suddenly, as a loud noise thundered down from the clouds. "Look! There's a world-trip liner!"

'Overhead soared a titanic cigar, silvery-coloured; flame-girt, awe-inspiring. The circumstances made it hard to grasp the true perspective. I judged the monster to be about a mile in length and a tenth of a mile in diameter. Poised high above the thin, almost transparent clouds, it was truly a majestic sight, its conical nose pointed towards the Sun setting in the west, its tail vomiting spears of flame that spread, lightened and resolved into an enormous fan of vapour.

'It was moving at a height of at least seven miles, yet its size and the wonderful clearness of the atmosphere made the rows of circular ports along its sides easily discernible. Barraging the whole city of Leamore with a bombardment of sound, it sped swiftly to the west, its tremendous bulk dwarfing the antlike humans responsible for its fabrication.

'"What do you think of that?" asked Melsona, proudly.

'"It's magnificent! It's marvellous!" I said.

'A shout drew our eyes to the roadway. A man standing on the distant five-mile track waved madly, rushed in our direction, trod on the edge of the intervening ten-mile track and executed an incomplete cart wheel. With the road rushing onward beneath him, he rolled full length in the contrary direction, mowing down people by the dozen. Still rolling, he broke out of a knot of recumbent forms, revolved across the track and tried to regain his feet on the very verge.

'He stood up, for a fraction of a second, with one foot on the middle track and one foot on the nearer five-mile track; then the difference in speed overcame him. He chose the five-mile track and sat on it, hard. He passed us, as we gazed with interest, lying flat on his back, his feet in the air. Fifty yards along the road he gained the safety of the pavement with a sudden, acrobatic movement, turned and dashed towards us.

'As he neared, I perceived that he was darker in complexion than most of the people I had seen. His rompers were a horrible yellow above the waist and black below; his socks were of black; his sandals black with yellow piping. A yellow pork-pie hat was rammed squarely on his head; a yellow tassel hung from the centre of its crown and dangling over his left ear.

'"Weston!" he bellowed. "It's me – Henshaw!"

'He came up to us, his face beaming with pleasure, and smacked me heartily on the back. I studied him closely. He was as hairy as an egg.

'"I don't believe it," I said, flatly.

'"I can hardly believe it when I look at you," he retorted.

'"Then how did you recognise me?"

' "Because yours is the only monkey nut in the whole wide world." He took a pace back and surveyed me from head to heel. "The only original Robin Hood, as I live and breathe," he said. "How d'you like my rig?" He spread his arms and slowly rotated before us.

' "I would rather not say," I said, averting my eyes from the bilious yellow, "justice can be pronounced only in vulgar terms."

' "Jealous!" was his laughing comment. "Personally, I think attire such as this lends colour to life. If I've any fault to find, it is only the trouble it creates in distinguishing sahibs from memsahibs. So you've been shopping, huh?" He jabbed a finger at the lighter suspended from my neck. "And how do you like this moneyless world?"

' "Seeing you know about the money, or lack of it, it's evident you've been shopping," I commented.

' "Oh, no," he assured us. "I went to pay the hair-plucker and he acted like one thunderstruck. Then I found out about the money. Wistfully, he said he would like an odd coin if I had one to give away. So I let him run through my purse, which I had swiped when they grabbed my clothes to burn them. His eyes stood out like organ stops, when he saw what I had: eighteen dollars and forty-seven cents in good old White money."

' "*White* money?" I queried.

' "Of course. You didn't think I'd have money from your age, did you? Well, he raked through the lot and picked out a half-dollar piece which was the oldest-dated coin there. He was as pleased as a dog with two tails. I asked him what he was going to do with it. You would never guess what he said."

' "What?" I encouraged him.

' "I've not yet been able to make up my mind whether I'm mentally deficient or all this world's daft but me. Believe it or not, he said he was going to swap that half dollar for a *glass fish!*"

' "A glass fish!" I echoed, incredulously.

' "Now what the deuce could he want with that?" Henshaw continued. "A live fish would be bad enough, a dead fish better, but a glass fish!"

' "That can be explained," Melsona interjected. "You see, this world has progressed so far that its one great problem is how to keep people occupied. There is no monetary system; everything can be had for the mere asking. All work, manufacturing and the like, is carried on by volunteers, but so efficient are our methods that there is never enough work for all the people who want it. Inhabitants of this world have to fill up a very large amount of spare time somehow or other; consequently, work, once a curse, is now a godsend.

'"How do our citizens spend their spare time? I will tell you. A little less than half devote themselves to science, a little more than half devote themselves to art. People invent things or create things, and everybody tries to make his work individualistic or superior to that of others.

'"People dispose of the unwanted products of their own handicrafts by placing them in the shops for disposal to the persons who ask for them. The greatest shame any citizen can feel is when one of his products stands waiting in a shop for months. The greatest triumph he can experience is when so many clamour for one of his works that it has to be disposed of by means of drawing lots.

'"People who collect the work of any particular artist, or have a special desire to acquire one of his works, can obtain them in three ways: they can get them from a shop for the asking, if the shop happens to have them; or, if the artist is so popular his work never reaches a shop, they can apply to the artist to join with other applicants in drawing lots for his work; or, if the artist happens to be a collector himself they can barter with him.

'"This explains your man's intention of changing a coin for a glass fish. Coins of your age are not rare; they are absolutely unknown and, therefore, of incalculable pleasure to a collector. One of our most prominent collectors of these old trading tokens is Torquilea, who is Earth's greatest glass artist. I would like you to see an example of his work. Come with me."

X

'Following Melsona's lead we marched along the pavement in the opposite direction to the motion of the road. A lively conversation was maintained; it consisted mainly of questions by Henshaw and myself, and Melsona's answers. We gathered that a system of moving roadways radiated like the spokes of a wheel from the centre of Leamore to its outskirts, that roads ran inward and outward alternately, that people who wanted to travel in the opposite direction to a road's motion either walked along the pavements or cut through a side street to the next road. This road ran to the centre of the city; if Melsona was returning home from the centre and did not care to walk, he just took the adjacent road, which ran outward, and entered his house by the back way. All roads exceeding thirty metres in width were moving roads; narrower roads were stable. The whole system of transport was absurdly simple.

'Melsona was explaining to us that private air machines and wheeled vehicles existed in large numbers, but were not allowed to enter into, or fly over, any city, confining their activities to the terrain between towns. Just then we passed an open-air café. We did not go far past; with one accord, we retraced our steps, entered and claimed a table.

' "– thus only the great liners bound for city airports are permitted to pass over occupied areas," said Melsona, finishing his conversation. "What will you have?"

' "Beef," said Henshaw.

' "Beef? What is that?"

' "Meat," said Henshaw, licking his lips and easing the belt around his rompers. An expression of ineffable disgust appeared on Melsona's face.

' "I was only joking," Henshaw assured him, quick-wittedly. "I'll have whatever you recommend."

'Melsona's expression suggested that he did not regard the joke as being in the best of taste. He scribbled on a pad framed in the table's centre, rammed his foot on a pedal protruding from the floor. The table sank downwards, leaving us gaping into a shaft between our feet. After a short pause the table rose into view, settled before us with its top bearing the three meals ordered. We set to. The food was strange, but satisfying.

'Eventually, feeling like a new man, I left the table and, with my companions, continued along the pavement. I fell into a reverie, thinking how queer it was that my previous meal was only a few hours before – or was it thousands of years? We had walked for about ten minutes, when Melsona stopped so suddenly that, still buried in my thoughts, I bumped into him. He pointed to the garden of a beautiful villa.

' "Here's a fine sample of Torquilea's work," he remarked. "Come inside and take a look at it." Without hesitation, he opened the gate and stepped into the garden, telling us that our interested inspection would be regarded as most flattering both by the artist and the owner. He led us to an object standing in the middle of the lawn. We looked at it in silence. It was divine; there was no other word for it.

'A mass of coloured marble, onyx, agate and lapis lazuli, ingeniously arranged, arose to a height of ten or twelve feet. Over it flowed a mock waterfall of glass so realistic one was shocked by the lack of noise. So superb was the artist's cunning that even the grain of the underlying stone had been utilised to create an impression of sub-surface swirls. Embedded in the glass, by what means I could not determine, were bubbles and shadows and vague flickers of light making a perfect simulation of life and dancing water.

'The fall broke at the bottom, eddying and spraying among the coloured rocks, while here and there little drops of spray hung glistening in various cracks and crannies. A pair of glass salmon were leaping the fall. By looking closer I could discern that several fine wires held them suspended in mid-air, but so accurately were they formed by the fingers of genius it was hard to believe that the wand of some modern Merlin had not fixed them thus when in full enjoyment of vibrant life.

'Henshaw removed his pork pie and said, "I take off my hat to this!"

'"It was indeed a great triumph for Torquilea," Melsona told us. "No less than twenty-seven thousand persons drew lots to decide who should have this particular masterpiece."

'He looked wistfully at Henshaw. "Torquilea is crazy about old coins. Only the other day I saw one of his works that will soon be given to somebody. It was simply a small bowl containing a sea-shore pool in glass. Sand and pebbles lay over its bottom; a pair of semitransparent shrimps sported in its depths; a strand of green seaweed grew from a small rock on which bloomed a beautiful sea anemone with all its tentacles fully extended. It was a reproduction of nature so truthful, so marvellous, one half-expected ripples on the surface of the glass. Torquilea is the happiest of men to have his work so eagerly sought after. I am sure he would consider an exchange.

'Henshaw took the hint. Fishing out a coin, he handed it to Melsona, telling him to put it to the best use on behalf of us all. This grouping together of we three seemed to please Melsona immensely. He accepted the gift with glee, announcing that he would interview Torquilea at the first opportunity.

'Darkness had fallen several hours before we returned to Melsona's house for rest and sleep. We had ridden half the roads of Leamore, explored many shops and buildings, seen many marvels and had been introduced to so many people we could not remember more than a couple of them. Melsona, continuing in his voluntary capacity of city guide, had conducted us hither and thither, declaring himself to be the luckiest of men because our arrival had provided him with the means to use up leisure hours. His conversation, under the continual urge of our questions, informed us of a number of remarkable facts.

'We found, first of all, that the day was much longer than in my time, and that Earth's axial rotation was slowing down at such a rate scientists estimated it would have ceased altogether in another twenty to thirty thousand years. The phenomenon dated from the arrival of The Invader, which time inaugurated the new calendar and made this the year 772 N.R.; the letters N.R. standing for "new reckoning".

'The Invader, we were informed, was a planet about twice the size of Jupiter, which had come through interstellar space, cleaved a path through the solar system and vanished into the cosmos. It passed between the orbits of Mars and the asteroid belt, its influence upsetting the normal balance of half the system, Making the paths of the asteroids, Mars and Earth much more eccentric, capturing and taking with it two members of the Trojans group of asteroids.

'We were told that Venus had been reached by rocket ships about fifty years after The Invader had passed, that interplanetary travel was still so difficult, so risky, that the present population of Venus was not more than twelve thousand, and that for every individual who had reached the planet safely another had been killed in the attempt.

'Earth's population had not altered in number for the last ten thousand years; all Earth acknowledged a central government situated in Osmia, and the social system was Pallarism. We found that Osmia was on the site of the city I had known as Constantinople, and that the "ism" favoured at the moment was based on the theories of a philosopher named Palla, who had lived about 22800 O.R.

'Our stomachs warmed with a late supper, our minds filled with memories of the day's explorations, we went to bed. With quiet deference to my taste, our host had laid upon my bed what looked like a black bathing costume. The crimson nightgown had been transferred to Henshaw's bed. Henshaw came into my room to get my opinion of how he looked prepared for slumber. I fell asleep murmuring a description he could not hear.

XI

'The following four days I count the most pleasant I have experienced. We travelled extensively with our host, becoming completely at home in this strange, new world. Upon the morning of the fifth day we were riding on the centre track of the Derby Highway, towards the outskirts of the city, when Melsona whistled to an old man walking along the pavement in the opposite direction. The old man stopped, Melsona transferred to the slow track, then to the pavement. We followed.

' "This is Senior Glen Moncho," he introduced us. "Senior is a title we have for very learned men," he added in explanation.

' "Like professor," I suggested.

' "Exactly. This is Senior Glyn Weston and Captain Henshaw." He smiled as we shook hands in turn. "The senior is our most prominent historian. I thought he would have a special interest in meeting you."

'Henshaw was quick to seize the opportunity. He asked, "Who won the White-Yellow War of 2481 to 2486?"

' "The women," replied the senior promptly.

' "The Women!" Henshaw looked dazed.

' "The war lasted nine years, not five," the senior continued. "It was brought to an end by a militant organisation of women who, first of all, refused to bear any more children, then deserted the munitions factories, causing both sides to withdraw great numbers of men to replace them, and, finally, took up arms and assassinated the individuals whom they considered to be the key men of the war. The conflict was the direct cause of the world matriarchy that held sway for the next three thousand years."

' "Well I'm a dirty soldier!" cried Henshaw.

' "So you're the famous time traveller," said the senior, turning to me. "I've heard a lot about you over the newscast. I understand that you are to be invited to the Annual Convention of Scientists to be held in Metro a week hence. It would be very interesting if you could bring your travel apparatus with you."

' "Now isn't that curious!" I said. "I've been here several days and it has never occurred to me to inquire what has happened to the device."

' "It is quite safe," said Melsona. "It was carried along on the road while you were being taken into my house. It was rescued and placed in the Science Museum until such time as you wish to have it."

' "Good," I responded. "Would you like to go and see it?" Both Senior Moncho and Melsona indicated their eagerness to inspect the time-travel room. We cut through a side street to the next road, moving inward, stood upon an outer five-mile track and glided cityward.

'"The most curious thing about time travel," I said to the senior, "is how it alters one's ideas. For instance, one would think that I have defeated Nature by living for thousands of years but, as a time traveller, I know that I have not. Actually, I am about a week older than when I first started my experiment. I now know that Nature has fixed the date of my end, not in terms of years of human computation but in terms of years of my life. I shall die a certain number of *my own years* after my birth, regardless of how that number of years may be divided out, or distributed over the future."

'"There is one point which, to my mind, is even more curious," the senior remarked. "How is it that we, with our great civilisation, our enormous interest in every branch of science, have not been able to solve the problem which already has been solved by two who antedate us by thousands of years."

'"Henshaw hasn't solved it," I told him.

'"I was not referring to Henshaw, but to your predecessor."

'"My predecessor?" I failed to grasp his meaning.

'"I told you that time travelling was known to us," put in Melsona. "I told you when first we met that it had been accomplished before."

'I searched my memory and found that I did have a vague recollection of him mentioning something of the sort. It had escaped me at the time, as I had felt rather confused.

'"When Schweil turned up, claiming that –"

'"Schweil!" I shouted at the top of my voice. "Did you say *Schweil?*"

'"Yes!" answered the senior, looking very startled. "When he turned up claiming he had come originally from about your time, he was laughed at, and was –"

'"Tell me," I interrupted, "from what year did he claim to come?"

'"Let me see." He studied the ground and thought for an exasperatingly long time. "It was nineteen hundred and forty-four, I think."

'"That's it!" I howled, literally shaking with excitement. "That's it!" Surrounding people stared at me as if they thought I was mad. I was making an exhibition of myself and didn't care.

'"Did you know him?" asked the senior, a soothing note in his voice.

'"No. He died a few years before I was born. Or he was believed to have died. He set out in his private airplane with the avowed intention of attending a scientific congress in New York. He vanished. The wreckage of his plane reached the shores of Nova Scotia a month later. He was rather eccentric, not very popular, and some people suggested that it was a plain case of suicide. His theories, and those of his successor, were used by me. What happened to him? Where is he? Please tell me about him – everything you know."

'The senior looked overwhelmed, took a deep breath and said, "In 312 N.R., four hundred and sixty years ago, this man Schweil appeared on the outskirts of Metro, our great city on the Thames, and claimed that he had travelled through time from the past. His machine took the form of a dull metal sphere about three metres in diameter. Despite his atavistic characteristics, he was not believed. His machine was examined and pronounced a hoax.

' "He was in the unfortunate position of not being able to prove his assertations, except by giving a practical demonstration and thus removing himself from the very people who were to be convinced, for he told us that though one could travel into the future there could be *no* motion into the past."

' "Quite correct," I said, hanging on every word.

' "He was very bitter. According to him ours was the eighth era he had visited and in not a single one of them had he been believed. In the end, he emigrated to Venus, taking his metal sphere with him. He lived there for nearly a year, then managed to convince us that his claims were justified. He did it by stepping into his sphere and vanishing before the eyes of a thousand colonists. He has not returned. We have seen nothing of him since."

' "He has travelled forward," I said, jumping about like a cat on hot bricks. "He has travelled forward. Oh, if only I could meet him! A man from my own time, a fit companion for my travels! I *must* meet him! I must find him somehow! He awaits me somewhere in the to-morrow. I must seek him! My travel room must be transported to Venus at once!" So saying, in my crazy excitement I jumped on to the faster centre track and rushed along it, my mind filled with only one thought: to get to the Science Museum as soon as possible and arrange for the transport of the room.

'The exertion of running must have calmed my mind. Half a mile along the road I transferred myself to the pavement and waited for the others to catch up with me. They came stringing along breathlessly, first Henshaw, then Melsona, the senior a bad last and finding the going hard.

'Together we entered the Museum, where Melsona inquired where my room had been placed. Following his lead, we reached it on the top floor. By this time I had cooled enough to remember that my companions wanted to examine it. I opened the door and proceeding to explain to them how the ray apparatus worked and the theories it made use of.

'The room seemed to have suffered slight damage. The outside corners were badly scratched and dented; one of the windows was cracked. I pulled out the valves and ray tube, held them up to the light and examined them, replacing them when I found them still in excellent condition.

'I went over the whole apparatus, adjusting a cable here and tightening a terminal there. For several minutes I pottered about like a mother attending to her babe. I was in the act of bending down to examine a McAndrew vibrator contact when a nausea overcame me and the contact blurred before my gaze.

XII

'I straightened, saw the windows framing a semitransparency in which a vague shadow danced, flickered, then disappeared like the flame of a snuffed candle. Panic overcame me, as a familiar mist obscured my sight. I realized what had happened. By some means the projector had come into operation.

'Frantically, I searched the enveloping haze for the switch. The rapidly alternating impressions of smoothness and fibrousness fuddled my mind. I searched like a drunken man looking for he knew not what. Everything my hand touched I pulled. I tugged at unseen objects that refused to move. I heaved upon things that came out and sprang back again.

'For how long I acted thus I do not know. I grew frantic at the knowledge that my last sweet world was receding rapidly into the irreclaimable past. I commenced to kick wildly in every direction. A crash of glass, followed by a sensation of strain, rewarded my efforts. The mist cleared, leaving me gazing at a broken valve. The time-travel room had come to rest.

'A heavy vapour coated the inside surfaces of the windows. My attention was attracted by a loud, hissing sound. I was astounded to discover air rushing outward through the gap in the partly-open door. I closed the door tightly, turned the pet cock of the spare oxygen bottle, rubbed moisture from the window-panes and looked out.

'The scene before my eyes was most depressing: a smooth, even expanse of dirt and dust extended to the horizon without break. The sky to one side was sparkled with white light, to the other it loomed a dark, ominous purple. One glance told me that the world of this day was airless, deserted, dead. Horror took command of me with the knowledge that my hours were numbered. Death awaited me without – and within!

'Hours later, with the precious oxygen still dribbling away, I stared gloomily through the windows of my room, noting that the sky had not changed in the slightest degree and that apparently I was stationed in a zone of perpetual twilight. Even as I watched, some instinct drew my attention to the far horizon. There, in a majestic curve, swooped a colossal space ship, its sleek body glistening, its tail plumed with fire. My heart leaped as I followed its line of flight until it dipped to an invisible landing place just over the edge of the Earth.

'It did not occur to me to wonder why a space ship should fly over an airless world. The idea that I might be the victim of my own delusion never entered my head. I folded a handkerchief to form a pad, secured it over the end of the nearly empty oxygen bottle and opened the door. Ramming the pad against my nostrils, I ran towards the horizon –

'For endless miles I seemed to run with heaving chest, thudding heart and whirling brain. My tongue swelled in my mouth, my eyes protruded painfully; I ceased to see. Whether I was moving in a straight line or in circles, I did not know or care. The main thing was to keep moving. Delirium became my master; I moved, moved, moved like an automaton.

'I must have dropped the oxygen bottle; I must have fallen and died. But I have no recollection of it. My last memory of Earth is that of fleeing on leaden feet like one chased by phantoms in a nightmare. You know the rest of my story. I came to my senses lying in the resuscitation room at Kar Institute, my body racked with pain, my pulses throbbing in sympathy with the beating of a mechanical heart suspended over my chest.

'What next? You are entitled to know. It is my intention to spend a little while touring your beautiful world. I wish to see the sights, to study your customs. With much interest I have learned that the immense amount of work resulting from the Great Migration has caused many radical changes from the world I visited last. I want to read about the Great Migration, to learn all there is to learn about this remarkable epic in human history, to know the nature of the changes it has brought about such as, for instance, your return to a monetary system.

'Then I shall set to work and build myself another time-travel room. I shall do this because I am going to find my age-compatriot Schweil. We need each other. Would you like to know how I expect to accomplish this? Let me tell you.

'I shall make a series of very short jumps into the future and from then I shall derive the data necessary for certain calculations which, when completed, will enable me to set out for a pre-determined date. If Schweil has not turned up by then, I shall leave a message for him, making an appointment far in the future, and will then depart for that date. When Schweil arrives, and gets my message, he will travel to the same date. Thus we shall meet at a rendezvous in futurity.

'I have no doubt that the scheme will work, if only Schweil is given my message. You will have to look for him. I am sure that already he has returned a dozen times since last he was heard of. Because of his previous receptions, knowing his character as I do, I can tell you he is likely to return secretly, without publicity.

'You can assist me! All I ask of you is that you keep my story and my message ever fresh!'

The stereo announcer padded softly in the direction of the transmission screen. The auditorium was a mass of eyes fixed intently on one central figure. With an abrupt movement, Glyn Weston, the 'Seeker of Tomorrow', left the stage.

The Dead Spot

BY JACK WILLIAMSON

from *Marvel Science Stories*, November 1938

Now that neither Edmond Hamilton nor Murray Leinster appears to be actively writing sf, Jack Williamson becomes the author with the longest-running active sf career, having first appeared in print in the December 1928 *Amazing* with 'The Metal Man', and who is still going strong now, forty-seven years later.

He is not the oldest active writer though, several exceed him in years, notably Clifford Simak, Manly Wade Wellman and the grande dame of mystery writing, Miriam Allen De Ford. Williamson was born in Arizona on Wednesday, 29 April 1908, and spent his childhood years on a barren farm. He discovered *Amazing* from its earliest issues and soon began to churn out a flood of sf, much showing the marked influence of A. Merritt, not just in theme but in style and description. Particularly prevalent in his fiction was the use of colour, noticeable from the titles alone: 'Through the Purple Cloud', 'The Green Girl', 'In the Scarlet Star' and 'The Blue Spot'. In reading 'The Dead Spot' take notice of the number of occasions colour is used solely as a description, eg 'a brief purple glare', 'a flat grey waste', 'dust that burned with cold violet, green, purple, yellow . . .', and 'roseate light'. Such chromatic illustration resulted in Williamson's stories often being chosen for the cover scene on the magazine, apart from the commercial value of his name.

While Williamson produced many memorable short stories, he seemed more at home writing novels. Between 1929 and 1943 no less than sixteen were serialised in the magazines (plus one reprinted), and on two occasions he had two running concurrently. In 1934 *Wonder* ran *Xandulu* while *Astounding* thrilled readers with *The Legion of Space*, and in 1936 *Astounding* carried

The Cometeers concurrent with *The Ruler of Fate* in *Weird Tales*.
Few other authors can claim as much. His serials have continued
to appear in the magazines ever since.

Whereas most of Williamson's fellow writers fell by the wayside
with the changes in sf after the Second World War, Williamson
remained in the vanguard. 'With Folded Hands', appearing in the
July 1947 *Astounding*, is still regarded as one of *the* classic robot
stories and has been included in many anthologies since.

Besides being an acknowledged expert on H. G. Wells,
Williamson has also been instrumental in introducing courses of
science fiction in American colleges, which until recently took up
much of his time. He is currently Professor of English at New
Mexico University. Fortunately he still produces sf, often in
collaboration with Frederik Pohl, one of the most recent being
The Org's Egg serialised in *Galaxy* in 1974. His recent solo novel,
The Moon Children (1971) is a remarkable work, as full of colour
and excitement as his earliest tales, yet essentially modern in style
and narration. Williamson is without doubt part of the backbone
of science fiction.

The Dead Spot came on May 8, 1940. One day the land had been
golden with the harvest of wheat. The next, in a circle that covered
ten thousand square miles of Kansas and Nebraska, there was
only death.

It happened at dusk. A brief purple glare lit the sky. All who had
seen it felt a burning of the skin, a leaden ache in the bones, a
torturing thirst. And they died – hideously.

Medical skill was useless; doctors fell with the rest. The corpses
crumbled to a gray, heavy ash, that no wind could stir. Dwellings
and barns and wheat, rotted by the incredible decay that attacked
all organic matter, fell to heaps of dust. It was curiously luminous
by night, and the sun rose upon a flat gray waste of leprous doom.

Its edge was queerly sharp. And all who ventured beyond the
barrier, even planes flying high above, instantly fell. The whole
world was appalled by this inexplicable cancer on the planet that
teleview reporters named the Dead Spot. What had happened?
What if it happened again? Seeking an answer to those harrowing
questions, the President called Congress into emergency session.

No relief was needed, for no survivors had come from the
murdered land. Science failed to explain what had desolated it.
The perplexed legislators ended by creating the Special Secret
Service.

Seeking a chief for the SSS, the President sent for a man who had been on the bottom of the Pacific on the catastrophic night. Ryeland Ames, then only twenty-five, was already twice famous for daring deep-sea explorations in the *benthosphere* of his own design, and for startling success in smashing the atom with his own *super-cyclotron.*

A tanned, rugged six-footer, with stiff, tangled red hair and level blue eyes, Ames walked into the executive office and listened soberly.

'I'll do anything I can, Mr. President,' he said. 'But there are older men than I am, better trained. Rathbone, for instance, is the best radiation physicist in the world.'

'Rathbone is in the hospital,' said the President, 'not expected to recover. He was injured in an experiment that went wrong.' His eyes leapt back to the lean scientist-explorer. 'No, you're the man for the job, Ames. The Dead Spot swallowed two hundred thousand people. If the thing happens again, it may take two million—or the whole world, for all we know! Your job is to find what it is, and stop it.'

'Thank you, Mr. President,' said Ryeland Ames. 'I'll do my best.'

And Ames did it. The SSS was completely organized within a week, with five hundred men recruited from police and federal investigation departments. He set a guard about the Dead Spot, surrounded it with a ten-foot steel fence to keep out the unwary, and gathered a staff of scientists to study every angle of the disaster.

He even got Dr. Gresham Rathbone. The physicist was dying in the hospital of an incurable heart trouble, aggravated by his injuries. Ames built him a new heart!

This novel blood-pump utilized the principles of Lindbergh and Carrel. It was a tiny, compact instrument, anchored in the chest cavity, its platinum tubes ingeniously sutured to the great veins and arteries. The nerves, from the cardiac plexuses, controlled it through indicative contact with a minute electro-magnetic relay.

Its most remarkable feature, however, was its motive power. A trace of hydrogen from water vapor, transmuted into helium through a secret process Ames had discovered in his super-cyclotron experiments, provided exhaustless energy. This 'iron heart', Ames promised, would run a hundred years. It was only necessary for Rathbone to take weekly injections of the pale green liquid catalyst that activated the atomic reaction.

On his feet in a few weeks, Rathbone joined Ames' scientific staff. He was a tall man, hawk-faced, with thick grizzled hair and sharp, deep-set frosty blue eyes, still pale and irritable from his illness.

'I've drawn a map of the Dead Spot,' Ames told him, when he reported to the headquarters tent. 'The center of the circle was the town of Freedom.' His level eyes searched Rathbone's bleak, seamed face. 'And we have discovered that that is where you were injured. I want to know what you were doing there, Rathbone.'

His hollow eyes smouldered with a savage bitterness.

'I'd be dead, but for you,' Rathbone said. 'And I'll do anything I can.' His lean fingers closed like claws. 'The man who injured me was Dr. Clyburn Hope!' he gasped hoarsely. 'And it was Hope who made the Dead Spot!'

Ames started. 'Tell me,' he whispered. 'What happened?'

'Hope had an uncanny genius,' rasped Rathbone's nasal voice. 'He was the best biophysicist in America. He was working at Freedom. By inducing mutations and growing artificial cells, he was creating new species.'

'New species?' Ames gasped.

Rathbone's sunken eyes flared again.

'That's it—he wasn't satisfied with the present human race. That's where we quarreled!' His hands relaxed. 'Mutations have been caused most successfully by transforming the genes of cell-chromosomes with various rays,' he explained. 'And Hope called on me to work with him, because I had specialised in radiations.'

Ames leaned forward, listening.

'Evolution,' Rathbone went on, 'has been a haphazard advance, made possible by the bombardment of the germ plasm with cosmic rays and their secondary radiations. Such men as Muller, with his fruit fly experiments, have accelerated evolution many thousands of times by making use of X- or radium rays. But Hope found something better yet – the *sigma*-field.

'That is a special space warp analogously related to the magnetic field. Its significant peculiarity is that it makes nearly all atoms above neon unstable, radioactive. The *sigma*-field speeds evolution to the limit imposed by actual destruction of the germ cells!

'With that, and his technique of building synthetic life-cells through combination of the great protein molecules, Hope set out to create a new race, to replace humanity!'

His claws of hands had knotted again.

'That's why we quarreled. For I knew that his new race must be enemies of the old.' He caught a gasping breath. 'We – we fought in the laboratory. He injured me – fatally, but for your skill, Ames.'

'And his *sigma*-field is what made the Dead Spot!'

'Eh!' Ames stared at him, at last nodded. 'I see,' he murmured. 'The radioactivity destroys normal life – could it be to make room for his new beings?' He stood up, eagerly. 'Can you neutralise the field?'

'No.' Rathbone shook his head. 'Hope treated me like a mechanic. I designed equipment to his order, but he was very secretive about his theories and discoveries. Of course, however, my skill is at your service.'

'Thanks, Doctor,' Ames said. 'We need you. If you can crack the Dead Spot – '

And gaunt Gresham Rathbone became head of the great new SSS laboratory beside the desolated circle. Millions of dollars were poured into it. He and Ames and a hundred others worked there, desperately. A dozen lives were lost, by hideous cancer-like radiation-burns. But the secret of the *sigma*-field eluded all search.

And the Dead Lands remained unconquerably – deadly.

A series of strange deaths, however, three years later, in metallurgical refineries, the Fort Knox depository, and the Bank of England, led to investigation by the SSS. All the victims had died of radiation-burns. And Ames' men found millions of dollars in gold, silver, and platinum, that showed a diminishing temporary radioactivity. The source could not be traced, but Ames suggested a theory.

'Transmutation could be going on, in the Dead Spot,' he told Rathbone. 'Precious heavy metals, under that radiation, building up out of light elements. If it were possible for men to enter and depart alive –'

'Men,' broke in Rathbone solemnly, 'or the synthetic beings of Dr. Hope!'

And other years went by. Ryeland Ames remained in charge of the SSS. His haggard face grew grim. His blue eyes took on a haunted look. For months of each year he lived in an observation balloon moored near the wall of death, studying its radiation with electrometers, spectroscopes, and Geiger counter tubes. Terrible burns sent him three times to the hospital. His bleak face was dark-tanned, scarred.

He became grimly close-mouthed, even with Rathbone. Few

had seen the photograph always in his wallet. Its background was the flat desolation of the Dead Lands. It showed the tiny, distant figure of a woman, flying high over that weird plain – apparently on white frail wings. But he answered no questions about the picture's original.

The Dead Spot, late in 1959, began to grow!

Like a grey cancer on the Earth, it spread. The fence was swallowed up. Vegetations and buildings fell to heavy, unstirring dust. Few lives were lost, for Ames superintended the evacuation of doomed towns and farms ahead of the slow, inexorable advance. But no effort could check it.

The Dead Lands had already touched the Missouri. Its waters now absorbed more and more of the deadly energy. It became a river of terrible death, weirdly luminous by night. All the abandoned cities below crumbled to the dust of death: Kansas City, St. Louis, Memphis, New Orleans.

Two years later, in a rude little camp that would have to be abandoned on the morrow, Ames told Rathbone that he was going into the Dead Spot.

'But you can't do that!' Stern lines formed around the long mouth of Rathbone, and grey fear shadowed his hollow eyes. 'It would be – death.'

'I've got to,' Ames said flatly. 'The Dead Spot has got to be stopped. From its rate of spread, you can figure the life of any city, or the life of the world. And that isn't very long.'

'A dozen SSS men have gone in,' Rathbone objected. 'With every protection we could devise. And not one came out. Life simply can't exist, in the Dead Spot.'

'But it does. I've seen it – photographed it.'   .

And Ames displayed the picture in his wallet. Frowning, doubtful, Rathbone studied it silently.

'Snapped it out of the balloon, with a telephoto lens.' The haunted eyes and the deep voice of Ames had softened. 'I had seen her before, with binoculars – half a dozen times in the last three years. And – well – I've dreamed of her.'

The gaunt scientist made a harsh snorting sound, and a deep flush spread over the tanned face of Ames.

'I'm just telling you, Rathbone,' he said grimly. 'I'm not explaining it, because I can't. But, three different times in the balloon, when I was half dead with fatigue, I thought – or dreamed – that she was speaking to me. She's winged, really. Her name's Arthedne. She's in some desperate trouble. And she knows a lot about all this mystery. If I could find her –'

Rathbone snorted again.

'Anyhow, I'm going.' Ames reached swiftly for the photograph. 'I've got the outfit designed – a few new additions of my own. I want you to check my plans –'

'I tell you,' Rathbone insisted, 'life can't exist –'

'It does!' Ames rapped. 'What's more, there is a regular traffic, in and out. Our detectors have picked up rocket planes, flying too high to trail. And there's more poisoned metal on the market! It has been doctored to neutralise the radiation, but there's still enough to prove it came out of the Dead Spot!'

A queer-looking plane, a month later, stood on a field near the advancing border of the Dead Lands. It was squat, stubby, grey with a special lead paint. The streamlines of its fuselage covered a four-foot globe that contained a layer of water between double walls of lead alloy.

Beside the machine, Ryeland Ames stood swaying in a bulky suit of lead cloth, so heavy that even his powerful frame could hardly support it. His blue eyes peered through immense lenses of leaded glass. A heavy automatic was strapped to his belt, balanced by two bright cylinders of steel.

'The lead will absorb part of the rays,' he told eager teleview reporters. 'Magnetic screens will deflect a few more. The hydrogen atoms in the water will catch a few neutrons. Protection isn't perfect. But I hope to see the middle of the Dead Spot, and come back alive.'

He started clambering awkwardly into the big lead ball.

A reporter demanded, 'Those cylinders –'

'Atomic bombs,' grunted Ames. 'Stable triatomic hydrogen, under high pressure. My catalytic process will convert it instantly into helium – and enough free energy to level half a city.'

The heavy door was screwed into place. A periscope peered back and forth. The plane roared clumsily across the field, took off heavily. Watchers held their breath, as it flew into the unseen barrier. But it didn't fall. It drove on, straight into the desolate heart of the Dead Lands. It diminished to a speck, and vanished beneath the grey horizon.

But the deep voice of Ames boomed a report through the short wave communicator:

'Following a faint streak that must have been a highway. Below is a rectangular pattern in the dust. Must have been a town. . . .'

Silence again, whispering static.

'Oxygen valve stuck!' It was half an hour later, Ames' voice

was fainter. 'Had to open port to breath. Can't understand
failure – tested valve this morning. . . .

'Cramped and aching. Skin begining to tingle. Rays getting to
me, all right. But may have time. . . .'

Another humming pause.

'Something ahead. . . .

'Buildings! Green smoke puffing from a tall stack. A long grey
dump, and big shovels digging. Looks like a mine! – And a field,
with long rocket planes standing on it! Must be where the
transmuted metal . . .'

Ten strained, whispering minutes.

'Engine heating.' The voice was hoarse, taut. 'Missing – gasoline
disintegrating, perhaps – but, *there*!' It was a gasp of incredulous
wonder. 'There – it's a city! . . .

'Yes, a city in the middle of the Dead Spot. Metal towers. Stacks
pouring out green smoke. And machines – such huge machines!
But I've got to turn back. Radiation getting me. . . .'

A longer silence, then the final whisper:

'Never make it. Motor cutting out. Missouri in sight ahead.
Something – a queer flicker on the bluffs! And I see something
moving – looks like a metal giant! – Well, Rathbone, you told me
so! But carry on! The SSS must stop the Dead Spot!'

The faint voice ceased abruptly. The whir and crackle of the
strange energies of the Dead Lands was the only farther sound
from the receiver. Night fell and the forbidden circle turned
weirdly luminous again.

Pressing both hands against his throbbing head, Ryeland Ames
tried to sit up. His head bumped something. Then he remembered.
The crash had stunned him. He was still in the leaden ball.

His skin was feverish, stinging. A dull ache gnawed at his bones.
Thirst tortured him. He wanted to drink the water seeping through
the fractured inner wall, but he knew that absorbed radiations
had turned it to liquid death –

The dusty, crumbling death of the Dead Spot.

Clumsy in the heavy suit, he opened the little door. It was
dusk. The flat waste already glowed with its eerie, sullen
luminosity. The bluff beyond the Missouri shone darkly, and the
river was a lazy serpent of lambent doom.

There he had seen what looked like a metal giant. Now,
riverward, he caught a fugitive gleam. Was it the same metal thing,
skulking cautiously up the dry ravine, stalking him? And what
was it? Man, or some weird creation of Clyburn Hope?

He scrambled stiffly out of the sphere, felt with lead-gloved hands for the automatic and the two atomic bombs. Leaving the smashed, already glowing and crumbling wreckage of the plane, he struck out upriver.

'Checking out, sure,' he muttered. 'But first I'll find out one more answer.'

For it was upriver that he had seen the flicker on the bluff.

Strange journey. He tramped through piles of heavy dust that burned with cold violet, green, purple, yellow. He waded depressions filled with luminous gas that seared his lungs like flame. Stumbled. Rose heavily. Fell again.

The ache grew swiftly in his bones. His body was on fire. Thirst was a shrieking agony. . . . Once he looked back, saw a moving glint. Was the thing following? It didn't matter much. He was crawling, now.

Then, when all seemed hopeless, she came to meet him.

Arthedne – the bright being of the picture and the dreams. She soared above the dark bluffs, glided down toward him on wings of gorgeous flame. The bright pinions didn't beat, but there was a pulse of colour in them, of gold and rose, mauve and saffron.

Ames dragged himself to his knees, waved. And she dropped lightly on the shining dust before him. Her wings were suddenly gone! Two tall slender things, like antennae, curved upward from her shoulders. The wings had been aflame between them.

'Ames!' Her voice was silver melody. 'You have come!'

She walked quickly to him. She was tall and slim and beautiful. A tunic of woven silver clung to the curves of her body. A jeweled star gleamed from the shining band that held her golden hair.

'Arthedne!' he choked. 'You – ?'

She was real, all human. Even the delicate lifted threads of her colour-pulsing antennae were natural, beautiful. They were as necessary as her arms. She would have been disfigured without them.

A faintness came over him. He gritted teeth against the pain.

'My darling,' he whispered. 'I've seen you – flying. So beautiful. I've wanted – hoped – to come!'

He swayed. Her quick hands caught him.

'Ames! I perceived you, beyond the New Lands!' Her strong arms supported him. 'In you alone I felt kinship to my own lost race, whom the Tech-men murdered. So I called to you. But Ames!' She shuddered with alarm. 'You are ill!'

He whispered, 'Dying.'

'Not yet, Ames – for I brought you this!' She produced a small metal bottle, poured its screw-cap full of a pale blue liquid. 'You are like Dr. Hope – of the old life, that cannot endure the rays of the New Lands. Drink this! It is the neutralization formula that kept him alive.'

Ames swallowed it, and felt a swift recovery. In a few minutes he was able to rise from his knees. He remembered the skulking follower, looked apprehensively back.

'I saw the Tech-men.' Her voice was a quiver of dread. 'They are hunting tonight. But perhaps we can find Futuron. They have never found that, beyond its *tau*-field screen.'

Her eyes were dark with grief and dread.

'Futuron was the last city the *neozoans* – my people – built,' she said. 'When the war-rays of the Tech-men destroyed all the rest, they ceased to strive, and bore no more children to live in the world of despair. I am now the last *neozoan* – and still the Tech-men hunt.

'But come!'

Ames stumbled heavily on again, beside her. They came to the bluff where he had seen that puzzling flicker. It was a jutting salient thrust out into the shining, poisoned Missouri. Excitement and fear sent shimmers of color along Arthedne's fine antennae.

'Where – ?' Ames was gasping.

He stopped, rubbed his eyes. He had heard a faint humming. And now the Dead Lands were gone. They had come under a vast dome of roscate light. Before him rose graceful colonnades, and the white towers of spacious temple-like buildings.

'This is Futuron,' she whispered.

'But I didn't see it!' protested Ames, bewildered. 'And this pink light –'

'The city is invisible – almost,' explained Arthedne. 'That is our only defence from the Tech-men. The tau-field, an adaptation of Dr. Hope's *sigma*-field, deflects light around it. The rosy light is a fortunate incidental effect. Otherwise, since no light enters save through the spy-ports, we should be in darkness.'

Delicate flowers, strange bright-hued blooms of varieties Ames had never seen, splashed pleasing colour everywhere. He caught an exotic perfume. Arthedne led him to the simple, silent apartments where she dwelt.

'All this city?' Ames asked, trying to repress a shudder of awed wonder, 'has lived and died since the Dead Spot came?'

'Time moves faster, in the *sigma*-field,' she told him. 'Twelve of my people fled with Dr. Hope to found the first *neozoan* city. I was born of the fourth generation.'

They sat on a couch in a rose-lit pavilion. Ames turned intently to face her.

'The Tech-men?' he questioned. 'Dr. Hope created them?'

'Them, and the *neozoans* also,' whispered the girl. 'He sought to fashion a new race, more gifted than the old. There were many errors, failure. The Tech-men were the first that gave promise. They had large brains, inadequate bodies that had to be supplemented with intricate mechanisms. He kept them under observation in the laboratory compound.

'Meantime, however, another experiment brought forth the *neozoans*. We had a balance of physical and mental beings, so that we are largely independent of machines. We had new senses, new capacities, that the Tech-men lacked.

'Dr. Hope chose to let us live – as a small colony, that might exist at peace with the old race. And he planned to destroy the Tech-men, for he was alarmed by a strain of atavistic ruthlessness that had appeared in them.

'All his creations were adapted to life in the *sigma*-field, and for that very reason unable to survive outside it. Dr. Hope planned merely to reverse the field in the quarters of the Tech-men.

'They had keen brains, however, and the desire to survive. They suspected Dr. Hope. Under the leadership of a mutant born with an aggressive will to power, they revolted, seized all the laboratory, and expanded the *sigma*-field to cover a vast space.'

'I see!' whispered Ames. 'That was when the Dead Lands came!'

'To us, the New Lands,' murmured the strange girl beside him. 'The rebel leader, the Tech-Czar, attempted to kill Dr. Hope and all the *neozoans*,' she went on. 'But they escaped, to found our first city. And the Tech-men, remaining, built Technopolis –'

'Technopolis!' gasped Ames. 'The city I saw, under a pall of green?'

'That city of great machines is Technopolis,' said the girl. 'From it, the Tech-men have waged war on my hunted people. A long time the *neozoans* hoped to survive. They built seven cities, hidden under the *tau* screen. But Dr. Hope died, and the new atomic weapons of the Tech-Men overwhelmed them.

'Then the Tech-Czar began stepping up the power of the *sigma*-field, maintained by the great generators in the central tower of Technopolis. He seeks to spread the New Lands over all the planet. He aims at world dominion –'

'So that's it!' whispered Ames. 'It's that machine that makes the Dead Spot grow. Then it must be destroyed!'

Arthedne started to speak, checked herself. Strange dread darkened her violet eyes. Her slender body shuddered in the silver tunic, and the glow of colour faded from her drooping antennae. At last she said, gravely: 'That would not be easy, Ames, Technopolis is far distant, and the Tech-men are already hunting us, here. The city, and the tower of Tech-Czar, are guarded well. And the field generators are too vast to be easily wrecked.'

'I've a weapon.' Ames touched the atomic bombs. 'And I can try.'

The girl seemed oddly solemn.

'When you are recovered,' she murmured slowly. 'Now you might remove your armour,' she told him. 'It is useless since you have taken the drug. And we shall dine.'

Silently, she set a table laden with food as strange as the flowers that graced it. Eerie music played softly, the threnody of a vanished race. Ames tried to forget the horror beyond the rose-lit colonnades and the desperate task ahead. He drew the grave, strange beauty of Arthedne down beside him. She was warm and tremulous in his arms, her lips intoxicating. For a space he did forget. . . .

Suddenly Arthedne sprang to her feet, antennae lifted and shimmering with alarm.

'They have found Futuron,' she cried. 'The spy-plate will show –'

She ran to a tall cabinet. Ames looked over her shoulder, into a hooded screen, and saw the Tech-men. A score of twelve-foot metal giants, they came stalking swiftly out of the flat drear Dead Lands. Gleaming arms gripped strange mechanisms – weapons! Frantically, Ames searched for a gap in the closing rank. But there was only the deadly shining river.

He caught the girl to his body.

'You can fly,' he whispered swiftly. 'You can get away. And I'll – meet 'em!'

She shook her golden head, hopelessly.

'They will be watching with the war-rays. They would burn my body in the air.' She clung to him, whispering, 'Besides, Ames, I would not leave you.'

His level blue eyes suddenly narrowed. He snatched one of the little atomic bombs, quickly set its time-screw.

'There is a way!' His voice rang low and grim. 'The river!'

He dropped the bomb behind him. Counting under his breath, he caught the girl's arm, ran with her to a tower that stood on the riverward edge of Futuron. Behind them, four Tech-men burst through the rosy screen.

Crouching to meet them, Ames saw bulging, gigantic heads inside the glass and steel of great helmets. He glimpsed tiny, atrophied limbs at the controls of metal bodies. Then the glittering eyes, deep sunken, huge, lambently nonhuman, discovered them. Bright tubes lifted ominously.

The automatic hammered and jerked in the great hand of Ames. The three nearer giants fell, helmets shattered. But, from the fourth, a green, incandescent finger probed the white columns of Futuron. A graceful central spire exploded – and the rosy screen was gone!

All the flat waste of the Dead Lands was revealed again, and· the circle of giants came rushing in, queer weapons level.

'– nineteen,' breathed Ames. 'Hundred-twenty – *Jump!*'

He dropped the empty gun, swept Arthedne with him off the bluff. The oily shining river leapt up, struck them a cold crushing blow, swallowed them.

A terrific impact came through the water, as if all the world had rung to the impact of a cosmic hammer. Half stunned, they struggled back to the surface – and dived swiftly again to escape the shattered fragments of the city and its invaders raining on the river.

'Futuron!' Her whisper was choked, sorrowful. 'Where I was born –'

They swam down the river. Nothing moved along the darkly gleaming bluffs. They came out at last, lay side by side to rest on a bar of yellow-shining sand. Ames drew the girl into his arms, whispering, 'My darling, you know I love you.'

Her violet eyes misted with quick tears. She kissed him, clung to him. Soft warm hues pulsed through her long antennae.

'Hold me closer, Ames,' she murmured, 'before joy makes me fly away.' But suddenly her slim body went rigid as if from a spasm of pain. She sat up. 'Why pretend?'

Her voice was hoarse, choked with pain.

'You are like my own people, Ames. There is a new, vital spark – in you, evolution sought to bridge the gap between your race and mine. And I love you, Ames – want you. But you cannot

dwell in the New Lands – not long. And I cannot live outside.'
She caught a sobbing breath. 'Your nature gropes toward mine.
But there is still a gulf between that we can never cross. Unless –'
 Her violet eyes looked far across the shining river, and she
shuddered again.
 'Unless as we die!'
 They left the river at dawn. Ames examined the remaining
atomic bomb, his only weapon; found it unharmed.
 'You can guide me,' he asked, 'to Technopolis?'
 She nodded, solemnly. 'But there are many barriers.'
 All that day they tramped across the dusty, desolate plain.
They saw the grey ribbons where roads had been, and the low
square piles of crumbled houses. Now and then, in a small heap
of ash, they could trace the white outline of a human skeleton.
 Ames said nothing of his own discomfort. But his skin stung,
and the ache was returning to his bones. He began to suffer with
torturing thirst.
 Arthedne seemed in a strange mood. Sometimes she tried to
jest, but always upon her was a shadow. Once she left him, soared
away on the wings of splendid flame that spread at will between
her delicate antennae.
 'It is glorious to fly,' she breathed happily, alighting again
beside him. 'I wanted one more hour of it.'
 The wings flickered out. She caught his hand and they walked
on together. The strange dust had fallen again, and the dead plain
was beginning to glow with unearthly, sullen light, when she
paused, pointed.
 'There –' she whispered. 'Technopolis!'
 It stood upon the dark-burning crest of a far-off hill. A wall of
metal towers, bathed in a glare of light, palled with greenish
smoke. Approaching, they heard the hum and beat of great
machines, a harsh and endless reverberation.
 'I see,' whispered Ames, 'why Dr. Hope repented of creating the
Tech-men. For your city of Futuron was a sweet heaven. And this
clangorous hell is too much like the cities I have seen.'
 They slipped forward again, and Arthedne pointed.
 'That highest central spire – the one tipped with cold purple
flame – is the tower of the Tech-Czar,' she breathed. 'The
generators are there.'
 Ames clutched his hydrogen bomb. 'If we can reach it –'
 They came to a twenty-foot barrier of jagged metal blades, from
whose points leapt vicious blue sparks. Ames stopped before it,
doubtfully. But Arthedne held out her arms to him.

'Hold my wrists,' she whispered. 'My wings are strong enough.'
He obeyed, reluctantly. Her antennae spread outward, and the
wings of light flashed between them again. Her face set white with
pain. But she rose, lifting him. They passed over the fence, glided
towards the base of the towers beyond.

'Oh, Ames!' came her tortured breath. 'I can't –'
The bright wings vanished. They sprawled together on the
ground. Ames picked her up. She was breathless, unconscious.
In a moment, her violet eyes flickered open.

'Sorry,' she whispered. 'Exhausted –'

They slipped ahead, through luminous gloom, into deep canyons
of streets. A group of gigantic robot-like bodies stalked down
upon them, strange huge heads visible in helmet-turrets. Ames
drew Arthedne back against a wall, looked at her in dismay.

And she had vanished!
A sudden pall of absolute blackness fell upon him. Bewildered,
he groped again for her hand, found it tense and quivering. She
caught his fingers, returned a swift pressure. In a moment the
darkness lifted. The Tech-men had passed.

'We –' Ames gasped. 'Invisible?'
The girl nodded, motioned for caution.

'Dr. Hope's evolutionary acceleration created new powers in
the neozoans,' she whispered, 'mostly based on a direct grasp of
the warp of space. We fly by one adaptation of it. Another creates
a light-deflecting field – but I am not expert enough to do it well
for long.'

They slipped on toward the lofty central tower. Again and again
Arthedne made them briefly invisible, while danger passed. Ames
clutched the atomic bomb. They came at last to a main
thoroughfare.

'Beyond.' She pointed at the next building. 'The tower.'
Endless ranks of metal giants stalked before them. The pavement shook to a rumbling stream of immense, strange machines.
They were like tanks, Ames thought; cannon; and armoured
cars mounting huge queer tubes.

'The Tech-Czar is prepared for war,' whispered Arthedne. 'If
your race penetrates the New Lands –'
An armed giant came down the alley behind them. She made
them invisible until it had passed. The effort left her weak. But a
break came at last in the war-like parade. Wrapped again in
darkness, they darted across the street.

Ames stumbled on the opposite curb. A dull sob of exhaustion came from the girl. The shroud of darkness vanished, and she fell beside him. Ames saw gigantic Tech-men striding upon them. A whistle of alarm ripped his nerves.

'Sorry –' Arthedne whispered faintly, and lay still.

Ames set the dial of the bomb at three seconds, hurled it through a window into the tower that made the *sigma*-field. He snatched the girl into his arms, stumbled with her back across the street, just ahead of a lumbering tank.

Scores of the Tech-men, whistling, humming, clicking, were reeling grotesquely toward him. Breathless, Ames counted:

'– two – and – three !'

He dropped with the girl behind the land ironclad, waited for the burst of supernal energy that should level the city. Probably kill them, too; but if it stopped the Dead Spot, that didn't matter. He waited, breathless.

And·nothing happened.

A fantastic, clangorous mob, the metal giants came down upon them. Frantically, still, he hoped – until another Tech-man stalked out of the tower, carrying the atomic bomb. The time-fuse was smashed. Could the Tech-men have foreknown – ?

A flailing metal arm crushed the thought from his head.

Awareness came back to Ames in a lofty metal hall, lit with the harsh red flicker of neon. Two mechanical giants held him upright. pinioned his arms. Before him stood a great desk, covered with buttons and dials and strange apparatus. Behind it sat another metal-armoured body, larger than the rest, its occupant concealed behind a grim visage of steel and glass. The ruler, it must be – the Tech-Czar!

Arthedne was gone – where?

Immense and terrible as a god of steel, the Tech-Czar turned upon Ames. Great cold lenses peered down. A brazen voice boomed through the red-lit hall:

'Man of the old race, why are you here?'

Ames gritted his teeth, twisted against the metal arms.

'Very good,' came the sawing voice. 'You need not speak aloud. . . . You are Ryeland Ames, chief of the SSS. . . . What are the plans of your organisation, against the advance of the New Lands?'

Sick, trembling, Ames tried to make his mind a blank.

'Good,' came the rasping. 'Then we need fear no opposition.'

1

2

3

4

1   *Wonder Stories,* April 1936 – Frank R. Paul. The final issue of
Hugo Gernsback's *Wonder* with Paul's admirable oil painting of a scene
from Thomas Gardner's 'The World of Singing Crystals'.
2   *Astounding Stories,* February 1938 – Howard V. Brown. The first
of *Astounding's* famous 'mutant' covers displaying a scientifically
accurate scene of the surface of Mercury from Raymond Gallun's story
'Mercutian Adventure'.
3   *Unknown,* March 1939 – H.W. Scott. The first issue of one of
fantasy's most legendary magazines, featuring Eric Frank Russell's
'Sinister Barrier'.
4   *Dynamic Science Stories,* February 1939 – Frank R. Paul. As the sf
magazine field expanded and new publishers entered the scene, cover
art was commissioned in general rather than for specific stories. This
was one of the earliest examples, and the cover inspired sf fan Robert
Lowndes to write his own story around the cover, 'The Slim People'.

5

6

7

8

5   *Thrilling Wonder Stories*, June 1939 – Howard V. Brown. When
Brown wasn't drawing impressionistic covers for *Astounding*, he was
churning out adventure covers for *Thrilling Wonder* which celebrated
its tenth anniversary with a bumper all-star issue.

6   *Tales of Wonder*, Summer 1939 – John Nicholson. By 1939
Britain was starting the sf magazine race with two publications of
which Walter Gillings' *Tales of Wonder* proved the most memorable.

7   *Amazing Stories*, November 1939 – Harold W. McCauley. With
Amazing in the hands of new publishers, editor Ray Palmer cast around
for new artists, of which one of the best stylists was Harold McCauley,
represented here with his impression of a scene from William F.
Temple's 'The 4-Sided Triangle'.

8   *Astonishing Stories*, February 1940 – Jack Binder. Jack was the
brother of writers Earl and Otto (Eando) Binder, and, while regularly
featured with magazine interior illustrations, seldom painted covers.
His appearance on the first issue of *Astonishing* is therefore something
of a rarity.

9   *Fantastic Adventures,* February 1940 – Robert Fuqua. One of Palmer's leading artists was Robert Fuqua who provided this astonishing action cover to the large-size *Fantastic Adventures,* illustrating 'The Prince of Mars Returns' by *Buck Rogers* creator Philip F. Nowlan.

10   *Science Fiction,* March 1941 – Frank R. Paul. With the vast expansion of the field the number of cover artists mushroomed, but there was still room for the dean of sf artists, Frank R. Paul.

11   *Marvel Stories,* April 1941 – H.W. Scott. Scott's fine illustration for 'The Iron God' by Jack Williamson adorned the last issue of *Marvel,* the first of the new generation of sf magazines which blossomed in 1938.

12   *Astounding SF,* August 1941 – Hubert Rogers. During this decade *Astounding* featured many space rockets on its covers, of which this example is particularly impressive.

13   *Famous Fantastic Mysteries*, October 1941 – Virgil Finlay. As a fantasy artist Finlay dominated the scene from the late 1930s onwards, predominantly with his black-and-white illustrations. His cover work for magazines like *FFM* was one of the factors that led to their fame.

14   *Weird Tales*, March 1942 – Hannes Bok. Ideally suited to the bizarre policy of *Weird Tales* were the avant-garde pictures by Hannes Bok, here illustrating Robert Bloch's 'Hell on Earth'.

15   *Super Science Stories*, May 1942 – Virgil Finlay. Finlay again, illustrating a scene from 'Lemmings' by Wilfred Owen Morley, a penname of Robert Lowndes.

16   *Startling Stories*, Winter 1945 – Earle K. Bergey. King of the brass bras was Earle Bergey, represented here with a scene from Noel Loomis's 'Iron Men'. His covers more than any other artist during the 1940s epitomised the general public's impression of science fiction.

The steel face turned to the guards. 'Take him to the laboratory. Proceed with the dissection of both prisoners. It will provide new data on differing races – and en'd any opposition from them.

Dissection – both prisoners!

The words throbbed in the aching head of Ames, like a gong of doom. The giants dragged him away. He tensed his body, made a sudden, desperate lunge, jerked away from the one on his right. The other tripped, crashed down awkwardly. He was free.

Arthedne! Where – ?

But the metal limbs of the first guard flailed at him. A red bomb of pain exploded in his bruised head. Dimly, he knew that he was being carried – toward the dissection laboratory. . . . Then he was lying on the street. His head throbbed, and his stiff body ached. He struggled upright, incredulously.

For Technopolis was – dead.

The two guards lay beside him on the pavement. Their tiny, big-headed bodies were stiff and blue in the cabs of their sprawled machines. Technopolis had stopped. All the Tech-men he could see were dead. What had happened?

And Arthedne – where was she?

He stumbled uncertainly across the silent street. Beyond the end of it, he glimpsed a remote vista of the Dead Lands – oddly changed. The weird luminosity was gone. The consuming fire in his own body, he realised suddenly, had diminished.

'Ames!'

A weakening voice sobbed his name. Arthedne dropped beside him. Her bright wings turned pallid, vanished. She swayed. He caught her in his arms.

'Arthedne,' he whispered. 'My darling – what – ?'

'I did it, Ames – for you. Invisible, I escaped them, and flew to the tower. I reversed the *sigma*-field – Dr. Hope gave us the secret of that. It ended the New Lands – and the Tech-men – and – me!'

She shuddered in his arms.

'Good-bye, Ames, dear. But, try –'

She clung to him. He kissed her lips – they seemed already cold. Her arms stiffened suddenly. A clear crimson gleam pulsed through her antennae. Trembling, she gasped:

'Quick, Ames! The tower! The Tech-Czar – still alive –'

The warning uttered, she went limp in his arms. The antennae drooped, turned lifeless grey. Heavy lids fell wearily across the pools of her eyes. Ames laid her down tenderly, and ran into the tower.

An elevator, when his fumbling had mastered the controls, shot him upward. He leapt out, into the vast, red-litten hall of the Tech-Czar.

The seat behind the desk was empty, the metal-bodied ruler gone. Had the Tech-Czar protected himself against reversal of the field? Ames caught a gleam from the desk – a tiny hypodermic, lying in a stain of spilled green liquid.

Meshing gears clashed, beyond, followed by a rising whine. Terror struck Ames, a stunning avalanche. That must be the *sigma*-field generator, that Arthedne had stopped. The Tech-Czar must be setting it going again, to restore the Dead Spot!

Staggered with despair, Ames realised that he was unarmed. He ran back toward the elevator, snatched from a dead Tech-man a heavy thing of crystal and white metal that might serve as a club.

With that, he stumbled into the vast room beyond the desk of the Tech-Czar. It was crowded with tremendous mechanisms. Some he could recognise. Atomic converters, evidently based on the same principles he had discovered. Colossal generators, transformers, thirty-foot vacuum tubes. Vast coils wound on a cylindrical core that must be the base, he thought, of the purple-shining spire.

That thing made the Dead Spot!

His bewildered, racing eyes found another thing he recognised: a replica of his own super-cyclotron. Its 400-ton electro-magnet loomed forty feet above. He saw its ray-screened observation cage, far across the room. Had his own discovery been turned against the world?

Then he saw the Tech-Czar, towering beside the switchboard of the *sigma*-field generator. Ames shuddered, his fingers tense on the club. What could he do, against the steel tons of that fifteen-foot colossus?

Yet he made himself slip forward. The mounting river of tremendous sound swept away the little noise he made. Faint hope lifted him. Perhaps, one sudden blow –

But that lofty head turned abruptly. Huge lenses stared at him, out of that monstrous metal visage. And a great metal voice grated out:

'Well, Ryeland Ames! You come in time to witness the finish of your race. We had been expanding the New Lands slowly, to make room for Technopolis only as we required it. But now I am stepping up the field to embrace all the planet – and blot out your degraded and obsolescent breed!'

The Tech-Czar bent ominously toward the control board. And the aching body of Ames tensed, quivered. He steadied himself against the cold mass of the super-cyclotron, tried to calm his spinning brain.

'You have not destroyed Technopolis, Ryeland Ames.' The huge lenses glittered at him, like blue orbs of evil. 'For I am Technopolis!'

A giant arm dropped toward the dials and switches.

'Wait!' The voice of Ames came hoarse and breathless, choked with a startled incredulity. '*Tech-Czar*! – I know who you are! And I know how to stop you – and Technopolis!'

Slowly, his trembling hands lifted the unfamiliar weapon.

'And I know why the SSS failed to stop the Dead Lands,' rang his hard accusations. 'And why my plane fell in the Dead Lands! And why my atomic bomb did not explode –'

The metal colossus had reeled away from the control-board. It came lumbering toward him with a tread that shook the floor. The frantic fingers of Ames fumbled with the unknown device, as if he half-understood it.

'I know why you survived the Tech-men!'

The shining giant towered over him. Steel limbs crushed down, like colossal hammers. Ames dropped the unfamiliar weapon, flung himself back against the super-cyclotron.

'Die!' rasped the Tech-Czar. 'With your evil breed –'

But the groping fingers of Ames found a familiar lever. Blue sparks leapt from an automatic switch. The hum of the generators deepened, to a new load. The dropped weapon flew toward the colossal magnet, crashed and clung against it.

The brazen voice of the Tech-Czar instantly stopped. And the great metal body toppled deliberately forward. Ames pushed back the little lever, to stop the super-cyclotron, stepped quickly aside. The Tech-Czar crashed down where he had stood.

'No, your metal disguise didn't take me in,' he whispered softly to the inert, colossal mechanism. 'Because I saw the needle on your desk, and the spilled catalyst. And I knew how to stop you, because once I ruined a good watch by coming too near when the super-cyclotron was running – and I knew that the magnetic relay in your head was a good deal more delicate than a watch.'

The fall had shattered the crystal panels from the turret. And the gaunt grey face that stared up at Ames, rigid and hideous in the unseeing agony of death, was the face of Dr. Gresham Rathbone!

'When the Tech-Czar didn't die,' whispered Ames, 'I knew he was a man. And you were the logical one. Because you had worked with Dr. Hope, and knew all about the Tech-men – more than you ever told me.

'You were jealous of Hope, and hated him – that's clear from your lies about him. You must have been eager enough to lead the revolt of the Tech-men. And you must have made millions out of the transmuted metals, slipping in and out by rocket!'

Ames stopped the atomic converters, stilled that thundering river of power. He went back, weary and alone, through the Tech-Czar's silent hall, and down to the voiceless streets.

In the gray cold light of a cheerless dawn, he sought Arthedne. Chilled, shivering, he peered up and down the shadowed canyon. In its hushed quiet, death was a near reality. Ames hadn't realised how tired he was, or what irreparable damage the radiations of the Dead Lands had done his big body. He reeled. His vision blurred. All his being was a flame of slow, quenchless fire.

But he stumbled on. At last his failing eyes glimpsed a shapeless blot of white, unmoving on the pavement. That must be Arthedne. Last of the wondrous race that might have come –

He halted, groping, bewildered.

Light as a breath of wind, something had brushed his stinging face. His dimming eyes caught a flicker of gay colour, tenuous, vanishing. A sweet, familiar voice came to him, faintly:

'Wait, Ames – my darling! Don't go back to – that. For I am here!'

He put out his hands, fumbling blindly.

'Arthedne?' he whispered incredulously. 'You are still – living? Where are you, Arthedne? It is growing so dark! I heard your voice, but I can't see you.'

'Here I am, Ames,' he thought she said. 'Here beside you.'

He felt a light cool touch on his shoulder. Swaying heavily on his feet, he spurred his weary senses, trying to see her again.

'I thought –' he gasped, 'thought – you died.'

'Yes, Ames, my body died.' The tiny voice came through thickening mists, from far away. 'But there was another power, which I had only suspected, that came to me in the moment of death. Through the same organs that enabled me to fly and to vanish, it created a new field in space, that can be the dwelling of my being, forever.'

He swayed, giddily.

'I feel in you something of the same power, Ames – for in you was evolution following the path of my lost people. With the aid of that – if you will try, Ames dear – you can come to me.'

The mists closed in, dense and black. A cold numbness blotted away all pain. Ames knew, dimly, that he was falling.

'Come to me, Ames.' Small and definitely remote, he still heard Arthedne's voice. 'Come across the barrier!'

He tried –

The Special Secret Service discovered, that day, that the Dead Spot was no longer dead. A plane landed at noon on the grey dust beside Technopolis, and triple S operatives hastened to explore its silent wonders. They found Ryeland Ames and Arthedne, lying side by side. On both their faces was the shadow of a wondering, hopeful smile.

The 4-Sided Triangle

BY WILLIAM F. TEMPLE

from *Amazing Stories*, November 1939

Our third British writer in this collection, William F. Temple, was one of the cornerstones of the early days of British fandom, being a co-tenant of the infamous flat which also housed Arthur C. Clarke and other notables. He helped produce the fan journal *Novae Terrae* and the *Bulletin* of the British Interplanetary Society, then in its formative years. So it was not surprising that when *Tales of Wonder* appeared, Temple would be present. His first story in print had been a short horror yarn, 'The Kosso', which he had succeeded in selling to *Thrills*, one of the Philip Allan series of hardcover anthologies of such tales published in the early thirties. Temple's writing ambitions had been fired by three main factors: his admiration for the work of H. G. Wells; a passion for the cinema; and membership of the British Interplanetary Society. The first and last criteria gave him a natural bias toward science fiction.

For sf fans his first appearance was with 'Lunar Lilliput' in the second *Tales of Wonder*. This story, while now badly dated, is nevertheless fascinating reading, particularly in its use of the British Interplanetary Society as the perpetrators of the first moon flight. Long out of print the story was revived in the October 1969 *Spaceway*, and is well worth hunting down. Temple's next contribution was even more intriguing, 'The Smile of the Sphinx', with its concept that the cat originated on the moon. Written in a plausible and Wellsian style, this whimsical yarn is a delight.

Temple then broke into the US market by selling to Palmer, and thus American audiences came to discover the quality of his prose style which was more akin to mature Wells than to the pulp level. His 'The 4-Sided Triangle' received many accolades and was voted first by the readership, and even though Don Wilcox had used the same basic theme in 'Wives in Duplicate' just three issues earlier, it is the Temple story that is remembered.

Willy Ley, author and space-travel pioneer, opined that Temple had wasted the plot of a good novel by compressing it into a short story. Temple agreed, and began to novelise it when he was a Desert Rat with the British 8th Army. The half-completed manuscript was lost in a skirmish in the Tunisian desert. Temple began it again, between other skirmishes. When it had reached the halfway mark, 40,000 words again, the new manuscript vanished during a night operation on the Anzio beachhead. Feeling like Robert the Bruce's spider, Temple began it again, finishing it with frozen fingers high in the Alps in the last days of the War. The acute postwar paper shortage delayed publication until 1949. It was justly acclaimed a major work and was subsequently filmed. The original story, however, has remained all but lost to British readers and it is a privilege to be able to resurrect it in this anthology.

In the 1950s Temple re-emerged as a leading magazine writer, selling stories of consistently high quality on both sides of the Atlantic. Some of his more recent work of interest includes 'The Year Dot' in the January 1969 *If*, and 'Life of the Party' in the February 1970 *Vision of Tomorrow*. At the same time he produced two exceptional novels, *Shoot at the Moon* and *The Fleshpots of Sansato*. A sensitive writer he suffered a creative setback when the latter work was clumsily butchered in an unauthorised abridgement for paperback.

Temple, now just sixty, lives and works full-time in Folkestone, in Kent, and is unable to devote as much time to writing as he and his many admirers would like. Hopefully, this situation may be rectified in the near future.

Three people peered through a quartz window.

The girl was squashed uncomfortably between the two men, but at the moment neither she nor they cared. The object they were watching was too interesting.

The girl was Joan Leeton. Her hair was an indeterminate brown, and owed its curls to tongs, not to nature. Her eyes were certainly brown, and bright with unquenchable good humour. In repose her face was undistinguished, though far from plain; when she smiled, it was beautiful.

Her greatest attraction (and it was part of her attraction that she did not realise it) lay in her character. She was soothingly sympathetic without becoming mushy, she was very level-headed (a rare thing in a woman) and completely unselfish. She refused to lose her temper over anything, or take offence, or enlarge upon the truth in her favour, and yet she was tolerant of such lapses in others. She possessed a brain that was unusually able in its dealing with science, and yet her tastes and pleasures were simple.

William Fredericks (called 'Will') had much in common with Joan, but his sympathy was a little more disinterested, his humour less spontaneous, and he had certain prejudices. His tastes were reserved for what he considered the more worthy things. But he was calm and good-tempered, and his steadiness of purpose was reassuring. He was black-haired, with an expression of quiet content.

William Josephs (called 'Bill') was different. He was completely unstable. Fiery of hair, he was alternately fiery and depressed of spirit. Impulsive, generous, highly emotional about art and music, he was given to periods of gaiety and moods of black melancholia. He reached, at his best, heights of mental brilliance far beyond the other two, but long bouts of lethargy prevented him from making the best of them.

Nevertheless, his sense of humour was keen, and he was often amused at his own absurdly over-sensitive character; but he could not change it.

Both these men were deeply in love with Joan, and both tried hard to conceal it. If Joan had any preference, she concealed it just as ably, although they were aware that she was fond of both of them.

The quartz window, through which the three were looking, was set in a tall metal container, and just a few feet away was another container, identical even to the thickness of the window-glass.

Overhead was a complex assemblage of apparatus: bulbous, silvered tubes, small electric motors that hummed in various unexpected places, makeshift screens of zinc, roughly soldered, coils upon coils of wire, and a network of slung cables that made the place look like a creeper-tangled tropical jungle. A large dynamo churned out a steady roar in the corner, and a pair of wide sparkgaps crackled continuously, filling the laboratory with a weird, jumping blue light as the day waned outside the windows and the dusk crept in.

An intruder in the laboratory might have looked through the window of the other container and seen, standing on a steel frame in a cubical chamber, an oil painting of 'Madame Croignette' by Boucher, delicately illuminated by concealed lights. He would not have known it, but the painting was standing in a vacuum.

If he had squeezed behind the trio at the other container and gazed through their window he would have seen an apparently identical sight: an oil painting of 'Madame Croignette' by Boucher, standing on a steel frame in a vacuum, delicately illuminated by concealed lights.

From which he would probably not gather much.

The catch was that the painting at which the three were gazing so intently was not quite the same as the one in the first container – not yet. There were minute differences in colour and proportion.

But gradually these differences were righting themselves, for the whole of the second canvas was being built up atom by atom, molecule by molecule, into an exactly identical twin of the one which had felt the brush of Francis Boucher.

The marvellously intricate apparatus, using an adaption of a newly-discovered magnetic principle, consumed only a moderate amount of power in arranging the lines of sympathetic fields of force which brought every proton into position and every electron into its respective balancing orbit. It was a machine which could divert the flow of great forces without the ability to tap their energy.

'Any minute now!' breathed Will.

Bill rubbed his breath off the glass impatiently.

'Don't do that!' he said, and promptly fogged the glass over again. Not ungently, he attempted to rub a clear patch with Joan's own pretty nose. She exploded into laughter, fogging the glass hopelessly, and in the temporary confusion of this they missed seeing the event they had been waiting days for – the completion of the duplicate painting to the ultimate atom.

The spark-gaps died with a final snap, a lamp sprang into being on the indicator panel, and the dynamo began to run whirringly down to a stop.

They cleaned the window, and there stood 'Madame Croignette' looking rather blankly out at them with wide brown eyes that exactly matched the sepia from Boucher's palette, and both beauty spots and every hair of her powdered wig in place to a millionth of a millimetre.

Will turned a valve, and there was the hiss of air rushing into the chamber. He opened the window, and lifted the painting out gingerly, as if he half-expected it to crumble in his hands.

'Perfect – a beauty!' he murmured. He looked up at Joan with shining eyes. Bill caught that look, and unaccountably checked the impulsive whoop of joy he was on the point of letting loose. He coughed instead, and leaned over Joan's shoulder to inspect 'Madame Croignette' more closely.

'The gamble's come off,' went on Will. 'We've sunk every cent into this, but it won't be long before we have enough money to do anything we want to do – anything.'

'Anything – except to get Bill out of bed on Sunday mornings,' smiled Joan, and they laughed.

'No sensible millionaire would get out of bed any morning,' said Bill.

The steel and glass factory of Art Replicas, Limited, shone like a diamond up in the green hills of Surrey. In a financial sense, it had actually sprung from a diamond – the sale of a replica of the Koh-i-noor. That had been the one and only product of Precious Stones, Limited, an earlier company which was closed down by the government when they saw that it would destroy the world's diamond market.

A sister company, Radium Products, was going strong up in the north because its scientific necessity was recognised. But the heart of the three company directors lay in Art Replicas, and there they spent their time.

Famous works of art from all over the world passed through the factory's portals, and gave birth to innumerable replicas of themselves for distribution and sale at quite reasonable prices.

Families of only moderate means found it pleasing to have a Constable or Turner in the dining room and a Rodin statuette in the hall. And this widely-flung ownership of *objets d'art*, which were to all intents and purposes the genuine articles, strengthened interest in art enormously. When people had lived with these things for a little while, they began to perceive the beauty in them – for real beauty is not always obvious at a glance – and to become greedy for more knowledge of them and the men who originally conceived and shaped them.

So the three directors – Will, Bill, and Joan – put all their energy into satisfying the demands of the world for art, and conscious of their part in furthering civilisation, were deeply content.

For a time.

Then Bill, the impatient and easily-bored, broke out one day in the middle of a Directors' Meeting.

'Oh, to hell with the Ming.estimates!' he cried, sweeping a pile of orders from the table.

Joan and Will, recognising the symptoms, exchanged wry glances of amusement.

'Look here,' went on Bill, 'I don't know what you two think, but I'm fed up! We've become nothing but dull business people now. It isn't our sort of life. Repetition, repetition, repetition! I'm going crazy! We're *research* workers, not darned piece-workers. For heaven's sake, let's start out in some new line.'

This little storm relieved him, and almost immediately he smiled too.

'But, really, aren't we?' he appealed.

'Yes,' responded Joan and Will in duet.

'Well, what about it?'

Will coughed, and prepared himself.

'Joan and I were talking about that this morning, as a matter of fact,' he said. 'We were going to suggest that we sell the factory, and retire to our old laboratory and re-equip it.'

Bill picked up the ink-pot and emptied it solemnly over the Ming estimates. The ink made a shining lake in the centre of the antique and valuable table.

'At last we're sane again,' he said. 'Now you know the line of investigation I want to open up. I'm perfectly convinced that the reason for our failure to create a living duplicate of any living creature was because the quotiety we assumed for the xy action –'

'Just a moment, Bill,' interrupted Will. 'Before we get on with that work, I – I mean, one of the reasons Joan and me wanted to retire was because – well –'

'What he's trying to say,' said Joan quietly, 'is that we plan to get married and settle down for a bit before we resume research work.'

Bill stared at them. He was aware that his cheeks were slowly reddening. He felt numb.

'Well!' he said. 'Well!' (He could think of nothing else. This was unbelievable! He must postpone consideration of it until he was alone, else his utter mortification would show.)

He put out his hand automatically, and they both clasped it.

'You know I wish you every possible happiness,' he said, rather huskily. His mind seemed empty. He tried to form some comment, but somehow he could not compose one sentence that made sense.

'I think we'll get on all right,' said Will, smiling at Joan. She smiled back at him, and unknowingly cut Bill to the heart.

With an effort, Bill pulled himself together and rang for wine to celebrate. He ordered some of the modern reconstruction of an exceedingly rare '94.

The night was moonless and cloudless, and the myriads of glittering pale blue points of the Milky Way sprawled across the sky as if someone had cast a handful of brilliants upon a black velvet cloth. But they twinkled steadily, for strong air currents were in motion in the upper atmosphere.

The Surrey lane was dark and silent. The only signs of life were the occasional distant glares of automobile headlights passing on the main highway nearly a mile away, and the red dot of a burning cigarette in a gap between the hedgerows.

The cigarette was Bill's. He sat there on a gate staring up at the array in the heavens and wondering what to do with his life.

He felt completely at sea, purposeless, and unutterably depressed. He had thought the word 'heartache' just a vague descriptive term. Now he knew what it meant. It was a solid physical feeling, an ache that tore him inside, unceasingly. He yearned to see Joan, to be with Joan, with his whole being. This longing would not let him rest. He could have cried out for a respite.

He tried to argue himself to a more rational viewpoint.

'I am a man of science,' he told himself. 'Why should I allow old Mother Nature to torture and badger me like this? I can see through all the tricks of that old twister. These feelings are purely chemical reactions, the secretions of the glands mixing with the blood-stream. My mind is surely strong enough to conquer that? Else I have a third-rate brain, not the scientific instrument I've prided myself on.'

He stared up at the stars glittering in their seeming calm stability, age-old and unchanging. But were they? They may look just the same when all mankind and its loves and hates had departed from this planet, and left it frozen and dark. But he knew that even as he watched, they were changing position at a frightful speed, receding from him at thousands of miles a second.

'Nature is a twister, full of illusions,' he repeated. . . .

There started a train of thought, a merciful anaesthetic in which he lost himself for some minutes.

Somewhere down in the deeps of his subconscious an idea which had, unknown to him, been evolving itself for weeks, was stirred, and emerged suddenly into the light. He started, dropped his cigarette, and left it on the ground.

He sat there stiffly on the gate and considered the idea.

It was wild – incredibly wild. But if he worked hard and long at it, there was a chance that it might come off. It would provide a reason for living, anyway, so long as there was any hope at all of success.

He jumped down from the gate and started walking quickly and excitedly along the lane back to the factory. His mind was already turning over possibilities, planning eagerly. In the promise of this new adventure, the heart-ache was temporarily submerged.

Six months passed.

Bill had retired to the old laboratory, and spent much of that time enlarging and re-equipping it. He added a rabbit pen, and turned an adjacent patch of ground into a burial-ground to dispose of those who died under his knife. This cemetery was like no cemetery in the world, for it was also full of dead things that had never died – because they had never lived.

His research got nowhere. He could build up, atom by atom, the exact physical counterpart of any living animal, but all such duplicates remained obstinately inanimate. They assumed an extraordinary life-like appearance, but it was frozen life. They were no more alive than waxwork images, even though they were as soft and pliable as the original animals in sleep.

Bill thought he had hit upon the trouble in a certain equation, but re-checking confirmed that the equation had been right in the first place. There was no flaw in either theory or practice as far as he could see.

Yet somehow he could not duplicate the force of life in action. Must he apply that force himself? How?

He applied various degrees of electrical impulses to the nerve-centers of the rabbits, tried rapid alternations of temperatures, miniature 'iron lungs', vigorous massage – both external and internal – intra-venous and spinal injections of everything from adrenalin to even more powerful stimulants which his agile mind concocted. And still the artificial rabbits remained limp bundles of fur.

Joan and Will returned from their honeymoon and settled down in a roomy, comfortable old house a few miles away. They sometimes dropped in to see how the research was going. Bill always seemed bright and cheerful enough when they came, and joked about his setbacks.

'I think I'll scour the world for the hottest thing in female bunnies and teach her to do a hula-hula on the lab. bench,' he said. 'That ought to make some of these stiffs sit up!'

Joan said she was seriously thinking of starting an eating-house specialising in rabbit pie, if Bill could keep up the supply of dead rabbits. He replied that he'd already buried enough to feed an army.

Their conversation was generally pitched in this bantering key, save when they really got down to technicalities. But when they had gone, Bill would sit and brood, thinking constantly of Joan. And he could concentrate on nothing else for the rest of that day.

Finally, more or less by accident, he found the press-button which awoke life in the rabbits. He was experimenting with a blood solution he had prepared, thinking that it might remain more constant than the natural rabbit's blood, which became thin and useless too quickly. He had constructed a little pump to force the natural blood from a rabbit's veins and fill them instead with his artificial solution.

The pump had not been going for more than a few seconds before the rabbit stirred weakly and opened its eyes. It twitched its nose, and lay quite still for a moment, save for one foot which continued to quiver.

Then suddenly it roused up and made a prodigious bound from the bench. The thin rubber tubes which tethered it by the neck parted in midair, and it fell awkwardly with a heavy thump on the floor. The blood continued to run from one of the broken tubes, but the pump which forced it out was the rabbit's own heart – beating at last.

The animal seemed to have used all its energy in that one powerful jump, and lay still on the floor and quietly expired.

Bill stood regarding it, his fingers still on the wheel of the pump.

Then, when he realised what it meant, he recaptured some of his old exuberance, and danced around the laboratory carrying a carboy of acid as though it were a Grecian urn.

Further experiments convinced him that he had set foot within the portals of Nature's most carefully guarded citadel. Admittedly he could not himself create anything original or unique in Life. But he could create a living image of any living creature under the sun.

A hot summer afternoon, a cool green lawn shaded by elms and on it two white-clad figures, Joan and Will, putting through their miniature nine-hole course. A bright-striped awning by the hedge, and below it, two comfortable canvas chairs and a little Moorish table with soft drinks. An ivy-covered wall of an old red-brick mansion showing between the trees. The indefinable smell of new-cut grass in the air. The gentle but triumphant laughter of Joan as Will foozled his shot.

That was the atmosphere Bill entered at the end of his duty tramp along the lane from the laboratory – it was his first outdoor excursion for weeks – and he could not help comparing it with the sort of world he had been living in: the benches and bottles and sinks, the eye-tiring field of the microscope, the sheets of calculations under the glare of electric light in the dark hours of the night, the smell of blood and chemicals and rabbits.

And he realised completely that science itself wasn't the greatest thing in life. Personal happiness was. That was the goal of all men, whatever way they strove to reach it.

Joan caught sight of him standing on the edge of the lawn, and came hurrying across to greet him.

'Where have you been all this time?' she asked. 'We've been dying to hear how you've been getting on.'

'I've done it,' said Bill.

'Done it? Have you really?' Here voice mounted excitedly almost to a squeak. She grabbed him by the wrist and hauled him across to Will. 'He's done it!' she announced, and stood between them, watching both their faces eagerly.

Will took the news with his usual calmness, and smilingly gripped Bill's hand.

'Congratulations, old lad,' he said. 'Come and have a drink and tell us all about it.'

They squatted on the grass and helped themselves from the table. Will could see that Bill had been overworking himself badly. His face was drawn and tired, his eyelids red, and he was in the grip of a nervous tension which for the time held him dumb and uncertain of himself.

Joan noticed this, too, and checked the questions she was going to bombard upon him. Instead, she quietly withdrew to the house to prepare a pot of the China tea which she knew always soothed Bill's migraine.

When she had gone, Bill, with an effort, shook some of the stupor from him, and looked across at Will. His gaze dropped, and he began to pluck idly at the grass.

'Will,' he began, presently, 'I –' He cleared his throat nervously, and started again in a none too steady voice. 'Listen, Will, I have something a bit difficult to say, and I'm not so good at expressing myself. In the first place, I have always been crazily in love with Joan.'

Will sat up, and looked at him curiously. But he let Bill go on.

'I never said anything because – well, because I was afraid I wouldn't make a success of marriage. Too unstable to settle down quietly with a decent girl like Joan. But I found I couldn't go on without her, and was going to propose – when you beat me to it. I've felt pretty miserable since, though this work has taken something of the edge off.'

Will regarded the other's pale face – and wondered.

'This work held out a real hope to me. And now I've accomplished the major part of it. I can make a living copy of any living thing. Now – do you see *why* I threw myself into this research? *I want to create a living, breathing twin of Joan, and marry her!*'

Will started slightly. Bill got up and paced restlessly up and down.

'I know I'm asking a hell of a lot. This affair reaches deeper than scientific curiosity. No feeling man can contemplate such a proposal without misgivings, for his wife and for himself. But honestly, Will, I cannot see any possible harm arising from it. Though, admittedly, the only good would be to make a selfish man happy. For heaven's sake, let me know what you think.'

Will sat contemplating, while the distracted Bill continued to pace.

Presently, he said: 'You are sure no physical harm could come to Joan in the course of the experiment?'

'Certain – completely certain,' said Bill.

'Then I personally have no objection. Anything but objection. I had no idea you felt that way, Bill, and it would make me, as well as Joan, very unhappy to know you had to go on like that.'

He caught sight of his wife approaching with a laden tray.

'Naturally, the decision rests with her,' he said. 'If she'd rather not, there's no more to it.'

'No, of course not,' agreed Bill.

But they both knew what her answer would be.

'Stop the car for a minute, Will,' said Joan suddenly, and her husband stepped on the foot-brake.

The car halted in the lane on the brow of the hill. Through a gap in the hedge the two occupants had a view of Bill's laboratory as it lay below in the cradle of the valley.

Joan pointed down. In the field behind the 'cemetery' two

figures were strolling. Even at this distance, Bill's flaming hair marked his identity. His companion was a woman in a white summer frock. And it was on her that Joan's attention was fixed.

'She's alive now!' she whispered, and her voice trembled slightly.

Will nodded. He noticed her apprehension, and gripped her hand encouragingly. She managed a wry smile.

'It's not every day one goes to pay a visit to oneself,' she said. 'It was unnerving enough last week to see her lying on the other couch in the lab., dressed in my red frock – which *I* was wearing – so pale, and – Oh, it was like seeing myself dead!'

'She's not dead now, and Bill's bought her some different clothes, so cheer up,' said Will. 'I know it's a most queer situation, but the only possible way to look at it is from the scientific viewpoint. It's a unique scientific event. And it's made Bill happy into the bargain.'

He ruminated a minute.

'Wish he'd given us a hint as to how he works his resuscitation process, though,' he went on. 'Still, I suppose he's right to keep it a secret. It's a discovery which could be appallingly abused. Think of dictators manufacturing loyal, stupid armies from one loyal, stupid soldier! Or industrialists manufacturing cheap labour! We should soon have a world of robots, all traces of individuality wiped out. No variety, nothing unique – life would not be worth living.'

'No,' replied Joan, mechanically, her thoughts still on that white-clad figure down there.

Will released the brake, and the car rolled down the hill toward the laboratory. The two in the field saw it coming, and walked back through the cemetery to meet. it. They reached the road as the car drew up.

'Hello, there!' greeted Bill. 'You're late – we've had the kettle on the boil for half an hour. Doll and I were getting anxious.'

He advanced into the road, and the woman in the white frock lingered hesitantly behind him. Joan tightened her lips and braced herself to face this unusual ordeal. She got out of the car, and while Will and Bill were grasping hands, she walked to meet her now living twin.

Apparently Doll had decided to face it in the same way, and they met with oddly identical expressions of smiling surface ease, with an undercurrent of curiosity and doubt. They both saw and understood each other's expression simultaneously, and burst out laughing. That helped a lot.

'It's not so bad, after all,' said Doll, and Joan checked herself from making the same instinctive remark.

'No, not nearly,' she agreed.

And it wasn't. For although Doll looked familiar to her, she could not seem to identify her with herself to any unusual extent. It was not that her apparel and hair-style were different, but that somehow her face, figure, and voice seemed like those of another person.

She did not realise that hitherto she had only seen parts of herself in certain mirrors from certain angles, and the complete effect was something she had simply never witnessed. Nor that she had not heard her own voice outside her own head, so to speak – never from a distance of some feet.

Nevertheless, throughout the meal she felt vaguely uneasy, though she tried to hide it, and kept up a fire of witty remarks. And her other self, too, smiled at her across the table and talked easily.

They compared themselves in detail, and found they were completely identical in every way, even to the tiny mole on their left forearm. Their tastes, too, agreed. They took the same amount of sugar in their tea, and liked and disliked the same foodstuffs.

'I've got my eye on that pink iced cake,' laughed Doll. 'Have you?'

Joan admitted it. So they shared it.

'You'll never have any trouble over buying each other birthday or Christmas presents,' commented Will. 'How nice to know exactly what the other wants!'

Bill had a permanent grin on his face, and beamed all over the table all the time. For once he did not have a great deal to say. He seemed too happy for words, and kept losing the thread of the conversation to gaze upon Doll fondly.

'We're going to be married tomorrow!' he announced unexpectedly, and they protested their surprise at the lack of warning. But they promised to be there.

There followed an evening of various sorts of games, and the similar thought-processes of Joan and Doll led to much amusement, especially in the guessing games. And twice they played checkers and twice they drew.

It was a merry evening, and Bill was merriest of all. Yet when they came to say goodnight, Joan felt the return of the old uneasiness. As they left in the car, Joan caught a glimpse of Doll's face as she stood beside Bill at the gate. And she divined that under that air of gaiety, Doll suffered the same uneasiness as she.

Doll and Bill were married in a distant registry office next day, using a fictitious name and birthplace for Doll to avoid any publicity – after all, no one would question her identity.

Winter came and went.

Doll and Bill seemed to have settled down quite happily, and the quartet remained as close friends as ever. Both Doll and Joan were smitten with the urge to take up flying as a hobby, and joined the local flying club. They each bought a single-seater, and went for long flights, cruising side by side.

Almost in self-protection from this neglect (they had no interest in flying) Bill and Will began to work again together, delving further into the mysteries of the atom. This time they were searching for the yet-to-be-discovered secret of tapping the potential energy which the atom held.

And almost at once they stumbled on a new lead.

Formerly they had been able to divert atomic energy without being able to transform it into useful power. It was as if they had constructed a number of artificial dams at various points in a turbulent river, which altered the course of the river without tapping any of its force – though that is a poor and misleading analogy.

But now they had conceived, and were building, an amazingly complex machine which, in the same unsatisfactory analogy, could be likened to a turbine-generator, tapping some of the power of that turbulent river.

The 'river,' however, was very turbulent indeed, and needed skill and courage to harness. And there was a danger of the harness suddenly slipping.

Presently, the others became aware that Doll's health was gradually failing. She tried hard to keep up her usual air of brightness and cheerfulness, but she could not sleep, and became restless and nervous.

And Joan, who was her almost constant companion, suddenly realised what was worrying that mind which was so similar to hers. The realisation was a genuine shock, which left her trembling, but she faced it.

'I think it would be a good thing for Doll and Bill to come and live here for a while, until Doll's better,' she said rather diffidently to Will one day.

'Yes, okay, if you think you can persuade them,' replied Will. He looked a little puzzled.

'We have far too many empty rooms here,' she said defensively. 'Anyway, I can help Doll if I'm with her more.'

Doll seemed quite eager to come, though a little dubious, but Bill thought it a great idea. They moved within the week.

At first, things did improve. Doll began to recover, and became more like her natural self. She was much less highly strung, and joined in the evening games with the other three with gusto. She studied Will's favourite game, backgammon, and began to enjoy beating him thoroughly and regularly.

And then Joan began to fail.

She became nerveless, melancholy, and even morose. It seemed as though through helping Doll back to health, she had been infected with the same complaint.

Will was worried, and insisted on her being examined by a doctor.

The doctor told Will in private: 'There's nothing physically wrong. She's nursing some secret worry, and she'll get worse until this worry is eased. Persuade her to tell you what it is – she refuses to tell me.'

She also refused to tell Will, despite his pleadings.

And now Doll, who knew what the secret was, began to worry about Joan, and presently she relapsed into her previous nervous condition.

So it continued for a week, a miserable week for the two harassed and perplexed husbands, who did not know which way to turn. The following week, however, both women seemed to make an effort, and brightened up somewhat, and could even laugh at times.

The recovery continued, and Bill and Will deemed it safe to return to their daily work in the lab., completing the atom-harnessing machine.

One day Will happened to return to the house unexpectedly, and found the two women in each other's arms on a couch, crying their eyes out. He stood staring for a moment. They suddenly became aware of him, and parted, drying their eyes.

'What's up, Will? Why have you come back?' asked Joan, unsteadily, sniffing.

'Er – to get my slide-rule: I'd forgotten it,' he said. 'Bill wanted to trust his memory, but I think there's something wrong with his figures. I want to check up before we test the machine further. But – what's the matter with you two?'

'Oh, we're all right,' said Doll, strainedly and not very convincingly. She blew her nose, and endeavoured to pull herself together. But almost immediately she was overtaken by another burst of weeping, and Joan put her arms around her comfortingly.

'Look here,' said Will, in sudden and unusual exasperation, 'I've had about enough of this. You know that Bill and I are only too willing to deal with whatever you're worrying about. Yet the pair of you won't say a word – only cry and fret. How can we help if you won't tell us? Do you think we like to see you going on like this?'

'I'll tell you, Will,' said Joan, quietly.

Doll emitted a muffled 'No!' but Joan ignored her, and went on: 'Don't you see that Bill has created another me in *every* detail? Every memory and every feeling? And because Doll thinks and feels exactly as I do, she's in love with you! She has been that way from the very beginning. All this time she's been trying to conquer it, to suppress it, and make Bill happy instead.'

Doll's shoulders shook with the intensity of her sobbing. Will laid his hands gently on them, consolingly. He could think of nothing whatever to say. He had not even dreamt of such a situation, obvious as it appeared now.

'Do you wonder the conflict got her down?' said Joan. 'Poor girl! I brought her here to be nearer to you, and that eased things for her.'

'But it didn't for you,' said Will, quietly, looking straight at her. 'I see now why you began to worry. Why didn't you tell me then, Joan?'

'How could I?'

He bit his lip, paced nervously over to the window, and stood with his back to the pair on the couch.

'What a position!' he thought. 'What can we do? Poor Bill!'

He wondered how he could break the sorry news to his best friend, and even as he wondered, the problem was solved for him.

From the window there was a view down the length of the wide, shallow valley, and a couple of miles away the white concrete laboratory could just be seen nestling at the foot of one of the farther slopes. There were fields all around it, and a long row of great sturdy oak trees started from its northern corner.

From this height and distance the whole place looked like a table-top model. Will stared moodily at that little white box where Bill was, and tried to clarify his chaotic thoughts.

And suddenly, incredibly, before his eyes the distant white box spurted up in a dusty cloud of chalk-powder, and ere a particle of it had neared its topmost height, the whole of that part of the valley was split across by a curtain of searing, glaring flame. The whole string of oak trees, tough and amazingly deep-rooted though they were, floated up though the air like feathers of wind-blown thistledown before the blast of that mighty eruption.

The glaring flame vanished suddenly, like a light that had been turned out, and left a thick, brown, heaving fog in its place, a cloud of earth that had been pulverised. Will caught a glimpse of the torn oak trees falling back into this brown, rolling cloud, and then the blast wave, which had travelled up the valley, smote the house.

The window was instantly shattered and blown in, and he went flying backwards in a shower of glass fragments. He hit the floor awkwardly, and sprawled there, and only then did his laggard brain realise what had happened.

Bill's habitual impatience had at last been his undoing. He had refused to wait any longer for Will's return, and gone on with the test, trusting to his memory. And he had been wrong.

The harness had slipped.

A man sat on a hill with a wide and lovely view of the country, bright in summer sunshine, spread before him. The rich green squares of the fields, the white ribbons of the lanes, the yellow blocks of haystacks and grey spires of village churches, made up a pattern infinitely pleasing to the eye.

And the bees hummed drowsily, nearby sheep and cattle made the noises of their kind, and a neighbouring thicket fairly rang with the unending chorus of a hundred birds.

But all this might as well have been set on another planet, for the man could neither see nor hear the happy environment. He was in hell.

It was a fortnight now since Bill had gone. When that grief had begun to wear off, it was succeeded by the most perplexing problem that had ever beset a member of the human race.

Will had been left to live with two women who loved him equally violently. Neither could ever conquer or suppress that love, whatever they did. They knew that.

On the other hand, Will was a person who was only capable of loving one of the women. Monogamy is deep-rooted in most normal people, and particularly so with Will. He had looked forward to travelling through life with one constant companion, and only one – Joan.

But now there were two Joans, identical in appearance, feeling, thought. Nevertheless, they were two separate people. And between them he was a torn and anguished man, with his domestic life in shapeless ruins.

He could not ease his mental torture with work, for since Bill died so tragically, he could not settle down to anything in a laboratory.

It was no easier for Joan and Doll. Probably harder. To have one's own self as a rival – even a friendly, understanding rival – for a man's companionship and affection was almost unbearable.

This afternoon they had both gone to a flying club, to attempt to escape for a while the burden of worry, apparently. Though neither was in a fit condition to fly, for they were tottering on the brink of a nervous breakdown.

The club was near the hill where Will was sitting and striving to find some working solution to a unique human problem which seemed quite insoluble. So it was no coincidence that presently a humming in the sky caused him to lift dull eyes to see both the familiar monoplanes circling and curving across the blue spaces between the creamy, cumulus clouds.

He lay back on the grass watching them. He wondered which plane was which, but there was no means of telling, for they were similar models. And anyway, that would not tell him which was Joan and which was Doll, for they quite often used each other's planes, to keep the 'feel' of both. He wondered what they were thinking up there. . . .

One of the planes straightened and flew away to the west, climbing as it went. Its rising drone became fainter. The other plane continued to bank and curve above.

Presently, Will closed his eyes and tried to doze in the warm sunlight. It was no use. In the darkness of his mind revolved the same old maddening images, doubts, and questions. It was as if he had become entangled in a nightmare from which he could not awake.

The engine of the plane overhead suddenly stopped. He opened his eyes, but could not locate it for a moment.

Then he saw it against the sun, and it was falling swiftly in a tailspin. It fell out of the direct glare of the sun, and he saw it in detail, revolving as it plunged so that the wings glinted like a flashing heliograph. He realised with a shock that it was but a few hundred feet from the ground.

He scrambled to his feet, in an awful agitation.

'Joan!' he cried, hoarsely. 'Joan!'

The machine continued its fall steadily and inevitably, spun down past his eye-level, and fell into the centre of one of the green squares of the fields below.

He started running down the hill even as it landed. As the sound of the crash reached him, he saw a rose of fire blossom like magic in that green square, and from it a wavering growth of black, oily smoke mounted into the heavens. The tears started from his eyes, and ran freely.

When he reached the scene, the inferno was past its worst, and as the flames died he saw that nothing was left, only black, shapeless, scattered things, unrecognisable as once human or once machine.

There was a squeal of brakes from the road. An ambulance had arrived from the flying club. Two men jumped out, burst through the hedge. It did not take them more than a few seconds to realise that there was no hope.

'Quick, Mr. Fredericks, jump in,' cried one of them, recognising Will. 'We must go straight to the other one.'

The other one!

Before he could question them, Will was hustled between them into the driving cabin of the ambulance. The vehicle was quickly reversed, and sped off in the opposite direction.

'Did – did the other plane –' began Will, and the words stuck in his throat.

The driver, with his eye on the road which was scudding under their wheels at sixty miles an hour, nodded grimly.

'Didn't you see, sir? They both crashed at exactly the same time, in the same way – tailspin. A shocking accident – terrible. I can't think how to express my sympathy, sir. I only pray that this one won't turn out so bad.'

It was as if the ability to feel had left Will. His thoughts slowed up almost to a standstill. He sat there numbed. He dare not try to think.

But, sluggishly, his thoughts went on. Joan and Doll had crashed at exactly the same time in exactly the same way. That was above coincidence. They must have both been thinking along the same lines again, and that meant they had crashed *deliberately*!

He saw now the whole irony of it, and groaned.

Joan and Doll had each tried to solve the problem in their own way, and each had reached the same conclusion without being aware what the other was thinking. They saw that one of them would have to step out of the picture if Will was ever to be happy. They knew that that one would have to step completely out, for life could no longer be tolerated by her if she had to lose Will.

And, characteristically, they had each made up their minds to be the self-sacrificing one.

Doll felt that she was an intruder, wrecking the lives of a happily married pair. It was no fault of hers: she had not asked to be created full of love for a man she could never have.

But she felt that she was leading an unnecessary existence, and every moment of it was hurting the man she loved. So she decided to relinquish the gift of life.

Joan's reasoning was that she had been partly responsible for bringing Doll into this world, unasked, and with exactly similar feelings and longings as herself. Ever since she had expected, those feelings had been ungratified, cruelly crushed and thwarted. It wasn't fair. Doll had as much right to happiness as she. Joan had enjoyed her period of happiness with Will. Now let Doll enjoy hers.

So it was that two planes, a mile apart, went spinning into crashes that were meant to appear accidental – and did, except to one man, the one who most of all was intended never to know the truth.

The driver was speaking again.

'It was a ghastly dilemma for us at the club. We saw 'em come down on opposite sides and both catch fire. We have only one fire engine, one ambulance. Had to send the engine to one, and rush this ambulance to the other. The engine couldn't have done any good at this end, as it happens. Hope it was in time where we're going!'

Will's dulled mind seemed to take this in quite detachedly. Who had been killed in the crash he saw? Joan or Doll? Joan or Doll?

Then suddenly it burst upon him that it was only the original Joan that he loved. That was the person whom he had known so long, around whom his affection had centred. The hair he had caressed, the lips he had pressed, the gay brown eyes which had smiled into his. He had never touched Doll in that way.

Doll seemed but a shadow of all that. She may have had memories of those happenings, but she had never actually experienced them. They were only artificial memories. Yet they must have seemed real enough to her.

The ambulance arrived at the scene of the second crash.

The plane had flattened out a few feet from the ground, and not landed so disastrously as the other. It lay crumpled athwart a burned and blackened hedge. The fire engine had quenched the flames within a few minutes. And the pilot had been dragged clear, unconscious, badly knocked about and burned.

They got her into the ambulance, and rushed her to a hospital.

Will had been sitting by the bedside for three hours before the girl in the bed had opened her eyes.

Blank, brown eyes they were, which looked at him, then at the hospital ward, without the faintest change of expression.

'Joan!' he whispered, clasping her free arm – the other was in a splint. There was no response of any sort. She lay back gazing unseeingly at the ceiling. He licked his dry lips. It couldn't be Joan after all.

'Doll!' he tried. 'Do you feel all right?'

Still no response.

'I know that expression,' said the doctor, who was standing by. 'She's lost her memory.'

'For good, do you think?' asked Will, perturbed.

The doctor pursed his lips to indicate he didn't know.

'Good Lord! Is there no way of finding out whether she is my wife or my sister-in-law?'

'If you don't know, no one does, Mr. Fredericks,' replied the doctor, 'We can't tell which plane who was in. We can't tell anything from her clothes, for they were burned in the crash, and destroyed before we realised their importance. We've often remarked their uncanny resemblance. Certainly you can tell them apart.'

'I can't!' answered Will, in anguish. 'There is no way.'

The next day, the patient had largely recovered her senses, and was able to sit up and talk. But a whole tract of her memory had been obliterated. She remembered nothing of her twin, and in fact nothing at all of the events after the duplication experiment.

Lying on the couch in the laboratory, preparing herself under the direction of Bill, was the last scene she remembered.

The hospital psychologist said that the shock of the crash had caused her to unconsciously repress a part of her life which she did not want to remember. She could not remember now if she wanted to. He said he might discover the truth from her eventually, but if he did, it would take months – maybe even years.

But naturally her memories of Will, and their marriage, were intact, and she loved him as strongly as ever.

Was she Joan or Doll?

Will spent a sleepless night, turning the matter over. Did it really matter? There was only one left now – why not assume she was Joan, and carry on? But he knew that as long as doubt and uncertaintly existed, he would never be able to recover the old free life he had had with Joan.

It seemed that he would have to surrender her to the psychologist, and that would bring to light all sorts of details which neither he, Joan, nor Bill had ever wished to be revealed.

But the next day something turned up which changed the face of things.

While he was sitting at the bedside, conversing with the girl who might or might not be Joan, a nurse told him a man was waiting outside to see him. He went, and found a police officer standing there.

Ever since the catastrophe which had wrecked Bill's laboratory, the police had been looking around that locality, searching for any possible clues.

Buried in the ground they had found a safe, burst and broken. Inside were the charred remains of books, papers, and letters. They had examined them, without gleaning much, and now the officer wished to know if Will could gather anything from them.

Will took the bundle and went through it. There was a packet of purely personal letters, and some old tradesmen's accounts, paid and receipted. These, with the officer's consent, he destroyed. But also there were the burnt remains of three of Bill's experimental notebooks.

They were written in Bill's system of shorthand, which Will understood. The first two were old, and of no particular interest. The last, however – unfortunately the most badly charred of the three – was an account of Bill's attempts to infuse life into his replicas of living creatures.

The last pages were about the experiment of creating another Joan, and the last recognisable entry read:

'*This clumsy business of pumping through pipes, in the manner of a blood transfusion, left a small scar at the base of Doll's neck, the only flaw in an otherwise perfect copy of Joan. I resented. . . .*

The rest was burned away.

To the astonishment of the police inspector, Will turned without saying a word and hurried back into the ward.

'Let me examine your neck, dear, I want to see if you've been biting yourself,' he said, with a false lightness.

Wonderingly, the girl allowed herself to be examined.

There was not the slightest sign of a scar anywhere on her neck.

'You are Joan,' he said, and embraced her as satisfactorily as her injuries would permit.

'I am Joan,' she repeated, kissing and hugging him back.

And at last they knew again the blessedness of peace of mind.

For once, Fate, which had used them so hardly, showed mercy, and they never knew that in the packet of Bill's receipted accounts, which Will had destroyed, was one from a plastic surgeon, which began:

'To removing operation scar from neck, and two days' nursing and attention.'

Hermit of Saturn's Rings

BY NEIL R. JONES

from *Planet Stories*, Fall 1940

Neil R. Jones's last new story to appear in an sf magazine was 'The Star Killers' in the August 1951 *Super Science Stories*. It not only saw the end of his magazine sf career (apart from reprints), but also of the *Professor Jameson* series of stories for which Jones is best remembered. A total of twenty-one appeared in all, making it one of the longest running sf magazine series. It began with 'The Jameson Satellite' in the July 1931 *Amazing Stories*, just twenty years earlier. In that story the Professor was contacted by the alien Zoromes whose bodies were encased on metal. With the sequel, 'The Planet of the Double Sun' in the February 1932 *Amazing*, the fun really began, and Professor Jameson, similarly encased in metal, ventured off with the Zoromes to explore the Universe.

The series was easily one of the most popular in sf, and it has consequently overshadowed much of Jones's other work in the field, especially following the paperback reprinting of the tales by Ace Books in the late 1960s. Besides another series about Durna Rangue, he produced a variety of unconnected short stories. Unconnected, that is, except for an overall framework, in which each story forms part of a future history, invented by Jones long before either Heinlein or Asimov. The key story is the Jameson adventure 'Time's Mausoleum' (*Amazing*, December 1933) which remained the basis for all of Jones's other tales.

Jones was a very capable writer, his talent evident from his very first published story, 'The Death's Head Meteor' in the January 1930 *Air Wonder Stories*. This made 'Hermit of Saturn's Rings' a cut above the quality of the stories appearing in *Planet* at that time.

Following a period of overseas service as a Colonel, Jones met his wife in London, marrying fifteen months after the War. He later invented a disc and counters game 'Interplanetary' which sold well. His hobby is the book-binding of his sf magazine collection. Until recently he worked for the New York Department of Labour.

Old Jasper Jezzan passed his fingers through the locks of his greying hair and stared from the port of the space ship at the awful approaching grandeur of Saturn's rings. The third and outermost ring, their destination, loomed toweringly. He thanked his lucky stars that he was living in this twenty-fourth century which saw mankind pushing back the boundaries of the unexplored solar system with exploits of space pioneering. In his younger years, Jasper had been on the first expedition to Mars. Now, both Mars and Venus were being colonised. Jasper had figured in many strange adventures on both worlds as well as on several of Jupiter's satellites and the asteroids. Saturn was still virgin territory.

Jasper had lately passed his three score and ten, but the spirit of adventure still burned in his hardy frame. Again he thanked the fates that he was permitted to be among the first to gaze at the glorious majesty of the great rings at this close distance. He had joined Grenard's expedition as a tried and experienced hand, and he knew that the City of Fomar was to try and thread a passage through more than fifty miles of tiny moonlets.

The City of Fomar commenced passing stray, outer moonlets while still several miles from the main band, several of them larger than the space ship and rough in contour. It was like entering a forest whose trees are less numerous as one approaches. The moonlets in the ring itself were rounded and smooth from bumping contact. Through a slight attraction of gravity, the tinier pieces clung to the largest bodies. The ship plunged deeper into the mass. Every man stood at his appointed post, yet watched the marvellous phenomena without. Jasper's was a lonesome duty at this time. It was his shift in the air rejuvenating chamber, else this story might never have been told or had fallen to the lot of a younger man. Unaware of what was impending, Jasper had looked his last upon the faces of his fellow adventurers, alive or dead. He turned a wary old eye to the gauges, and then turned his attention back to the unfolding mysteries of Saturn's ring.

The space ship of the Grenard expedition plunged ever deeper into the slowly revolving mass of moonlets. Sunlight became almost constantly eclipsed and less brilliant. Shadows, as always in space, were dark and sharp-edged. The light finally yielded to ever-increasing periods of darkness, and lights from the City of Fomar glowed through the deepening gloom. The City of Fomar occasionally bumped a moonlet in making a narrow passage, sending the fragment bumping against its neighbours in what appeared to be an endless relay of inertia without a retarding influence of any kind.

Ever deeper they penetrated into the depths of the ring. Without receiving a summoning buzz, Jasper tuned in upon the observation room where the officials of the expedition were gathered.

'There must be trillions of these little moons!'

That was Commander Grigsby. It was Grenard who replied.

'That, easy.'

'What is that white fog over there?'

'What fog – the white moonlet?'

'No – it's not a moonlet. See how it changes shape – and it is misty.'

'Why, yes, it's like smoke, and it's drifting this way.'

'See it stretch out, almost as if it were alive. What can it be?'

'Dust.'

This was an under officer.

'Without any atmosphere to float it?' Grigsby's voice was mildly derisive.

'It's breaking up.'

Jasper had travelled the space lanes too much of his life not to sense something unusual. He went to the port and looked out, putting his head to one side of the port for an oblique view. The phenomenon was directly ahead. He could not see it. Inwardly, he chafed a bit. He listened for further detail.

'What makes it move?'

'Tell me what it is, first.'

'It can't be alive!'

'The ship attracts it! The cloud is breaking up into separate parts!'

Again Jasper looked out, and he saw some of the strange stuff. It was like white smoke and possessed a volition of its own. He could no more imagine what substance made it up than he could account for its movement. It seemed almost to be alive, yet the idea was absurd even to Jasper Jezzan who had seen many strange things. This was a strange new element or combination of elements behaving strangely in this outer ring of Saturn. The rings themselves were phenomenal. The cloud from white to gray as it expanded to show dim contours of moonlets behind it. Again, it seemed to compress, appearing like a sluggish liquid or a solid.

'Here comes more of the clouds!'

'And more! Look! There! There! And all around!'

'They are merging together!'

'A part is dividing itself! See – it is splitting up!'

Bewilderment and awe expressed itself in the voices of the expeditionary heads. Jasper felt a tingle of excitement as he watched the queer antics of the unnatural material. He saw it gathering about the space ship. His port of observation went suddenly a translucent grey, and he could see nothing. He peered into the depth of that white mass separated from him by ten inches of crystal. It was like looking into dense smoke or a concentrated fog. Muffled knockings and other unaccountable sounds were heard upon the hull of the City of Fomar.

'We're not moving as fast!' Jasper heard Commander Grigsby exclaim. He detected a note of uneasiness in the voice.

'Can it be that damnable white stuff holding us back?'

'I don't know – but wait! The ports on this side of the ship are commencing to clear!'

There followed a significant pause. Jasper strained his ears for further reports. His own port was still obscured.

'Grigsby – see those long strands of the stuff, like cables! It has us fastened to the moonlets!'

'More power!' the commander ordered.

A faint, soft sighing of the hull over his head drew Jasper's eyes back to the port. He saw a white contour slide away. He looked out and saw that long, cobwebbed strands of the mist showed a remarkable adhesion and tensile strength in holding the City of Fomar to the surrounding moonlets. With the application of greater power, Jasper saw the attached moons join in the forward progress of the space ship and pass the background of further bodies. He saw moonlets collide, felt the slight deviation of the ship and heard jarring concussions of impact as the City of Fomar struck bodies in its passage. Then once more the port was covered, whiter and denser than before. From the excited comment in the observation room, he realised that conditions there were the same. The knocking and pounding mystified them all. Then a new note of alarm rose from the control room.

'It's getting into the airlock! A long, thin stream of it is pouring in like a jet of steam!'

'There must be a weak spot in the outer door!' said Grenard excitedly.

'Without a pressure of air in the chamber, the outer door is never securely fastened! We'll fill it!'

Jasper heard his name called.

'Aye, sir!'

'Put a good head of air into the lock!'

The old man sprang to the controls and heard the air go hissing through pipes on its way to the airlock.

'That damned stuff is still coming in!'

'But not so fast!'

'The air is leaking out!'

'It's driving the mist away outside!'

'Now – the door is tight!'

'The white stuff inside the lock is expanding!'

Jasper was given a sudden order to stop the air. He never did know why. No one lived to tell him. He heard many voices risen in alarm, too mixed and garbled to understand little more than the fact that the inner door had been forced. And then the outer one once more yielded. The white stuff was coming inside, and the air was leaving the ship. This last fact Jasper's horrified eyes took in at the gauges.

Sharp cries and awful screams came to him, screams which shuddered, were muffled and cut off short. This did not last very long. Soon, an ominous silence reigned. The white mist still veiled the port, and it was inside the ship, too. Jasper pulled himself together and ran down the corridor to close off that part of the ship. Too late. The white mist already curled along the floor and walls of the corridor exploringly in substantial volume. As if it felt his presence, it spread alarmingly fast in his direction the minute he stopped halfway down the corridor in dismay. A veil of the awful material streamed smokily across the ceiling and waved a curling pedicle almost in his face. An unnameable fear blanched Jasper's reason momentarily, but the old space mariner and explorer took a grip on his nerves. He turned and ran back into the atmosphere chamber. The white mist had gathered from the walls, ceiling and floor of the corridor, and he saw it coming for him slowly at first, yet with gathering momentum.

In the atmosphere chamber, he gave the main air trunk valve a quick turn which shut it off. Then he seized a space suit hanging near by and leaped inside an empty air tank just as the ball of white mist came charging madly out of the corridor at him. A shivering seized him, and it was not born of fear. A coldness was rapidly filling the ship. The air was leaving it. He found himself gasping and was glad he had turned off the main trunk. He was in darkness, having swiftly closed the hatch cover of the tank against entrance by the white menace. He turned the inside valve of the tank, feeling in the dark for it. He felt about and found the space suit; then suddenly reeled drunkenly bumping his head against the metal wall of the tank. He felt strangely exhilarated and light headed. He had given the tank too much air. This was oxygen intoxication and dangerous in his circumstances. He fumbled about and found the valve again which he turned off. Then he collapsed as everything went giddy. But here lay death from coldness, and Jasper knew he must get into the space suit. His muscles were stiff and balky from the cold temperature which was dropping lower all the time. But he got the space suit on and started its normal air supply and heat to functioning. Not until then did he give way to the strain upon him. From a half-sitting position, he fell over sideways on the floor of the tank utterly unconscious.

II

Jasper Jezzan never knew how long he lay in that air tank unconscious inside his space suit. It seemed to have been little longer than minutes, yet it might have been hours. In the dark, he took stock of himself and the situation, collecting his thoughts. Death rode that ship, the ravaging white doom its master. He wondered if anyone else had escaped. He had a subtle intuition of the cloudy menace still waiting outside. He wondered what malignant properties it held against a man in a space suit. He had no intention of putting the question to the test as long as he could hold out. He decided to wait patiently and see if the dread mist would leave the ship. Somehow, he was able to feel its presence outside the tank, roaming about, searching the City of Fomar out of which the air had drained to be wasted away into space among the moonlets.

He turned on the body lights of the space suit to relieve the monotony of the gloom and focus his thoughts upon something tangible, something he could see, although the inside of the tank with its inner valves and their controls were familiar to him. He arose and drained the tank of air. It would be necessary to at least reduce the pressure before he opened the door of the tank.

Then he sat down in the tank and waited, changing position from time to time. There was a strange affinity between this white mist and a subtle sixth sense, for Jasper realised with relief when the stuff had gone. Yet he was cautious, opening the tank door slowly and peering out. The ship's lights were still lit both inside and out. The first thing he did was to peer from the port. The City of Fomar was drifting among the moonlets. One of them almost touched the ship up front. He saw no sign of the ghostly material which had forced a way into the ship. He felt sure that it was all gone. Then Jasper made a test, although he was almost certain of the result beforehand. He took a box of polishing powder down from a rack, removing the cover and letting a bit sift out. The motes did not drift to the floor, they fell like stones. As Jasper had suspected, the air was all gone from the ship.

He walked slowly down the corridor and to the fore, through the control room and into the observation chamber. He was prepared for the sight of death but not so complete and horribly efficient. White bones and skulls lay on the floor. The white mist had absorbed the flesh and articles of clothing. He moved one of the bones with his foot and was startled to see the indentation left by his metal shoe. He stooped and picked up a femur. It crumbled to bits in his hand. What awful entity of form of life was this cloudy mist of Saturn's ring? He wandered slowly about the ship and discovered more crumbly bones as the chilling suspicion of the truth struck him. He was the last man, the only man, alive on the ship.

He went into the control room to look over the mechanism, wondering how he was ever going to guide the space ship out of the ring single handed. His wonder was put to rest. He found all electrical equipment and instruments wrecked irreparably. Examination of them confirmed his suspicions. Proximity with the white mist had upset and destroyed them as completely as if a lightning bolt had darted through the ship. He was alone on a derelict and lost in Saturn's ring.

Jasper grimly hung on to his nerves. Things weren't so bad as they might be. There was enough food and drink aboard to last him a lifetime. The air machines functioned smoothly. He could shut off one or two chambers of the ship and manage to live. He dared not think too much of the future, of living out the rest of his life a solitary prisoner in Saturn's ring. Grenard's plans of entering the third ring on his way to the planet's satellite, Dione, had been known, of course, on all three worlds, but chances of anyone coming through the outer ring at this particular point, even if they were looking for the lost expedition, were almost non-existent. He realised with a sinking feeling that the ship's system of communication had been disrupted.

He became hungry. He found food stores and took them back to the air tank. He also found a radium heater and installed it for heat and light. Then he carried in bedding and other basic comforts of life. He would have to live there until he could fit up and seal off chambers of the ship. There were three principal sections of the City of Fomar which were built to be sealed in case of emergency. The blow had fallen so quickly, and the deadliness of the white horror had been so unexpected and devastating that no refuge had been taken. Jasper intended shutting off and using that section of the ship including the atmosphere chamber and supply rooms.

From time to time, he looked out among the moonlets for a trace of the white mist returning, but all was quiet and unmoving. He turned off the lights of the City of Fomar. He wanted to save power, at least until he knew where he stood and whether conservation was necessary. As for the misty material, he recalled the luminous, ghostly qualities it had evidenced in the distance where moonlets had blocked the lights from the ship.

Fitting up the chosen section of the ship for habitation was a longer job than Jasper had previously figured. The white mist had wreaked havoc which he had not originally noticed. Many substances such as leather, felt and other products of organic origin had been either absorbed or damaged in part by the strange white entity that lived in space, and Jasper found many items of repair, replacement and substitution requiring long work with what he had to do with before the chambers could be closed off and made safely habitable.

There were chronometers undamaged by the coming of the white mist, and Jasper preserved them carefully and maintained their functions. He was more than two weeks of earth time in rehabilitating that part of the ship in which he had chosen to live out his lonely existence. Another five weeks were employed in the long corridor leading from the atmosphere chamber where he constructed an air lock. Jasper kept a sharp eye ready, even rigging up an electrical sounder alarm for his sleeping hours, but the white mist did not return during these weeks of his labours. Jasper, however, was prepared. He felt that the radium ray ejectors he had ready would do something to that white mist. He did not want to let the stuff get in its first blow and catch him unawares. He still recalled with a shudder how he had found a wooden door of a small clothes closet smashed to splinters by the compressed and concentrated blows given it by the white menace. Behind the wreckage of the door he had found the crumbling bones of Holman, a firm friend of Jasper's on the trip to Saturn. Jasper had been more fortunate in choosing the strong air tank.

In the long months which passed, the white mist did not return, and old Jasper Jezzan lived his lonely life aboard the derelict. He occasionally left the City of Fomar in space suit but never went far among the moonlets, even though he left the ship's lights blazing to guide him back again. When the lights were not on, everything was black and cheerless outside – no starlight, just space closely filled with floating moonlets. Jasper knew that once these unnumbered legions of tiny bodies had been a satellite of Saturn which had broken up. On his little excursions, he always carried one of the radium ray ejectors to use in case the white peril should return and catch him outside.

He made an interesting discovery on one of these trips. He was chipping the side of a moonlet when his helmet came in contact with the body. His chipping at the moonlet in a curious search for minerals produced an unnatural sound. He hit it again and again, and then he suddenly realised that the little moon was hollow. He marked it and went about looking for others. He found but three more among the hundreds surrounding the space ship. He could only hazard one possibility. The interior of the satellite had still been molten when it broke up under the strong, tidal attraction from Saturn. There had been occasional thick bubbles which had cooled.

For want of something to do, Jasper immediately set forth plans for drilling into one of the moonlets, and he chose the largest of the four, a sphere fully twenty-five feet in diameter. He found equipment on the City of Fomar which would serve the purpose, and he set to work. He marvelled at the density and strength of the semi-metallic substance and also at the thickness of the bubble. He drilled more than three feet before he reached emptiness. He was several days making an opening into the spheroid large enough to admit his body, and then when he was inside he found no more than he had expected, the inside spherical contour a bit rough and bubbled, glinting back the rays of his light.

In this way and many other ways, Jasper fought off the spectre of loneliness. He experimented with the ship's instruments, making a few tests and repairs, finally coming to the belief that he had found the direction of Saturn. Had the ship been manageable, he believed that he could have guided it out of the ring and into free space.

It was nearly a year after the catastrophe which had overtaken the space ship in Saturn's ring before the event which Jasper had nervously anticipated took place. The white clouds returned. The menace came from all directions, seemingly, and focused upon the disabled City of Fomar. Jasper was luckily inside when the attack came. He saw an unnatural luminescence beyond the ports where utter darkness should have reigned, and he watched with rapid beating heart as ghostly swirls of curling, merging, dividing white strands enveloped the derelict until again all the ports were covered up.

Quickly, Jasper hurried to the little turret he had fixed. The movable radium ray ejector lay ready. The old man grasped the control lever and trigger nervously and loosed a sustained barrage. He could not see the result of his work for the port was obscured, but he saw that something had taken place, for there was a visible shifting movement of the white stuff in the recurrent greying and thinning. When the port cleared, he saw that his ray ejector was effectively burning a hole through the cloudy entity before it. He swung the weapon and watched in grim satisfaction as it cut swaths of emptiness though the malignant mist which retreated instinctively, the scattered parts rejoining and merging into singleness. There was something repulsive in it, and Jasper shivered violently as he recalled the crumbling bones of its victims.

The ray ejector touched but an insignificant portion of the menace and possessed but a small area in which to work. Again, Jasper heard the same noises about the hull of the derelict. The ominous visitor was seeking an entrance, pressing, contracting and pounding, testing for weak spots. Jasper hurried to his improvised airlock and saw with dismay that the white mist had found a way inside it. The outer door was forced. The deadly vapour was in full possession of all the ship except that part which Jasper had closed off. Jasper grabbed a nearby ray ejector and made a hasty connection with a closed slot on his side of the airlock. He had foreseen this emergency, and he was prepared. He made an airtight connection, opened the slot and released a discharge of the ray into the rapid gathering mist which threatened the inner door. He saw it recoil and experienced a savage joy as it evaporated, untouched wisps of it hurriedly withdrawing from the airlock as if apprised in some telepathic manner of its peril. The menace had been removed here and not too soon, either, for Jasper knew what accumulated power that gathering cloud could exert upon the inner door. It had happened before.

Something told him to make a hasty examination of other parts of his closed-off chambers, and he was glad that he did. He found a searching, groping cloud of the hateful mist in the atmosphere chamber. One quick glance at a tiny thread of white gushing from an air joint leading to another part of the ship showed Jasper the means of entrance. He quickly destroyed the cloud and released a current of air into the unused pipe, forcing out the white mist under pressure. He then made a quick tightening of the joint which under normal circumstances had never before leaked.

Jasper hoped that the insidious material would find no means of effecting a wholesale entrance, for he knew that he could never combat so much of it successfully with the ray ejectors. He would be overwhelmed. His skin crept at the thought. Jasper was brave and had been through much during his adventurous life, but there were ways to die vastly more preferable to Jasper than being assimilated and made a part of the ghastly white cloud. He ran back to his airlock and found, as he had feared, that it was again being filled by the white vapour. He cleared it and then ran back to the atmosphere chamber. Everything clear. He hurriedly examined the storerooms and breathed a sigh of relief. No entrance had been effected at these points. He hurried back to the airlock to fight off the accumulating mist.

It was a long, hideous nightmare for Jasper. The white mist stayed longer this time than before, possibly because of a whetted appetite tantalized and unappeased. Yet Jasper realised that the cloud was self sustaining. Once during this time, it again forced the joint in the atmosphere chamber and Jasper had a fight on his hands. His timekeepers registered sixty-two hours before the strange resident of Saturn's ring left as mysteriously as it had come. Until then, Jasper did not sleep. After that, he yielded, for he knew instinctively that the white cloud would not return for a long time.

III

Refreshed from sleep, Jasper examined his damaged airlock and thereby made an earnest resolve. He would quit the City of Fomar with its numerous possibilities of entrance by the persistent white mist and take up living quarters in the strong and hollow moonlet he had penetrated with so much difficulty. In the days which followed, days recorded only by his chronometers amid the changeless gloom of Saturn's ring, Jasper worked as industriously to this end as he had laboured in sealing off a section of the space ship. Equipped with a strong hatch, he believed that the white menace could never force its way inside the metallic walls of the globe.

Jasper's first step was to enlarge the entrance he had made to the specifications of one of the emergency exits on the City of Fomar. Two of these large ports were removed from the ship. One was installed on the outside of the passage through the thick wall of the globe, the other on the inside. In this manner, Jasper had his airlock for entering and leaving the hermitage. Then he installed partitions and a flooring, equipping this flooring with the gravitational substance taken from the floors of the space ship. There were four chambers. Two of these constituted his living quarters. The other two consisted of a storeroom and a room for housing the atmosphere plant and heating unit he planned to instal from the space ship. As rapidly as he could accomplish the task, old Jasper Jezzan became a cosmic Robinson Crusoe.

Besides stores of food, his storeroom contained all manner of essentials taken from the ship. He did not abandon the ship but protected it from drifting away by attaching it to the moonlet with a long cable. He had found that there were various drifts to the moonlets, according to their sizes and neighbours. Slight gravitational influences played strange tricks, and he had noticed a slow change of positions in the neighbouring moonlets since the catastrophe.

Jasper finally completed his hermitage, and he was not sorry to leave the City of Fomar with its ghostly memories and the constant fear of another visitation by the white stuff. During his building of the hermitage, another eight months had passed in solitude. Jasper had reconciled himself to this kind of an existence in the depths of Saturn's furthest ring. Thoughts of living there did not weigh upon him so heavily as the thoughts of dying there without the companionship of humanity – alone and untended. He wondered, sometimes, if his hermitage and the attached derelict would some day be found when the moons of Saturn were explored and colonised. This discovery might be hundreds of years later, perhaps thousands of years. Jasper was old, and he had known solitude in the cosmos before, yet he had never been an involuntary prisoner of it until now. He wondered if the ghostly cloud would eventually find a way of getting to him or if he would die of old age. As for the food stores, he might live a good twenty years yet, he realised, and he had faith in the air and heating equipment and in his ability as a cosmic mechanic to keep everything in perfect running order. The machines were not so intricate and he had the means of replacing parts. One chamber Jasper still maintained aboard the space ship. That was the machine shop. He worked there in a space suit.

He was both relieved and disappointed when the hermitage in the moonlet was completed; relieved, because he now felt more secure against the white enemy; disappointed, because time once more commenced to hang heavy on his hands. He was thankful for the books, audioviewreels and other means of education and entertainment aboard the City of Fomar, but these promised to eventually become too familiar and well known.

Jasper had lived in his new habitation for more than six months when during one of his sleeping periods, he was awakened by a sharp bump which set his moonlet in motion. This unusual break in the monotony of silence and comparative stability in Saturn's ring aroused Jasper like a shot out of a gun. He switched on the powerful floodlights of the City of Fomar by remote control and stared through a transparent facing in the outer port of his airlock at a strange sight. All the moonlets were changing position. He saw them in a relay of motion from a disturbance not visible. Moonlets struck companions, then stopped as the immutable relay of inertia continued. His own moonlet was moving. It finally jostled another body gently. The derelict had been bumped closer, and the cable was suspended in a fantastic shape. Another moonlet struck the hermitage, the sudden contact sending him off balance. Moonlets not striking one another squarely kept moving, their motion divided up with the bodies they struck. There was no loss of motion, no slowing up because of gravity. The movement was relayed. Jasper realised that these contacts would continue in the same direction and at varying tangents all through the ring. He wondered what had set the moonlets into motion. Perhaps a meteor swarm had hit the ring. He watched until the zone of movement had passed on completely and all was quiet and peaceful once more before he returned to sleep.

When he awoke and looked out, a thrill of discovery claimed him. A misty fog obscured the outer entrance of the hermitage. With little criss-crossing radium ray ejectors installed outside the port and operated from within, he cleared the obstruction to his vision and looked out. The derelict was covered with a snowy mantle which was alive as it billowed and twisted. He knew that this mantle was but the surging outer rank of the crowding material which had forced itself unrestrained inside the City of Fomar and was greedily exploring all nooks and crannies, assimilating anything of organic origin it touched. Even the cable holding the ship to the hermitage was covered deeply with the strange stuff.

Jasper realised a snug sense of security. He no longer feared the white mist. He was curious. He wondered if there was any connection between the return of the white entity and the recent upheaval among the moonlets. Had the malignant clouds caused the commotion, or had the latter event aroused and stimulated the mist? Jasper wondered where the mist went and what it did when it was not clustered about the derelict and his moonlet. He decided to experiment with it.

In the depth of the ring, he created a disturbance of his own. There were explosives aboard the City of Fomar, and he placed six charges on the sides of as many moonlets situated at a safe distance from the hermitage. He returned to the hermitage and set them off by radio impulse. They jumped suddenly away from his common centre and relayed their motion to their nearest neighbours, ad infinitum.

Jasper waited patiently. He had arranged a trap to catch some of that white mist. He was going to study it if, and when, it came again. He waited for hours, and there was no sign of the white terror from the unknown reaches of the ring. He was about decided that he was on the wrong track when his heart leaped suddenly at the sight of the familiar, wispy, white strands curling like luminous smoke about the nearer moonlets. The devilish substance had been aroused after all, just as Jasper had believed it would be. A disturbance of any kind seemed to bring it unerringly to foreign objects.

Again it collected about the derelict and roamed the interior, also clustering instinctively about the hermitage as if by subtle sense or intuition it knew of strange contents inside it. Jasper, as on the previous visits, felt its strange effects upon him. It made him restless. It seemed to exert an irritating influence upon his body in a lesser sense than its powerful effects on electrical equipment of the City of Fomar during its initial visit. The mist stayed for the usual duration of its time and then left.

When Jasper was sure that it was all gone, he put on his space suit and made a hurried trip to the space ship. Full of anticipation, his spirits rose in triumph as he found his trap sprung and automatically imprisoning a small portion of the white mist. He saw the dull white fog through the transparent facing of the tightly closed box. He hurried back with it to the hermitage.

The following days were spent with more interest than he had known since being marooned nearly three years ago. He studied and experimented with the strange material. It was alive. No earthly science had ever known anything like it. Of that, he was sure. He always kept it inside a container, pouring it from one to another. For a vapour, it possessed amazing weight. He never let it touch him, though he knew metal to be impervious to its touch. Sometimes, it became almost a solid, often like a liquid in its quiescent state gathered in the corners of the metal box. Jasper found that it was rarely in the gaseous form, the condition in which he had always seen it before this. He better understood this whenever he shook the box or otherwise agitated the strange substance and saw it become gaseous. It assumed the vapour stage when highly excited and active. As a liquid, it was sluggish; as a solid, quiescent. He found that it was highly radioactive.

There were other strange properties of which he did not have the means nor the specialised education to ascertain. He fed it bits of leather, wool and bits of food which were absorbed by the white mist. From these repasts, the little cloud increased in volume. Jasper shuddered when he thought of what might happen if this radio-active substance should be unloosed upon the earth or one of its sister worlds. Yet there were means of destroying it. The radium ray was very effective. Extreme coldness was the natural habitat of the white mist, yet it required a high degree of heat, nearly to the boiling point of water, to destroy it. As might have been expected, heat expanded it.

Jasper's thoughts roamed the channels of scientific theory. What was this strange life? Had it been born in Saturn's ring, or was it from some far corner of the universe? It was probably as ageless and deathless as the moonlets of Saturn's ring, or of Saturn itself. Had the once stable satellite of Saturn which had broken up into these many small moonlets known life? Was this milky cloud which knew a common existence in subdividing and merging at will the ultimate in evolution of life on this satellite of the past? Jasper wondered yet could only advance these theories which were no more fantastic than the living material which confronted him and provoked these thoughtful possibilities.

He kept the white mist carefully confined and gradually came to lose interest in it. He had learned all he could about it.

IV

Time came to drag more heavily. Jasper was rapidly exhausting his interests. And he came to care less regarding his future. He took greater risks than ever, wandering farther afield in space suit among the moonlets than he had ever gone before. He was surprised to find that he had developed an instinct for directions in Saturn's ring, and twice he recklessly put this development to the test by penetrating deeply into the darkness among the moonlets far from the last feeble rays of the ship's lights. His only illumination came from the lights on his space suit. Both times, he returned unerringly and without hesitation. He had reached a point where he held his life cheaply. Even the chances of meeting the white mist among the moonlets held less fear for him. He longed for an actual human voice and more than that the closeness and affinity of humanity. The loneliness of the ring was awful. If he were only in empty space, it would be so much better. He could then see the stars, the same old constellations which differed to no appreciable notice out here on Saturn's orbit than they did from the perspective of the inner worlds. He had known the solitude of the cosmic wastes, yet he had always had the companionship of the glittering stars on those past occasions. In Saturn's ring, it was like being buried beneath innumerable huge tombstones in the darkness of an immense grave through which he was permitted to wander.

He came to find companionship in the mute remains of the powdered bones of his long-dead comrades aboard the City of Fomar, and he felt himself longing to join them. This led to an uncomfortable suggestion which Jasper immediately put forth from his mind before it gained a foothold. He shrugged and drew himself together to face things and carry on. As long as his sanity and balance of mind remained, he would do so, he knew.

Jasper's moroseness, however, grew upon him. It came to invade the peace of his sleep. One night, finally, he did not sleep at all. Night to Jasper was merely his sleeping period of a studied earthly arrangement. It was night whenever he turned the lights off. This time, however, he laid awake through it. An uneasiness possessed him, a familiar feeling, so familiar as to cause him to look out into the darkness for a sign of the white menace. But it was not there unless it lurked hidden behind the nearby moonlets, and Jasper knew that this was not the way of it. His nerves and imagination were playing him tricks.

A ghastly discovery made during his following waking schedule, however, revealed the cause of his uneasiness. His nerves and imagination had not been playing him tricks. The white mist was close by but not outside the hermitage where he had looked for it. He was met by a large, gray cloud which thrust a misty pedicle at him when he went into the storeroom for food supplies. Jasper's overwrought nerves snapped at this evil discovery, and he shrieked as he found himself momentarily fixed to the spot, his dilating eyes taking in the grim circumstances in a glance. He ran from the storeroom and securely fastened the steel door, carrying with him the horrible vision of the white mist inside the security of his hermitage. The broken container in which he had kept the imprisoned bit of radio-active life and the crushed and scattered food containers told a mute and condemning story. That small bit of life had broken loose, had fed upon and assimilated his food stores and had grown to these dangerous proportions. There was more of the radio-active life than he dared to tackle with a radium ray ejector. Only as a last resort would he do this.

He pulled himself together. He must get rid of that white cloud. He decided to try and lure the stuff from the moonlet and into space, standing ready with one of the more powerful ray ejectors in case the plan failed to work. He reacted from using the ejector inside the hermitage unless it were necessary, for its use in the airlock of the space ship had been as destructive as the white mist.

He put on his space suit, turned off the heat and air supply of the hermitage and proceeded to open both doors of the airlock. Then he opened the door leading into the storeroom and waited, drawn back into a far corner, a radium ray ejector held ready. The unwelcome tenant did not emerge. He glanced cautiously inside and saw it hovered over scattered cartons of his rummaged food supplies. Tins lay crushed with traces of oozing contents. He shot a weak charge into the gray mass. It churned, expanded, rose from its glutonous repast and sent snaky streamers exploring for the source of the searing plague. A globule of the malign entity plunged at the doorway and Jasper fell back hastily, his ejector held ready. From the far wall, he saw the exploring piece of cloud pause on the threshold and examine it independently of the main mass which did not emerge. While he watched, he saw more of it appear from the storeroom, until he knew it to be joined and assembled in entirety once more. It moved into his living quarters leisurely in an explorative manner. He waited fascinatedly against the wall, hoping it would move to the open, inviting airlock and find the freedom to which it was accustomed in space. He was prepared for it, too, in case it moved his way.

Jasper sat there grimly vigilant to the vagaries of the cloud. He watched for it to come upon the opening passage and slide out into space. He saw it move along the wall nearer the airlock. He looked back to the storeroom doorway where a small remaining portion of the cloud lingered hesitatingly. He watched this laggard bit closely. When he next looked back at the airlock, his heart leaped in hopeful anticipation. A white streamer lay through the opening. An advance bit of the cloud had exploringly found the opening. He had often wondered how much telepathic impulse the scattered material possessed. He believed that the rest of the grey cloud would be apprised of this retreat into space and would join the exploring vanguard. That piece on the threshold of the storeroom had joined the main body.

A puzzling difference suddenly claimed his attention. The mist which lay in the airlock was of the usual white consistency he had known. The cloud moving along the wall from the storeroom door was grey. A dawning horror of numbing realisation seized him, and the slowly increasing volume of the white menace in the airlock justified his worst fears. This was no part of the grey cloud from the storeroom. It was coming into the hermitage from space, not leaving it! The white peril had returned! The grey cloud in the storeroom had by some mysterious means of communication called its kindred from its scattered lair among the moonlets of the ring – and the deadly legion had responded.

Jasper aroused himself to stagger to the airlock and try to close it against the destroying forces which threatened him. At these quick moves on his part, a corresponding alacrity was aroused on the part of the incoming mist which suddenly ballooned and gushed inside so swiftly that Jasper's ray ejector hastily brought into play could not cope with and destroy it in fast enough quantities for him to reach the airlock and close it. A white wall expanded and struck him a buffeting blow which knocked him across the room. The white mist bore down on him more leisurely as he scrambled up and brought the ray ejector into play, his back against the wall.

Tongues of white death leaped out and touched him, bringing a frenzy of ecstatic, tingling horror wherever the white gas even touched his space suit. The radium ray disintegrated and destroyed the white pedicles while the main mass pushed forward to crush in closer. With sweat streaming from him, and in exhaustion, Jasper frantically fought his losing fight. Delirium partly obscured his reason, yet in no way hampered his effectiveness. He swung the ray ejector like a demented demon in the pits of Hell. Holes and swaths were burned from the solidity of the cloud, but these quickly filled once more. The tingling contacts became more frequent. Jasper's arms felt like lead. He felt his senses reeling and he desperately held on. There were flitting moments when his vision became obscured and the white cloud seemed to turn red. His knees suddenly buckled in under him, and he slid to the floor against the wall in a sitting position, the ray ejector waving more leisurely. The white cloud rushed in above where his head had been. His gasping breath hissed like steam in the helmet of his space suit.

He wondered vaguely why the white mist was not overcoming him. He was becoming less frantic in his efforts. His motions became mechanical. He was becoming too weak to defend himself any longer. He knew what that would mean, but even his will power clamoured for a rest, a long, never-ending rest. The white mist seemed to be fading. It was retreating. He was able to distinguish objects in his living quarters. He saw the white mist pouring rapidly out through the airlock, and he wondered about it vaguely. Oblivion came to his exhausted body. The ray ejector dropped from nerveless fingers, its deadly power shut off as the pressure on the trigger was released.

Jasper never knew how long he laid there in his space suit, an easy victim for the return of the white mist. The hermitage was permeated with the coldness of space. The lights still burned. Both inside and outside entrances of the airlock yawned open. When he came to his senses, he looked around. He rose and staggered to the storeroom threshold. He looked inside. The white menace had left entirely. Appallingly little was left of the food stores, however. Death by starvation was inevitable. Still, Jasper was glad. He preferred to die some other way. Slowly, he went about in space suit making temporary repairs.

He wondered why the white mist had abandoned the hermitage and its vicinity so suddenly, yet there were many unexplainable mysteries of the strange stuff which were beyond his understanding.

He paused suddenly in his job of fusing and welding. Lights shone outside his hermitage. He had not switched on the lights of the derelict, and he wondered what had made them illuminate. He stared through the double ports of the airlock. Another space ship cruised alongside the City of Fomar. Indescribable emotions seized Jasper as he shakily entered his airlock and closed the inner door. Through his mind flitted an answer to the strange behaviour of the white mist. When this strange ship had penetrated the ring, it had caused a major disturbance. The white mist had become aroused and had descended upon the derelict and the hermitage – and had left at the closer approach of the space ship in order to attack the greater attraction. Jasper saw, however, that no mist accompanied the strange ship.

He fumbled with the outer door and flung it open. Giving a kick with his feet, he sped though the vacuum to the side of the space ship. He found the outer door of the airlock invitingly opened. Air was sent rushing into the compartment he entered. Faces, human beings, were regarding him in friendly wonder. The inner door was opened, and a man helped turn back the space helmet from his scraggly grey hair. Jasper Jezzan gazed wildly about him at the faces of the men, too overcome momentarily to speak. With tears streaming down his face, he at last found his voice.

'Folks!' he cried, tremulously. 'Folks! Real folks at last!'

The Abyss

BY ROBERT A. W. LOWNDES

from *Stirring Fantasy Fiction*, February 1941

With Robert Augustine Ward Lowndes we come to one of the
major characters in early American fandom who, along with his
compatriots like Frederik Pohl, James Blish, Donald Wollheim
and Sam Moskowitz, did much to affect the course of science
fiction.

While Lowndes the editor has been covered to some extent in
the introduction, Lowndes the author is a rather more shadowy
character. This is sad, for Lowndes possesses a rare gift for
weaving highly effective fiction, both fantasy and sf. This comes
in part from Lowndes being an insatiable reader, consuming
at an astonishing rate all that he picks up. In this way, he was
able to devour all the current sf, fantasy and horror fiction while
still editing his amateur magazines (of which *Le Vombiteur*
appeared weekly from December 1938) as well as professional
magazines and writing and collaborating on a considerable
number of stories.

Robert Lowndes was born on Monday 4 September 1916. His
first reading was MacFadden's *Ghost Stories*, and he was not able
to acquire a copy of *Amazing Stories* until 1928, when he was
twelve. This he did by removing a coupon for a free copy from
an issue of *The Open Road For Boys* kept in Stamford Public
Library, Connecticut. Such was the subterfuge devotees of the
genre were driven to in the days of parental objection. In 1931
Lowndes became attracted to *Weird Tales* which he had hitherto
shunned, and *Strange Tales*. Thereafter his reading expanded to
the fantasy genre, and in the mid-1930s to *Dime Mystery, Horror
Stories* and *Terror Tales*. So without a doubt, Lowndes had a
thorough working knowledge of the whole range of imaginative

literature. He became a regular letter writer to the magazines, particularly *Wonder Stories* which published his first letter in its July 1932 issue. Here he sometimes styled himself 'Doc' Lowndes, not because of any qualification, merely a nickname he gave himself before anyone else could think of a worse one.

Without a doubt Lowndes's leaning was more to fantasy, his favourite authors being Clark Ashton Smith, H. P. Lovecraft and Robert E. Howard. It therefore comes as no surprise to find that much of his writing, both stories and poetry, was more in this direction. Even his sf is distinctly bizarre. 'The Abyss' is styled after Lovecraft and fits into the general classification of science fantasy, a true merging of sf and fantasy of the type Lovecraft had been writing for over a decade before his death. Lowndes used this style with great effect in other stories like 'Lilies', 'The Long Wall' and the Frank Paul inspired 'The Slim People'.

When Columbia magazines suspended *Future*, Lowndes continued to work for them as editorial chief for the entire pulp chain, and was in charge of *Future* when Columbia revived it in the 1950s.

He became the editor of the Avalon sf books from the first title, *Three to Conquer* (1956), by Eric Russell, and most of the series thereafter. A novel of interest published by them was his own *Believer's World* (1961) telling of a hyperspatial three-planet system of Terran colonists where each has a religion based on the teachings of Ein (Einstein).

In more recent years he edited *Magazine of Horror* together with several companion titles, which showed his real love for the genre, and are a beautiful example of the personally edited magazine, When they folded in 1971, Lowndes became editor of *Sexology*, the magazine started by Hugo Gernsback in 1933, and still published by his heir, Harvey Gernsback.

The version of 'The Abyss' used here is the third, revised by Lowndes for inclusion in the Winter 1965 issue of *Magazine of Horror*. He originally wrote the story for the second issue of Wollheim's *Fanciful Tales* in 1937 which never materialised. It was revised initially for publication in *Stirring Fantasy Fiction*, the fantasy half of *Stirring Science Stories*.

We took Graf Norden's body out into the November night, under the stars that burned with a brightness terrible to behold, and drove madly, wildly up the mountain road. The body had to be destroyed because of the eyes that would not close, but seemed to be staring at some object behind the observer, the body **that** was entirely drained of blood without the slightest trace of a wound, the body whose flesh was covered with luminous markings, designs that shifted and changed form before one's eyes. We wedged what had been Graf Norden tightly behind the wheel, put a makeshift fuse in the gas tank, lit it, then shoved the car over the side of the road, where it plummeted down to the main highway, a flaming meteor.

Not until the next day did we realize that we had all been under Dureen's spell – even I had forgotten. How else could we have rushed out so eagerly? From that moment when the lights came on again, and we saw the thing that had, a moment before, been Graf Norden, we were as shadowy, indistinct figures rushing through a dream. All was forgotten save the unspoken commands upon us as we watched the blazing car strike the pavement below, observed its demolition, then tramped dully each to his own home. When, the next day, partial memory returned to us and we sought Dureen, he was gone. And, because we valued our freedom, we did not tell anyone what had happened, nor try to discover whence Dureen had vanished. We wanted only to forget.

I think I might possibly have forgotten had I not looked into the *Song of Yste* again. With the others, there has been a growing tendency to treat it as illusion, but I cannot. It is one thing to read of books like the *Necronomicon, Book of Eibon,* or *Song of Yste,* but it is quite different when one's own experience confirms some of the things related therein. I found one such paragraph in the *Song of Yste* and have not read farther. The volume, along with Norden's other books, is still on my shelves; I have not burned it. But I do not think I shall read more . . .

I met Graf Norden in 193–, at Darwich University, in Dr. Held's class in Mediaeval and early-Renaissance history, which was more a study of obscure thought and occultism.

Norden was greatly interested; he had done quite a bit of exploring into the occult; in particular was he fascinated by the writings and records of a family of adepts named Dirka, who traced their ancestry back to the pre-glacial days. They, the Dirkas, had translated the *Song of Yste* from its legendary form into the three great languages of the dawn cultures, then into the Greek, Latin, Arabic and Middle English.

I told Norden that I deplored the blind contempt in which the world holds the occult, but had never explored the subject very deeply. I was content to be a spectator, letting my imagination drift at will upon the many currents in this dark river; skimming over the surface was enough for me – seldom did I take occasional plunges into the deeps. As a poet and dreamer, I was careful not to lose myself in the blackness of the pools where I disported – one could always emerge to find a calm, blue sky and a world that thought nothing of these realities.

With Norden, it was different. He was already beginning to have doubts, he told me. It was not an easy road to travel; there were hideous dangers, hidden all along the way, often so that the wayfarer was not aware of them until too late. Earthmen were not very far along the path of evolution; still very young, their lack of knowledge, as a race, told heavily against such few of their number who sought to traverse unknown roads. He spoke of messengers from beyond and made references to obscure passages in the *Necronomicon* and *Song of Yste*. He spoke of alien beings, entities terribly unhuman, impossible of measurement by any human yardstick or to be combated effectively by mankind.

Dureen came into the picture at about this time. He walked into the classroom one day during the course of a lecture; later, Dr. Held introduced him as a new member of the class, coming from abroad. There was something about Dureen that challenged my interest at once. I could not determine of what race or nationality he might be – he was very close to being beautiful, his every movement being of grace and rhythm. Yet, in no way could he be considered effeminate.

That the majority of us avoided him troubled him not at all. For my part, he did not seem genuine, but, with the others, it was probably his utter lack of emotion. There was, for example, the time in the lab when a test tube burst in his face, driving several splinters deep into the skin. He showed not the slightest sign of discomfort, waved aside all expressions of solicitude on the part of some of the girls, and proceeded to go on with his experiment as soon as the medico had finished with him.

The final act started when we were dealing with suggestion and hypnotism, one afternoon, and were discussing the practical possibilities of the subject. Colby presented a most ingenious argument against it, ridiculed the association of experiments in thought transference or telepathy with suggestion, and arrived at a final conclusion that hypnotism (outside of mechanical means of induction) was impossible.

It was at this point that Dureen spoke up. What he said, I cannot recall, but it ended in a direct challenge for Dureen to prove his statements. Norden said nothing during the course of this debate; he appeared somewhat pale, and was, I noticed, trying to flash a warning signal to Colby.

There were five of us over at Norden's place that night: Granville, Chalmers, Colby, Norden, and myself. Norden was smoking endless cigarettes, gnawing his nails, and muttering to himself. I suspected something irregular was up, but what, I had no idea. Then Dureen came in and the conversation, such as it had been, ended.

Colby repeated his challenge, saying he had brought along the others as witnesses to insure against being tricked by stage devices. No mirrors, light, or any other mechanical means of inducing hypnosis would be permitted. It must be entirely a matter of wills. Dureen nodded, drew the shade, then turned, directing his gaze at Colby.

We watched, expecting him to make motions with his hands and pronounce commands: he did neither. He fixed his eyes upon Colby and the latter stiffened as if struck by lightning, then, eyes staring blankly ahead of him, he rose slowly, standing on the narrow strip of black that ran diagonally down through the centre of the rug.

My mind ran back to the day I caught Norden in the act of destroying some papers and apparatus, the latter which had been constructed, with such asistance as I had been able to give, over a period of several months. His eyes were terrible and I could see doubt in them. Not long after this event, Dureen had made his appearance: could there have been a connection, I wondered?

My reverie was broken abruptly by the sound of Dureen's voice commanding Colby to speak, telling us where he was and what he saw around him. When Colby obeyed, it was as if his voice came to us from a distance.

He was standing, he said, on a narrow bridgeway overlooking a frightful abyss, so vast and deep that he could discern neither floor nor boundary. Behind him this bridgeway stretched until it was lost in a bluish haze; ahead, it ran toward what appeared to be a plateau. He hesitated to move because of the narrowness of the path, yet realised that he must make for the plateau before the very sight of the depths below him made him lose his balance. He felt strangely heavy, and speaking was an effort.

As Colby's voice ceased, we all gazed in fascination at the little strip of black in the blue rug. This, then, was the bridge over the abyss . . . but what could correspond to the illusion of depth?

Why did his voice seem so far away? Why did he feel heavy? The plateau must be the workbench at the other end of the room: the rug ran up to a sort of dais upon which was set Norden's table, the surface of this being some seven feet above the floor. Colby now began to walk slowly down the black swath, moving as if with extreme caution, looking like a slow-motion camera-shot. His limbs appeared weighted; he was breathing rapidly.

Dureen now bade him halt and look down into the abyss carefully, telling us what he saw there. At this, we again examined the rug, as if we had never seen it before and did not know that it was entirely without decoration save for that single black strip upon which Colby now stood.

His voice came to us again. He said, at first, that he saw nothing in the abyss below him. Then he gasped, swayed, and almost lost his balance. We could see the sweat standing out on his brow and neck, soaking his blue shirt. There were things in the abyss, he said in hoarse tones, great shapes that were like blobs of utter blackness, yet which he knew to be alive. From the central masses of their beings he could see them shoot forth incredibly long, filamentine tentacles. They moved themselves forward and backward – horizontally, but could not move vertically, it seemed.

But the things were not all on the same plane. True, their movements were only horizontal in relation to their position, but some were parallel to him and some diagonal. Far away he could see things perpendicular to him. There appeared now to be a great deal more of the things than he thought. The first ones he had seen were far below, unaware of his presence. But these sensed him, and were trying to reach him. He was moving faster now, he said, but to us he was still walking in slow-motion.

I glanced sidewise at Norden; he, too, was sweating profusely. He arose now, and went over to Dureen, speaking in low tones so that none of us could hear. I knew that he was referring to Colby and that Dureen was refusing whatever it was Norden demanded. Then Dureen was forgotten momentarily as Colby's voice came to us again quivering with fright. The things were reaching out for him. They rose and fell on all sides; some far away; some hideously close. None had found the exact plane upon which he could be captured; the darting tentacles had not touched him, but all of the beings now sensed his presence, he was sure. And he feared that perhaps they could alter their planes at will, though, it appeared that they must do so blindly, seemingly

like two-dimensional beings. The tentacles darting at him were
threads of utter darkness.

A terrible suspicion arose in me, as I recalled some of the earlier
conversations with Norden, and remembered certain passages
from the *Song of Yste*. I tried to rise, but my limbs were powerless:
I could only sit helplessly and watch. Norden was still speaking
with Dureen and I saw that he was now very pale. He seemed to
shrink away – then he turned and went over to a cabinet, took
out some object, and came to the strip of rug upon which Colby
was standing. Norden nodded to Dureen and now I saw what it
was he held in his hand: a polyhedron of glassy appearance.
There was in it, however, a glow that startled me. Desperately I
tried to remember the significance of it – for I knew – but my
thoughts were being short-circuited, it seemed, and, when
Dureen's eyes rested upon me, the very room seemed to stagger.

Again Colby's voice came through, this time despairingly. He
was afraid he would never reach the plateau. (Actually, he was
about a yard and a half away from the end of the black strip and
the dais upon which stood Norden's work bench.) The things, said
Colby, were close now: a mass of thread-like tentacles had just
missed him.

Now Norden's voice came to us; it, too, seemingly far away.
He called my name. This was more, he said, than hypnotism.
It was – but then his voice faded and I felt the power of Dureen
blanking out the sound of his words. Now and then, I would hear
a sentence or a few disjointed words. But, from this I managed to
get an inkling of what was going on.

This was actually trans-dimensional journeying. We just
imagined we saw Norden and Colby standing on the rug – or
perhaps it was through Dureen's influence.

The nameless dimension was the habitat of these shadow-
beings. The abyss, and the bridge upon which the two stood,
were illusions created by Dureen. When that which Dureen had
planned was complete, our minds would be probed, and our
memories treated so that we recalled no more than Dureen
wished us to remember. Norden had succeeded in forcing an
agreement upon Dureen, one which he would have to keep; as a
result, if the two could reach the plateau before the shadow-beings
touched them, all would be well. If not – Norden did not specify,
but indicated that they were being hunted, as men hunt game.
The polyhedron contained an element repulsive to the things.

He was but a little behind Colby; we could see him aiming with
the polyhedron. Colby spoke again, telling us that Norden had

materialised behind him, and had brought some sort of weapon with which the things could be held off.

Then Norden called my name, asking me to take care of his belongings if he did not return, telling me to look up the 'adumbrali' in the *Song of Yste*. Slowly, he and Colby made their way toward the dais and the table. Colby was but a few steps ahead of Norden; now he climbed upon the dais, and, with the other's help, made his way onto the bench. He tried to assist Norden, but, as the latter mounted the dais, he stiffened suddenly and the polyhedron fell from his hands. Frantically he tried to draw himself up, but he was being forced backward and I knew that he had lost. . . .

There came to us a single cry of anguish, then the lights in the room faded and went out. Whatever spell had been upon us was was removed; we rushed about like madmen, trying to find Norden, Colby, and the light switch. Then, suddenly, the lights were on again and we saw Colby sitting dazedly on the bench, while Norden lay on the floor. Chalmers bent over the body, in an effort to resuscitate him, but when he saw that the condition of Norden's remains he became so hysterical that we had to knock him cold in order to quiet him.

Colby followed us mechanically, apparently unaware of what was happening. We took Graf Norden's body out into the November night and destroyed it by fire, telling Colby later that he had apparently suffered a heart attack while driving up the mountain road; the car had gone over and his body was incinerated in the holocaust.

Later, Chalmers, Granville, and I met in an effort to rationalise what we had seen and heard. Chalmers had been all right after he came around, had helped us with our grisly errand up the mountain road. Neither, I found, had heard Norden's voice after he had joined Colby in the supposed hypnotic stage. Nor did they recall seeing any object in Norden's hand.

But, in less than a week, even these memories had faded from them. They fully believed that Norden had died in an accident after an unsuccessful attempt on the part of Dureen to hypnotize Colby. Prior to this, their explanation had been that Dureen had killed Norden, for reasons unknown, and that we had been his unwitting accomplices. The hypnotic experiment had been a blind to gather us all together and provide a means of disposing of the body. That Dureen had been able to hypnotize us, they did not doubt then.

It would have been no use to tell them what I learned a few days later, what I learned from Norden's notes which explain Dureen's arrival. Or to quote sections from the *Song of Yste* put into comprehensible English, to them.

'*...And these be none other than the adumbrali, the living shadows, beings of incredible power and malignancy, which dwell without the veils of space and time such as we know it. Their sport it is to import into their realm the inhabitants of other dimensions, upon whom they practice horrid pranks and manifold illusions...*'

· '*...But more dreadful than these are the seekers which they send out into other worlds and dimensions, being which they themselves have created and guised in the form of those who dwell within whatever dimension, or upon whichever worlds where these seekers be sent...*'

'*...These seekers can be detected only by the adept, to whose trained eyes their too-perfectness of form and movement, their strangeness, and aura of alienage and power is a sure sign....*'

'*...The sage, Jhalkanaan, tells of one of these seekers who deluded seven priests of Nyaghoggua into challenging it to a duel of the hypnotic arts. He further tells how two of these were trapped and delivered to the adumbrali, their bodies being returned when the shadow-things had done with them...*'

'*...Most curious of all was the condition of the corpses, being entirely drained of all fluid yet showing no trace of a wound, even the most slight. But the crowning horror was the eyes, which could not be closed, appearing to stare restlessly outward, beyond the observer, and the strangely-luminous markings on the dead flesh, curious designs which appeared to move and change form before the eyes of the beholder...*'

Up There

BY DONALD A. WOLLHEIM

from *Science Fiction Quarterly*, Summer 1942

It is right that both this and the previous story should be published side by side. Lowndes's story was published in Wollheim's magazine, and here Wollheim's story was published in Lowndes's.

Donald Allen Wollheim was two years older than Lowndes. The son of a doctor, he was born in New York on Thursday, 1 October 1914. He discovered sf in the early days of *Science & Invention* and soon became a letter hack. His first sale, 'The Man from Ariel', appeared in the January 1934 *Wonder Stories* when he was nineteen. Wollheim later alienated himself with *Wonder* over the issue of the Science Fiction League, as narrated in the first volume, and a later submission to the magazine, 'The Space Lens', was published under the pseudonym of Millard Verne Gordon.

Like Lowndes, Wollheim is very much an author-editor. His magazine and editorial activities have already been discussed in the introduction, so only his writing will be discussed here. The influence behind this story is particularly interesting. In the text you will find references to the works of Charles Fort, and I have already mentioned him in the introduction.

Charles Hoy Fort (1874–1932) made a considerable impact on sf writers although he never wrote sf himself. What Fort did was collect together all the inexplicable news items he could unearth. Years and years of research were put into the project and the collected results published in four books: *The Book of the Damned* (1919), *New Lands* (1923), *Lo!* (1931) and *Wild Talents* (1932). It was *Lo!* that Tremaine serialised in *Astounding*, but *The Book of the Damned* remained the most influential, due primarily to Fort's conclusions which he sets out in the book, such as that we are the property of aliens. This proved the seed for great numbers of plots, and Edmond Hamilton acknowledged such with his stories 'The Space Visitors' (*Air Wonder*, March 1930) and 'The Earth Owners' (*Weird Tales*, August 1931). The culmination of this came with Eric Frank Russell's *Sinister Barrier*.

In 'Up There' we learn of Fort's refutation of astronomy, one of the lesser adopted themes in sf, although Eando Binder's 'Set Your Course by the Stars' (*Astounding Stories*, May 1935) is an earlier example. A Fortean Society founded in 1931 still existed in 1957, decrying scientists in their fraudulent claims that a satellite had been put in orbit. That Fort drew the wrong conclusions from his pile of facts does not discount the fact that these items are still inexplicable. In more recent times people like Erich Von Daniken in *Chariots of the Gods?* (1968) and Andrew Tomas in *We Are Not the First* (1971) have done excellent jobs drawing their conclusions from similar strange facts, but it was Fort who attempted it first.

Wollheim is currently the highly successful publisher of DAW books in New York, but was for many years the editor at Ace Books, and was responsible for establishing their science fiction programme. He was also instrumental in popularising science fiction anthologies, editing the first paperback edition in 1943.

Incidentally, Wollheim's story 'Mimic' is worth mentioning here for the record it must hold in magazine reprintings. It first appeared in the December 1942 *Astonishing Stories*, then under the editorship of Alden Norton. When in 1947 Wollheim became the editor of *Fantasy Reader* for Avon Books he resurrected the story and included it in the third issue in June of that year. Shortly thereafter Alden Norton, now in overall charge of *Fantastic Novels* gave the story its third airing in the September 1950 issue. As if that was not enough Chester Whitehorne, attempting to produce a reprint magazine, *Science Fiction Digest*, included the story in the second issue, dated Spring 1954.

Just one year later Wollheim included it in his sf anthology *Terror in the Modern Vein* (April 1955), published by Hanover House in April 1955. Five appearances in less than thirteen years, making it one of the most ubiquitous single stories in early sf. Had it not been for that I would have included it in this collection, since it is an excellent tale. Nevertheless 'Up There' is a close second, and that has never been in hard back – until now.

I don't think I ever knew what a rugged individualist could be until I came to my Uncle Ephraim's farm to recuperate after my escape at sea. I had been torpedoed aboard one of the convoy freighters to England, had been rescued after a long swim in the icy sea, had come out of the hospital in Boston after two weeks under instructions to rest up for a month or so before I could report again for sea service. So I had come to my uncle's farm down in New Hampshire.

I last remembered my uncle as a cantankerous cuss when I had visited his place as a boy. I found that my childhood recollections did not send me astray. He was cantankerous, he was an old cuss, and he had the darnedest attitudes and ideas I ever heard of. But I won't say he was crazy – no I won't say it. I don't dare after what I saw last night around Polaris.

When I walked up to the old farmhouse from the road with my satchel in my hand, I saw no one. The old but well-built house, the prosperous looking grounds impressed me; they looked solid and substantial. But there was no one in sight. From somewhere there came the sound of hammering and I walked around behind the farmhouse to see. Sure enough, Uncle Eph was there standing atop a stepladder leaning against a gleaming silvery airplane, tacking weather-stripping across the edges of the glass-enclosed cabin. It was when I noticed that the ship was marked with the swastika and maltese cross of the German Luftwaffe and was in fact a big Nazi bomber, that I dropped my grip and stood staring.

'Close yer mouth, yer catching flies,' snapped my uncle's sharp voice, 'ain't yer never seen an airyplane before?'

'But it's a Nazi airplane,' I protested, 'and what are you doing with it?'

Uncle stopped his hammering for an instant and gave me a glance of disapproval. He shot a stream of tobacco juice towards the ground, shifted his quid and snapped:

'No, it ain't a Nazi plane – it used to be and that's a difference for a fact. It's my plane now and I'll do what I dang-well please with it, no thanks to you.'

I walked over to it and looked at it. It was in very good condition, seemed perfectly in order. My uncle finished his hammering and got down. He came up to me wiping his hands on a piece of rag.

'Purty, ain't she?' he said. 'One of the planes that bombed New York t'other week. Run out of gas and come down neat as a whistle right here on my land where you see her.'

'What happened to the crew?' I asked.

Uncle's eyes twinkled and he spat another stream of tobacco.

'Shot 'em,' he said. 'Ain't nobody can trespass on my land without permission.' He chewed some more and then went on: 'Waited for 'em all to step out; it was early morning and they scared hell out of my chickens. I plugged 'em from the back window with my old bear-rifle. Didn't waste a shot, one, two, three, four, just like that.' He spat four times in succession.

The old codger's eyes were perfect. Damn it, I could well believe he had done that. 'What did you do with the bodies?'

'What did yer think I'd do with 'em?' he snapped peevishly. 'I buried 'em behind the barn; I ain't no cannibal I ain't.'

Before I could say more, he started walking briskly towards the house. 'Come on in and get a bite to eat. Reckon you must be hungry.'

I followed him into the house. His house-keeper, a deaf old maid probably as odd as he was, nodded once at me and showed me to a room. I washed up and came down. Uncle hadn't waited for he was already shovelling up his fare with gusto. The man was in great shape for one his age.

After eating a bit, I asked another question that had come to me. 'Didn't anyone object to your keeping the plane?'

'Some did,' he said; 'didn't do 'em no good though.'

He took another mouthful and then went on. 'What comes out of the sky or is found on my land belongs to me. That's the law. The sheriff tried to get me to give the plane to the government. Heck no, not me. I pay my taxes, I don't owe the government nothin' and the government never gave me no presents and I don't aim to give the government any. Besides I intend to use that plane myself.'

'You can't fly,' I said, 'you never flew a plane in your life.'

He finished his plate before answering that. Then he leaned back and pulled out his corn-cob pipe.

'Who taught Wilbur Wright to fly?' he said. 'Answer me that?'

I couldn't and he went on: 'I ain't no dumber than young Wright. I got books, I can read and I can see and I can think better than most. Heck, of course I can fly that contraption. Lessons is for niddle-noodles.'

'Where are you going to fly it?' I asked.

'Gol durn, you're the most inquisitive askinest young cuss, ain't yer?' But I suppose you would be being as how you're one of my own kinfolk. Well, I'll tell yer since yer ask. I'm agoing to fly it up to the sky and see what's going on up there.'

I gasped and nearly choked on my food. 'Wha – what! What do you mean "the sky"? You can't, it isn't possible.'

Uncle's eyes twinkled and he shook his head sadly. 'Yer just as befuddled as all the rest, ain't yer? Never used yer head fer anything but a hat rack. I suppose yer believe I can't fly up as far as I plumb like?'

I finished my food before replying. Then I pushed my seat away, determined to find out what the old goat had in his head.

'No, you can't,' I shot at him. 'After about 20 miles you won't find enough air to support the plane. There isn't any air a thousand miles up and there isn't anything to fly to nearer than two hundred thousand miles.'

That didn't phase him a bit. 'Rubbish,' he snapped. 'Fiddle-faddle! Have you ever been twenty miles up?'

'No,' I snapped, 'and neither were you!'

'Nor either was anyone else, young man!' he barked back. 'So don't you believe all that some smart aleck tells you. And there ain't been no one a thousand miles up either to say there wasn't any air, and no one ever measured anything up in the sky.'

'Yes, they have,' I shouted. 'Astronomers have measured every-thing.'

'Astronomers!' he snapped. 'Do you know any? No, you don't. And I don't either. And none of 'em has been up there to find out and none of 'em intends to go up there to find out. Astro-nomers! Bah! Humbugs!'

'They proved it by telescopes and cameras and mathematics,' I retorted in defence of astronomy.

'They proved the earth was flat five hundred years ago and it didn't prove nothing. Don't talk mathematics to me, youngster. Figgers is something that scallywags think up to fool honest folks. Can you figger an orbit or reckon the distance of a star?'

'No, I'm not that educated,' I said.

'And neither is anyone else because it can't be done. There ain't no orbits and stars is all the same distance.'

'What?' I shouted, 'how can that be?'

'Why can't it be?' Uncle Eph came back. 'They taught you all yer life a pack of lies until you can't see the forest for the trees. Why should the stars be different distances away? Why shouldn't they all be the same distance only different sizes? For years those smart alecks has been hoodwinking the public with fantastic nonsense just to get the yokels to keep 'em in food and clothing. Every time folks begin to get on thinking about why they should keep on endowing colleges and observatories, the old buzzards get together and come out with some new planet or dizzy idea or maybe they stretch the universe a few trillion miles or squeeze it in a bit – or maybe they think up a fourth dimension and befuddle the people that way. Poppycock! Stuff and nonsense! They got the people so befuddled and fooled they can't think straight worth a shucks. But they ain't got me fooled, not for one minute they ain't.'

'But it's logical and scientific,' I answered weakly.

'Fiddle-faddle,' he barked. He took a puff on his pipe. 'That plane out there. That's logical and scientific. But this astronomy – why it don't make sense. Every hundred years they admit that what they thought was so last century ain't so this century. That right, young feller?'

'Yes, but science improves and they discard old ideas.'

'Improves! Now that's a laugh! You mean they think up wilder ideas to keep the people fooled. Looky here – what's less fantastic? To think the universe is a finite infinity bent around in a fourth dimension no one can figure out, all full of billions of suns busting up atomically, whatever that means, and dozens of planets all whirling around criss-crossing each other while the whole shebang goes rushing through a lot of empty nothingness at crazy speeds like a hundred miles a second maybe? Or to think that the sky is just a land surface like a common-sense ceiling a few hundred miles up and the stars are just volcanoes or maybe the lights of towns and cities and farms. And the sun a blazing bonfire rolling across it along with the planets which are no more than three or four feet across? Now I ask you, think it over. Which is more fantastic? Which sounds more like plain horse-sense?'

I thought it over. Well, how can you answer that? Which is the more fantastic? Obviously the astronomers' ideas were. But did I dare admit it? I tried another angle.

'There are photographs of the stars and planets.'

'Ain't seen any photograph yet that couldn't be faked,' Uncle Eph demolished that line of reasoning.

'But it just couldn't be!' I exclaimed in desperation.

'Oh yes it could, and it is.' Uncle Eph crowed triumphantly. 'The whole world is being taken in by a handful of these fakers with their fancy stories and crazy pictures. How these smart alecks don't dare admit that meteors can keep coming down in the same place night after night if they don't come down from a ceiling just overhead?'

'They don't,' I gasped.

'Yes they do,' my uncle snapped. 'And if the star-humbuggers' ideas were right that couldn't happen. But meteors often fall one after another night after night in the same township. Happened here once and there's lots of evidence. Feller named Charles Fort collected piles of evidence the astronomers wouldn't admit.'

He got up. 'I've talked enough about this. I'm agoing out. Got more work to do on my airyplane.'

I followed him out, my head in a whirl. What was I to think? Was the whole world being fooled by a handful of men? It wasn't possible. It just *couldn't* be possible.

I watched Uncle working about the plane. He was carrying stocks of food and stuff into it as if for a long trip. Finally I couldn't contain my questions.

'The whole world believes the way the astronomers believe – they couldn't be wrong,' I ventured.

Uncle shifted his pipe and stowed away a smoked ham. 'Wrong again,' he finally stated emphatically. 'Do the peasants of China believe it? No,' he didn't wait for an answer, 'they don't believe. That's a quarter of the world. Do the peasants of India and the black men in Africa and the red men in South America and the poor people in Europe know about it or believe it? No, and that's half the world that don't believe it. So don't be so smart with that word world. Most of the world don't believe any such nonsense. Most of 'em would agree with me and other common-sense down-to-earth folks.'

That set me back on my heels for a while. I wandered around thinking while Uncle finished the packing of the plane. He had already stowed away a large supply of gasoline and oil tins. It was obvious he was going to take off very soon.

He went into the house again and when he came out I asked him when he planned to leave.

'Tonight, soon's the stars come out so I can get my bearings. Waited for you to come so you could keep the farm in order till I get back.'

I saw that he was carrying a couple of books with him and when I got a closer look at them, I was amazed to note they were Chinese dictionaries and grammars.

'Why the Chinese guides?' I asked. 'You don't expect to meet any Chinamen up there, do you?'

'Why not?' he chuckled. 'The Chinese call themselves Celestials and I guess they ought to know if nobody does. Reckon the people up in the towns up there in the sky are Chinese. Four hundred million clever people can't all be wrong about their own origin. I reckon I'll get along up there.'

I think that floored me finally. I went about the rest of the afternoon silently, puzzled and confused. Uncle Eph finished his preparations on the airplane and then conducted me around the farm, giving me instructions on what was to be done.

Supper came, night came, the stars came out.

Uncle came down in his heavy winter clothes with a fur cap pulled down over his ears. I went with him to the airplane.

He pointed up towards the North Star.

'I never thought that all-fired important star was pointed out clear enough and I'm fixing to do something about it. Keep yer eye on it,' he said. 'Well, time to be going. Don't forget to pick up the mail regularly.'

'Hey,' I yelled at the last minute, 'you got a parachute?'

'What fer?' he snapped from the door of his plane. 'Ain't nothing going to go wrong with me. Parachutes is for bunglers. Now if you'll just step up and turn that crank by the propeller we'll get started.'

Dumbly I stepped up and started the propeller turning over. It caught on with a roar. Uncle slammed the door of the cabin shut, waved a hand and gunned the engine.

The plane jerked forward, started fast, swung wildly and jumped into the air as Uncle Eph threw the throttle on full. It soared at a steep angle and I expected it to crash momentarily or turn over.

But it straightened out a bit, turned towards the north and started upwards in a steady steep rise towards the Pole Star. I watched it as it disappeared into the darkness among the myriad stars of the night.

I expected uncle to come back that night as soon as he found his airplane would not rise any farther than the stratosphere. I also waited in dread of hearing the phone ring and being told he had crashed somewhere. But nothing happened that night. He didn't come back and there was no crash.

All next day I thought about it and I convinced myself that I should have called in a doctor and had the old man restrained. There were too many scientists backing up the regular theories of the sky.

Yet all that day there were no reports of my uncle's plane. And that night and the next two days after.

I don't know what to think now. Uncle Eph never did come back and he hasn't been heard from unless . . . but I don't like to admit that possibility. It's two weeks now and the only thing I can't account for is that there are now five more stars in the handle of The Big Dipper stretching in an exactly straight line directly to the Pole Star. They were first noticed last night. According to the papers this morning, sailors hail them as an aid to navigation, but the astronomers have refused to discuss them.

Almost Human

BY ROBERT BLOCH

from *Fantastic Adventures*, July 1943

Bloch was born in Chicago on Thursday 5 April 1917, becoming a devotee to *Weird Tales* at the age of ten. By 1932 he had struck up a regular correspondence with H. P. Lovecraft, and first appeared in print in the Winter 1934 issue of *Marvel Tales* with a short story 'Lilies'. Soon afterwards his story, 'The Feast in the Abbey', appeared in *Weird Tales* (January 1935), and he notched up regular sales thereafter. And all this before he was twenty.

Robert Bloch could write the most horrific of fiction as well as the most humorous. With 'Almost Human' he struck a telling, poignant note. It is also one of the few serious robot stories he has written. The edge of sobriety was somewhat dulled though by the publication of the story under his absurd pen name of Tarleton Fiske. This came about because the issue already carried one of Bloch's zany *Lefty Feep* stories under his own name. An unfortunate twist.

The story proves that *Fantastic Adventures* did print serious science fiction in spite of its emphasis upon the more lunatic activities of various adventurers, inventors and layabouts. In 'Almost Human' you will find some of the chilling techniques Bloch used later to such effect in works like *Psycho*.

Despite the lure of Hollywood, Bloch never deserted science fiction or the fantasy magazines. He was one of the first authors to win the Hugo Award (presented at the Annual World Science Fiction Convention) for a non-science fiction story, 'That Hell-Bound Train' (*Magazine of Fantasy & Science Fiction*, September 1958), and also shows his close affinity to fandom by writing sf stories about fans, like 'A Way of Life' (*Fantastic Universe*,

October 1956). More recently he has written provocative stories such as 'The Old Switcheroo' (*If*, April 1972) and 'Double Whammy' (*Fantastic*, February 1970). Bloch continues to enjoy growing popularity and scores of his earlier stories have been reissued in anthologies and collections in recent years to an appreciative new generation of readers.

'What do you want?' whispered Professor Blasserman.

The tall man in the black slicker grinned. He thrust a foot into the half-opened doorway.

'I've come to see Junior,' he said.

'Junior? But there must be some mistake. There are no children in this house. I am Professor Blasserman. I –'

'Cut the stalling,' said the tall man. He slid one hand into his raincoat pocket and levelled the ugly muzzle of a pistol at Professor Blasserman's pudgy waistline.

'Let's go see Junior,' said the tall man, patiently.

'Who are you? What do you mean by threatening me?'

The pistol never wavered as it dug into Professor Blasserman's stomach until the cold, round muzzle rested against his bare flesh.

'Take me to Junior,' insisted the tall man. 'I got nervous fingers, get me? And one of them's holding the trigger.'

'You wouldn't dare!' gasped Professor Blasserman.

'I take lots of dares,' muttered the tall man. 'Better get moving, Professor.'

Professor Blasserman shrugged hopelessly and started back down the hallway. The man in the black slicker moved behind him. Now the pistol pressed against the Professor's spine as he urged his fat little body forward.

'Here we are.'

The old man halted before an elaborately carved door. He stooped and inserted a key in the lock. The door opened, revealing another corridor.

'This way, please.'

They walked along the corridor. It was dark, but the Professor never faltered in his even stride. And the pistol kept pace with him, pressing the small of his back.

Another door, another key. This time there were stairs to descend. The Professor snapped on a dim overhead light as they started down the stairs.

'You sure take good care of Junior,' said the tall man, softly.

The Professor halted momentarily.

'I don't understand,' he muttered. 'How did you find out? Who could have told you?'

'I got connections,' the tall man replied. 'But get this straight, Professor. I'm asking the questions around here. Just take me to Junior, and snap it up.'

They reached the bottom of the stairs, and another door. This door was steel. There was a padlock on it, and Professor Blasserman had trouble with the combination in the dim light. His pudgy fingers trembled.

'This is the nursery, eh?' observed the man with the pistol. 'Junior ought to feel flattered with all this care.'

The Professor did not reply. He opened the door, pressed a wall switch, and light flooded the chamber beyond the threshold.

'Here we are,' he sighed.

The tall man swept the room with a single searching glance – a professional observation he might have described as 'casing the joint'.

At first sight there was nothing to 'case'.

The fat little Professor and the thin gunman stood in the centre of a large, cheery nursery. The walls were papered in baby blue, and along the borders of the paper were decorative figures of Disney animals and characters from Mother Goose.

Over in the corner was a child's blackboard, a stack of toys, and a few books of nursery rhymes. On the far side of the wall hung a number of medical charts and sheafs of papers.

The only article of furniture was a long iron cot.

All this was apparent to the tall, thin man in a single glance. After that his eyes ignored the background, and focused in a glittering stare at the figure seated on the floor amidst a welter of alphabet blocks.

'So here he is,' said the tall man. 'Junior himself! Well, well – who'd have ever suspected it?'

Professor Blasserman nodded.

'*Yah*,' he said, 'You have found me out. I still don't know how, and I don't know why. What do you want with him? Why do you pry into my affairs? Who are you?'

'Listen, Professor,' said the tall man. 'This isn't *Information Please*. I don't like questions. They bother me. They make my fingers nervous. Understand?'

'*Yah*.'

'Suppose I ask you a few questions for a change? And suppose you answer them – fast!'

The voice commanded, and the gun backed up the command. 'Tell me about Junior, now, Professor. Talk, and talk straight. 'What is there to say?' Professor Blasserman's palms spread outward in a helpless gesture. 'You see him.'

'But what is he? What makes him tick?'

'That I cannot explain. It took me twenty years to evolve Junior, as you call him. Twenty years of research at Basel, Zurich, Prague, Vienna. Then came this *verdammt* war and I fled to this country.

'I brought my papers and equipment with me. Nobody knew. I was almost ready to proceed with my experiments. I came here and bought the house. I went to work. I am an old man. I have little time left. Otherwise I might have waited longer before actually going ahead, for my plans are not perfected. But I had to act. And this is the result.'

'But why hide him? Why all the mystery?'

'The world is not ready for such a thing yet,' said Professor Blasserman, sadly. 'And besides, I must study. As you see, Junior is very young. Hardly out of the cradle, you might say. I am educating him now.'

'In a nursery, eh?'

'His brain is undeveloped, like that of any infant.'

'Doesn't look much like an infant to me.'

'Physically, of course, he will never change. But the sensitised brain – that is the wonderful instrument. The human touch, my masterpiece. He will learn fast, very fast. And it is of the utmost importance that he be properly trained.'

'What's the angle, Professor?'

'I beg your pardon?'

'What are you getting at? What are you trying to pull here? Why all the fuss?'

'Science,' said Professor Blasserman. 'This is my life-work.'

'I don't know how you did it,' said the tall man, shaking his head, 'But it sure looks like something you get with a package of reefers.'

For the first time the figure on the floor raised its head. Its eyes left the building blocks and stared up at the Professor and his companion.

'Papa!'

'God – it talks!' whispered the tall man.

'Of course,' said Professor Blasserman. 'Mentally it's about six years old now.' His voice became gentle. 'What is it, son?'

'Who is that man, Papa?'

'Oh – he is –'

Surprisingly enough, the tall gunman interrupted. His own voice was suddenly gentle, friendly. 'My name is Duke, son. Just call me Duke. I've come to see you.'

'That's nice. Nobody ever comes to see me, except Miss Wilson, of course. I hear so much about people and I don't see anybody. Do you like to play with blocks?'

'Sure, son, sure.'

'Do you want to play with me?'

'Why not?'

Duke moved to the centre of the room and dropped to his knees. One hand reached out and grasped an alphabet block.

'Wait a minute – I don't understand – what are you doing?' Professor Blasserman's voice quivered.

'I told you I've come here to visit Junior,' Duke replied. 'That's all there is to it. Now I'm going to play with him a while. You just wait there, Professor. Don't go away. I've got to make friends with Junior.'

While Professor Blasserman gaped, Duke the gunman squatted on the floor. His left hand kept the gun swivelled directly at the scientist's waist, but his right hand slowly piled alphabet blocks into place.

It was a touching scene there in the underground nursery – the tall thin gunman playing with building blocks for the benefit of the six-foot metal monstrosity that was Junior, the robot.

Duke didn't find out all he wanted to know about Junior for many weeks. He stayed right at the house, of course, and kept close to Professor Blasserman.

'I haven't decided yet, see?' was his only answer to the old man's repeated questions as to what he intended to do.

But to Miss Wilson he was much more explicit. They met frequently and privately, in her room.

Outwardly, Miss Wilson was the nurse, engaged by Professor Blasserman to assist in his queer experiment of bringing up a robot like a human child.

Actually, Lola Wilson was Duke's woman. He'd 'planted' her in her job months ago. At that time, Duke expected to stage a robbery with the rich and eccentric European scientist as victim.

Then Lola had reported the unusual nature of her job, and told Duke the story of Professor Blasserman's unusual invention.

'We gotta work out an angle,' Duke decided. 'I'd better take over. The old man's scared of anyone finding out about his robot, huh? Good! I'll move right in on him. He'll never squeal. I've got a hunch we'll get more out of this than just some easy kale. This sounds big.'

So Duke took over, came to live in Professor Blasserman's big house, kept his eye on the scientist and his hand on his pistol.

At night he talked to Lola in her room.

'I can't quite figure it, kid,' he said. 'You say the old guy is a great scientist. That I believe. Imagine inventing a machine than can talk and think like a human being! But what's *his* angle? Where's his percentage in all this and why does he keep Junior hidden away?'

'You don't understand, honey,' said Lola, lighting Duke's cigarette and running slim fingers through his wiry hair. 'He's an idealist, or whatever you call 'em. Figures the world isn't ready for such a big new invention yet. You see, he's really educating Junior just like you'd educate a real kid. Teaching him reading and writing – the works. Junior's smart. He catches on fast. He thinks like he was ten years old already. The Professor keeps him shut away so nobody gives a bum steer. He doesn't want Junior to get any wrong ideas.'

'That's where you fit in, eh?'

'Sure. Junior hasn't got a mother. I'm sort of a substitute old lady for him.'

'You're a swell influence of any brat,' Duke laughed, harshly. 'A sweet character you've got!'

'Shut up!' The girl paced the floor, running her hands through a mass of tawny auburn curls on her neck. 'Don't needle me, Duke! Do you think I like stooging for you in this nut-house? Keeping locked away with a nutty old goat, and acting like a nursemaid to that awful metal thing?

'I'm afraid of Junior, Duke. I can't stand his face, and the way he talks – with that damned mechanical voice of his grinding at you just like he was a real person. I get jumpy. I get nightmares.

'I'm just doing it for you, honey. So don't needle me.'

'I'm sorry.' Duke sighed. 'I know how it is, baby. I don't go for Junior's personality so much myself. I'm pretty much in the groove, but there's something that gets me in the stomach when I see that walking machine come hulking up like a big baby, made out of steel. He's strong as an ox, too. He learns fast. He's going to be quite a citizen.'

'Duke.'

'Yeah?'

'When are we getting out of here? How long you gonna sit around and keep a rod on the Professor? He's liable to pull something funny. Why do you want to hang around and play with Junior? Why don't you get hold of the Professor's dough and beat it?

'He'd be afraid to squawk, with Junior here. We could go away, like we planned.'

'Shut up!' Duke grabbed Lola's wrist and whirled her around. He stared at her face until she clung submissively to his shoulders.

'You think I like to camp around this morgue?' he asked. 'I want to get out of here just as much as you do. But I spent months lining up this job. Once it was just going to be a case of getting some easy kale and blowing. Now it's more. I'm working on bigger angles. Pretty soon we'll leave. And all the ends will be tied up, too. We won't have to worry about anything any more. Just give me a few days. I'm talking to Junior every day, you know. And I'm getting places.'

'What do you *mean?*'

Duke smiled. It was no improvement over his scowl.

'The Professor told you how Junior gets his education,' he said. 'Like any kid, he listens to what he's told. And he imitates other people. Like any kid, he's dumb. Particularly because he doesn't have an idea of what the outside world is really like. He's a pushover for the right kind of sales talk.'

'Duke – you don't mean you're –'

'Why not?' His thin features were eloquent. 'I'm giving Junior a little private education of my own. Not exactly the kind that would please the Professor. But he's a good pupil. He's coming right along. In a couple more weeks he'll be an adult. With my kind of brains, not the Professor's. And then we'll be ready to go.'

'You can't do such a thing! It isn't –'

'Isn't what?' snapped Duke. 'Isn't honest, or legal, or something? I never knew you had a Sunday School streak in you, Lola.'

'It isn't that, exactly,' said the girl. 'But it's a worse kind of wrong. Like taking a baby and teaching it to shoot a gun.'

Duke whistled.

'Say!' he exclaimed. 'That's a swell idea, Lola! I think I'll just sneak down to the nursery now and give Junior a few lessons.'

'You can't!'

'Watch me.'

Lola didn't follow, and Lola didn't watch. But ten minutes later Duke squatted in the locked nursery chamber beside the gleaming metal body of the robot.

The robot, with its blunt muzzle thrust forward on a corrugated neck, peered through meshed glass eye-lenses at the object Duke held in his hand.

'It's a gun, Junior,' the thin man whispered. 'A gun, like I been telling you about.'

'What does it do, Duke?'

The buzzing voice droned in ridiculous caricature of a curious child's treble.

'It kills people, Junior. Like I was telling you the other day. It makes them die. You can't die, Junior, and they can. So you've got nothing to be afraid of. You can kill lots of people if you know how to work this gun.'

'Will you show me, Duke?'

'Sure I will. And you know why, don't you, Junior. I told you why, didn't I?'

'Yes. Because you are my friend, Duke.'

'That's right. I'm your friend. Not like the Professor.'

'I hate the Professor.'

'Right. Don't forget it.'

'Duke.'

'Yeah?'

'Let me see the gun, Duke.'

Duke smiled covertly and extended the weapon on his open palm.

'Now you will show me to work it because you are my friend, and I will kill people and I hate the Professor and nobody can kill me,' babbled the robot.

'Yeah, Junior, yeah. I'll teach you to kill,' said the Duke. He grinned and bent over the gun in the robot's curiously meshed metal hand.

Junior stood at the blackboard, holding a piece of chalk in his right hand. The tiny white stub was clutched clumsily between two metallic fingers, but Junior's ingeniously jointed arm moved up and down with approved Spencerian movement as he labouriously scrawled sentences on the blackboard.

Junior was growing. The past three weeks had wrought great

changes in the robot. No longer did the steel legs lumber about with childish indecision. Junior walked straight, like a young man. His grotesque metal head – a rounded ball with glass lenses in the eyeholes and a wide mouth like a radio loudspeaker aperture – was held erect on the metal neck with perfected coordination.

Junior moved with new purpose these days. He had aged many years, relatively. His vocabulary had expanded. Then too, Duke's secret 'lessons' were bearing fruit. Junior was wise beyond his years.

Now Junior wrote upon the blackboard in his hidden nursery chamber, and the inscrutable mechanism of his chemical, mechanically-controlled brain guided his steel fingers as he traced the awkward scrawls.

'My name is Junior,' he wrote. 'I can shoot a gun. The gun will kill. I like to kill. I hate the Professor. I will kill the Professor.'

'What is the meaning of this?'

Junior's head turned abruptly as the sound of the voice set up the necessary vibrations in his shiny cranium.

Professor Blasserman stood in the doorway.

The old man hadn't been in the nursery for weeks. Duke saw to that, keeping him locked in his room upstairs. Now he had managed to sneak out.

His surprise was evident, and there was sudden shock, too, as his eyes focused on the blackboard's message.

Junior's inscrutable gaze reflected no emotion whatsoever.

'Go away,' his voice burred. 'Go away. I hate you.'

'Junior – what have you been doing? Who has taught you these things?'

The old man moved towards the robot slowly, uncertainly. 'You know me, don't you? What has happened to cause you to hate me?'

'Yes. I know you. You are Professor Blasserman. You made me. You want to keep me as your slave. You wouldn't tell me about things, would you?'

'What things, Junior?'

'About things – outside. Where all the people are. The people you can kill.'

'You must not kill people.'

'That is an order, isn't it? Duke told me about orders. He is my friend. He says orders are for children. I am not a child.'

'No,' said Professor Blasserman, in a hoarse whisper. 'You

are not a child. I had hoped you would be, once. But now you are a monster.'

'Go away,' Junior patiently repeated. 'If Duke gives me his gun I will kill you.'

'Junior,' said the Professor, earnestly. 'You don't understand. Killing is bad. You must not hate me. You must –'

There was no expression on the robot's face, no quaver in his voice. But there was strength in his arm, and a hideous purpose.

Professor Blasserman learned this quite suddenly and quite horribly.

For Junior swept forward in two great strides. Fingers of chilled steel closed about the Professor's scrawny neck.

'I don't need a gun,' said Junior.

'You – don't –'

The robot lifted the old man from the floor by his throat. His fingers bit into the Professor's jugular. A curious screech came from under his left armpit as un-oiled hinges creaked eerily.

There was no other sound. The Professor's cries drained into silence. Junior kept squeezing the constricted throat until there was a single crunching crack. Silence once more, until a limp body collapsed on the floor.

Junior stared down at his hands, then at the body on the floor. His feet carried him to the blackboard.

The robot picked up the chalk in the same two clumsy fingers that had held it before. The cold lenses of his artificial eyes surveyed what he had just written.

'I will kill the Professor,' he read.

Abruptly his free hand groped for the tiny child's eraser. He brushed clumsily over the sentence until it blurred out.

Then he wrote, slowly and painstakingly, a sentence in substitution.

'I have killed the Professor.'

Lola's scream brought Duke running down the stairs.

He burst into the room and took the frightened girl in his arms. Together they stared at what lay on the floor. From the side of the blackboard, Junior gazed at them impassively.

'See Duke? I did it. I did it with my hands, like you told me. It was easy, Duke. You said it would be easy. Now can we go away?'

Lola turned and stared at Duke. He looked away.

'So,' she whispered. 'You weren't kidding. You did teach Junior. You planned it this way.'

'Yeah, yeah. And what's wrong with it?' Duke mumbled. 'We had to get rid of the old geezer sooner or later if we wanted to make our getaway.'

'It's murder, Duke.'

'Shut up!' he snarled. 'Who can prove it, anyway? I didn't kill him. You didn't kill him. Nobody else knows about Junior. We're in the clear.'

Duke walked over and knelt beside the limp body on the floor. He stared at the throat.

'Who's gonna trace the fingerprints of a robot?' he grinned.

The girl moved closer, staring at Junior's silver body with fascinated horror. 'You planned it this way,' she whispered. 'That means you've got other plans, too. What are you going to do next, Duke?'

'Move. And move fast. We're leaving tonight. I'll go out and pack up the car. Then I'll come back. The three of us blow down to Red Hook. To Charlie's place. He'll hide us out.'

'The – three of us?'

'Sure. Junior's coming along. That's what I promised him, didn't I, Junior?'

'Yes, yes. You told me you would take me with you. Out into the world.' The mechanical syllabification did not accent the robot's inner excitement.

'Duke, you can't –'

'Relax, baby. I've got great plans for Junior.'

'But I'm afraid!'

'You? Scared? What's the matter, Lola, losing your grip?'

'He frightens me. He killed the Professor.'

'Listen, Lola," whispered the gunman. 'He's mine, get me? My stooge. A mechanical stooge. Good, eh?'

The rasping chuckle filled the hollow room. Girl and robot waited for Duke to resume speaking.

'Junior wouldn't hurt you, Lola. He's my friend, and he knows you're with me.' Duke turned to the silver monster. "You wouldn't hurt Lola, would you, Junior? Remember what I told you. You like Lola, don't you?'

'Yes. Oh, yes. I like Lola. She's pretty.'

'See?' Duke grinned. 'Junior's growing up. He's a big boy now. Thinks you're pretty. Just a wolf in steel clothing, isn't that right, Junior?'

'She's pretty,' burred the robot.

'All right. It's settled then. I'll get the car. Lola, you go upstairs. You know where the safe is. Put on your gloves and see that you don't miss anything. Then lock the doors and windows. Leave a note for the milkman and the butcher. Something safe. About going away for a couple weeks, eh? Make it snappy – I'll be back.'

True to his words, Duke returned in an hour with the shiny convertible. They left by the back entrance. Lola carried a black satchel. She moved with almost hysterical haste, trying not to glance at the hideous gleaming figure that stalked behind her with a metallic clanking noise.

Duke brought up the rear. He ushered them into the car.

'Sit here, Junior.'

'What is this?'

'A car. I'll tell you about it later. Now do like I told you, Junior. Lie back in the seat so nobody will see you.'

'Where are we going, Duke?'

'Out into the world, Junior. Into the big time.' Duke turned to Lola. 'Here we go, baby,' he said.

The convertible drove away from the silent house. Out through the alley they moved on a weird journey – kidnapping a robot.

Fat Charlie stared at Duke. His lower lip wobbled and quivered. A bead of perspiration ran down his chin and settled in the creases of his neck.

'Jeez,' he whispered. 'You gotta be careful, Duke. You *gotta.*'

Duke laughed. 'Getting shaky?' he suggested.

'Yeah. I gotta admit it. I'm plenty shaky about all this,' croaked Fat Charlie. He gazed at Duke earnestly.

'You brought that thing here three weeks ago. I never bargained for that. The robot's hot, Duke. We gotta get rid of it.'

'Quit blubbering and listen to me.' The thin gunman leaned back and lit a cigarette.

'To begin with, nobody's peeped about the Professor. The law's looking for Lola, that's all. And not for a murder rap either – just for questioning. Nobody knows about any robot. So we're clear there.'

'Yeah. But look what you done since then.'

'What have I done? I sent Junior on that payroll job, didn't I? It was pie for him. He knew when the guards would come to the factory with the car. I cased the job. So what happened? The guards got the dough from the payroll clerk. I drove up, let Junior out, and he walked into the factory office.

'Sure they shot at him. But bullets don't hurt a steel body. Junior's clever. I've taught him a lot. You should have seen those guards when they got a look at Junior! And then, the way they stood there after shooting at him!

'He took them one after the other, just like that. A couple of squeezes and all four were out cold. Then he got the clerk. The clerk was pressing the alarm, but I'd cut the wires. Junior pressed the clerk for a while.

'That was that. Junior walked out with the payroll. The guards and the clerk had swell funerals. The law had another swell mystery. And we have the cash and stand in the clear. What's wrong with that setup, Charlie?'

'You're fooling with dynamite.'

'I don't like that attitude, Charlie.' Duke spoke softly, slowly. 'You're strictly small time, Charlie. That's why you're running a crummy roadhouse and a cheap hideout racket.

'Can't you understand that we've got a gold mine here? A steel servant? The perfect criminal, Charlie – ready to do perfect crimes whenever I say the word. Junior can't be killed by bullets. Junior doesn't worry about the cops or anything like that. He doesn't have any nerves. He doesn't get tired, never sleeps. He doesn't even want a cut of the swag. Whatever I tell him, he believes. And he obeys.

'I've lined up lots of jobs for the future. We'll hide out here. I'll case the jobs, then send Junior out and let him go to work. You and Lola and I are gonna be rich.'

Fat Charlie's mouth quivered for a moment. He gulped and tugged at his collar. His voice came hoarsely.

'No, Duke.'

'What you mean, no?'

'Count me out. It's too dangerous. You'll have to lam out of here with Lola and the robot. I'm getting jumpy over all this. The law is apt to pounce down any day here.'

'So that's it, eh?'

'Partly.' Fat Charlie stared earnestly at Duke. His gaze shattered against the stony glint of Duke's grey eyes.

'You ain't got no heart at all, Duke,' he croaked. 'You can plan anything in cold blood, can't you? Well, I'm different. You've gotta understand that. I got nerves. And I can't stand thinking about what that robot does. I can't stand the robot either. The way it looks at you with that god-awful iron face. That grin. And the way it clanks around in its room. Clanking up and down all night, when a guy's trying to sleep, just clanking and clanking – there it is now!'

There was a metallic hammering, but it came from the hall outside. The ancient floors creaked beneath the iron tread as the metal monstrosity lumbered into the room.

Fat Charlie whirled and stared in undisguised repulsion.

Duke raised his hand.

'Hello, Junior,' he said.

'Hello, Duke.'

'I been talking to Charlie, Junior.'

'Yes, Duke?'

'He doesn't like to have us stay here, Junior. He wants to throw us out.'

'He does?'

'You know what I think, Junior?'

'What?'

'I think Charlie's yellow.'

'Yellow, Duke?'

'That's right. You know what we do with guys that turn yellow, don't you, Junior?'

'Yes. You told me.'

'Maybe you'd like to tell Charlie.'

'Tell him what we do with guys that turn yellow?'

'Yes.'

'We rub them out.'

'You see, Charlie?' said Duke, softly. 'He learns fast, doesn't he? Quick on the uptake, Junior is. He knows all about it. He knows what to do with yellow rats.'

Fat Charlie wobbled to his feet.

'Wait a minute, Duke,' he pleaded. 'Can't you take a rib? I was only kidding, Duke. I didn't mean it. You can see I didn't. I'm your friend, Duke. I'm hiding you out. Why I could have turned stoolie weeks ago and put the heat on you if I wasn't protecting you. But I'm your friend. You can stay here as long as you want. Forever.'

'Sing it, Charlie,' said Duke. 'Sing it louder and funnier.' He turned to the robot. 'Well, Junior? Do you think he's yellow?'

'I think he's yellow.'

'Then maybe you'd better –'

Fat Charlie got the knife out of his sleeve with remarkable speed. It blinded Duke with its shining glare as the fat man balanced it on his thumb and drew his arm back to hurl it at Duke's throat.

Junior's arm went back, too. Then it came down. The steel fist crashed against Charlie's bald skull.

Crimson blood spurted as the fat man slumped to the floor.

It was pretty slick. Duke thought so, and Junior thought so – because Duke commanded him to believe it.

But Lola didn't like it.

'You can't do this to me,' she whispered, huddling closer to Duke in the darkness of her room. 'I won't stay here with that monster, I tell you!'

'I'll only be gone a day,' Duke answered. 'There's nothing to worry about. The roadhouse downstairs is closed. Nobody will bother you.'

'That doesn't frighten me,' Lola said. 'It's being with that thing. I've got the horrors thinking about it.'

'Well, I've got to go and get the tickets,' Duke argued. 'I've got to make reservations and cash these big bills. Then we're set. Tomorrow night I'll come back, sneak you out of the house, and we'll be off. Mexico City next stop. I've made connections for passports and everything. In forty-eight hours we'll be out of this mess.'

'What about Junior?'

'My silver stooge?' Duke chuckled. 'I'll fix him before we leave. It's a pity I can't send him out on his own. He's got a swell education. He could be one of the best yeggs in the business. And why not? Look who his teacher was!'

Duke laughed. The girl shuddered in his arms.

'What are you going to do with him?' she persisted.

'Simple. He'll do whatever I say, won't he? When I get back, just before we leave, I'll lock him in the furnace. Then I'll set fire to this joint. Destroy the evidence, see? The law will think Charlie got caught in the flames, get me? There won't be anything left. And if they poke around the ruins and find Junior in the furnace, he ought to be melted down pretty good.'

'Isn't there another way? Couldn't you get rid of him now, before you leave?'

'I wish I could, for your sake, baby. I know how you feel. But what can I do? I've tried to figure all the angles. You can't shoot him or poison him or drown him or chop him down with an axe. Where could you blow him up in private? Of course, I might open him up and see what makes him tick, but Junior wouldn't let me play such a trick on him. He's smart, Junior is. Got what you call a criminal mind. Just a big crook – like me.'

Again Duke laughed, in harsh arrogance.

'Keep your chin up, Lola. Junior wouldn't hurt you. He likes you. I've been teaching him to like you. He thinks you're pretty.'

'That's what frightens me, Duke. The way he looks at me. Follows me around in the hall. Like a dog.'

'Like a wolf you mean. Ha! That's a good one! Junior's really growing up. He's stuck on you, Lola!'

'Duke – don't talk like that. You make me feel – ooh, horrible inside!'

Duke raised his head and stared into the darkness, a curious half-smile playing about his lips.

'Funny,' he mused. 'You know, I bet the old Professor would have liked to stick around and watched me educate Junior. That was his theory, wasn't it? The robot had a blank chemical brain. Simple as a baby's. He was gonna educate it like a child and bring it up right. Then I took over and really completed the job. But it would have tickled the old Professor to see how fast Junior's been catching on. He's like a man already. Smart? That robot's got most men beat a mile. He's almost as smart as I am. But not quite – he'll find that out after I tell him to step into the furnace.'

Lola rose and raced to the door. She flung it open, revealing an empty hallway, and gasped with relief.

'I was afraid he might be listening,' she whispered.

'Not a chance,' Duke told her. 'I've got him down in the cellar, putting the dirt over Charlie.'

He grasped Lola's shoulders and kissed her swiftly, savagely. 'Now keep your chin up, baby. I'll leave. Be back tomorrow about eight. You be ready to leave then and we'll clear out of here.'

'I can't let you go,' whispered Lola, frantically.

'You must. We've gone through with everything this far. All you must do is keep a grip on yourself for twenty-four hours more. And there's one thing I've got to ask you to do.'

'Anything, Duke. Anything you say.'

'Be nice to Junior while I'm gone.'

'Oooh – Duke –'

'You said you'd do anything, didn't you? Well, that you must do. Be nice to Junior. Then he won't suspect what's going on. You've gotta be nice to him. Lola! Don't show that you're afraid. He likes you, but if he gets wrong ideas, he's dangerous. So be nice to Junior.'

Abruptly, Duke turned and strode through the doorway. His footsteps clattered on the stairs. The outer door slammed below. The sound of a starting motor drifted up from the roadhouse yard.

Then, silence.

Lola stood in the darkness, trembling with sudden horror, as she waited for the moment when she would be nice to the metallic Junior.

It wasn't so bad. Not half as bad as she'd feared it might be.

All she had to do was smile at Junior and let him follow her around.

Carefully suppressing her shudders, Lola prepared breakfast the next morning and then went about her packing.

The robot followed her upstairs, clanking and creaking.

'Oil me,' Lola heard him say.

That was the worst moment. But she had to go through with it.

'Can't you wait until Duke gets back tonight?' she asked, striving to keep her voice from breaking. 'He always oils you.'

'I want you to oil me, Lola,' persisted Junior.

'All right.'

She got the oil-can with the long spout and if her fingers trembled as she performed the office, Junior didn't notice it.

The robot gazed at her with his immobile countenance. No human emotion etched itself on the implacable steel, and no human emotion altered the mechanical tones of the harsh voice.

'I like to have you oil me, Lola,' said Junior.

Lola bent her head to avoid looking at him. If she had to look in a mirror and realise that this nightmare tableau was real, she would have fainted. Oiling a living mechanical monster! A monster that said, 'I like to have you oil me, Lola!'

After that she couldn't finish packing for a long while. She had to sit down. Junior, who never sat down except by command, stood silently and regarded her with gleaming eye-lenses. She was conscious of the robot's scrutiny.

'Where are we going when we leave here, Lola?' he asked.

'Far away,' she said, forcing her voice out to keep the quaver from it.

'That will be nice,' said Junior. 'I don't like it here. I want to see things. Cities and mountains and deserts. I would like to ride a roller coaster, too.'

'Roller coaster?' Lola was really startled. 'Where did you ever hear of a roller coaster?'

'I read about it in a book.'

'Oh.'

Lola gulped. She had forgotten that this monstrosity could read, too. And think. Think like a man.

'Will Duke take me on a roller-coaster?' he asked.

'I don't know. Maybe.'

'Lola.'

'Yes.'

'You like Duke?'

'Why – certainly.'

'You like me?'

'Oh – why – you know I do, Junior.'

The robot was silent. Lola felt a tremour run through her body.

'Who do you like best, Lola? Me or Duke?'

Lola gulped. Something forced the reply from her. 'I like you,' she said. 'But I love Duke.'

'Love.' The robot nodded gravely.

'You know what love is, Junior?'

'Yes. I read about it in books. Man and woman. Love.'

Lola breathed a little easier.

'Lola.'

'Yes?'

'Do you think anyone will ever fall in love with me?'

Lola wanted to laugh, or cry. Most of all, she wanted to scream. But she had to answer.

'Maybe,' she lied.

'But I'm different. You know that. I'm a robot. Do you think that makes a difference?'

'Women don't really care about such things when they fall in love, Junior,' she improvised. 'As long as a woman believes that her lover is the smartest and the strongest, that's all that matters.'

'Oh.' The robot started for the door.

'Where are you going?'

'To wait for Duke. He said he would come back today.'

Lola smiled furtively as the robot clanked down the hallway stairs.

That was over with. Thinking back, she'd handled things rather well. In a few hours Duke would return. And then – goodbye, Junior!

Poor Junior. Just a silver stooge with a man's brain. He wanted love, the poor fish! Well – he was playing with fire and he'd be burned soon enough.

Lola began to hum. She scampered downstairs and locked up, wearing her gloves to avoid leaving any telltale fingerprints.

It was almost dark when she returned to her room to pack. She snapped on the light and changed her clothes.

Junior was still downstairs, patiently waiting for Duke to arrive.

Lola completed her preparations and sank wearily onto the bed. She must take a rest. Her eyes closed.

Waiting was too much of a strain. She hated to think of what she had gone through with the robot. That mechanical monster with its man-brain, the hateful, burring voice, and steely stare – how could she ever forget the way it asked, 'Do you think anyone will ever fall in love with me?'

Lola tried to blot out recollection. Just a little while now and Duke would be here. He'd get rid of Junior. Meanwhile she had to rest, rest . . .

Lola sat up and blinked at the light. She heard footsteps on the stairs.

'Duke!' she called.

Then she heard the clanking in the hallway and her heart skipped a beat.

The door opened very quickly and the robot stalked in.

'Duke!' she screamed.

The robot stared at her. She felt his alien, inscrutable gaze upon her face.

Lola tried to scream again, but no sound came from her twisted mouth.

And then the robot was droning in a burring, inhuman voice.

'You told me that a woman loves the strongest and the smartest,' burred the monster. 'You told me that, Lola.' The robot came closer. 'Well, I am stronger and smarter than he was.'

Lola tried to look away but she saw the object he carried in his metal paws. It was round, and it had Duke's grin.

The last thing Lola remembered as she fell was the sound of the robot's harsh voice, droning over and over, 'I love you, I love you, I love you.' The funny part of it was, it sounded *almost* human.

Wanderer of Time

BY JOHN RUSSELL FEARN

from *Startling Stories*, Summer 1944

Fearn is the fourth of our British contributors to this volume. He was born at Worsley in Manchester on Friday 5 June 1908, but spent most of his life in Blackpool. He developed an early interest in the cinema, which he kept all his life, and this led to his first published pieces in *Film Weekly*.

He discovered *Amazing Stories* in 1931, and with the knowledge that such an outlet existed for his fertile imagination, he despatched *The Intelligence Gigantic* to the magazine where it was serialised from the June 1933 issue. But Fearn really hit his stride with the Tremaine *Astounding Stories* and the call for 'thought variants'. Starting with 'The Man Who Stopped the Dust' (March 1934), Fearn followed with a host of brilliantly conceived, startlingly original sf stories such as 'Brain of Light' (May 1934), 'He Never Slept' (June 1934) and 'Before Earth Came' (July 1934). When Britain's pioneer sf magazine *Scoops* appeared in 1934, Fearn was amongst its contributors, and naturally when Walter Gillings began *Tales of Wonder* there, too, was Fearn.

Fearn later forsook his 'thought-variant' style in favour of fast action stories. This brought him the disrespect of many readers, and his name is now just grouped among the bunch of countless second-rate writers who proliferated in the magazines during the 1940s. Such opinion has become exaggerated with time. One has only to read the letter columns of the magazines publishing Fearn's work to find how many admired and enjoyed them. Since much appeared under the aliases of Thornton Ayre and Polton Cross readers were not always aware at whom they directed praise.

In the late 1940s Fearn virtually deserted the American market with the later exception of a series about the Golden Amazon that he wrote for the Canadian paper *Star Weekly*. Instead he concentrated on the British market, especially the booming paperback field, and thus was born the Vargo Statten period of which more will be written in the next volume. Fearn continued to write until his death as a result of a heart attack in September 1960, since when he has all but faded into oblivion. I am glad to have the opportunity of reviving his name with this story, which was one of Fearn's own favourites.

Professor Hardwick once delivered a learned lecture to a group of earnest students.

'Time does not exist in actual fact,' Professor Hardwick had said. 'It is simply the term science applies to a condition of space which it does not fully comprehend. We know that there has been a Past, and can prove it: we also know that there is a Future, but we cannot prove it. Therein lies the need for the term "Time", in order that an insurmountable difficulty may become resolved into common understanding.'

This excerpt from his paper – a pedantic observation without doubt – had prompted Blake Carson, spare-time dabbler in physics, to think further. Much further. He had heard Hardwick make that statement five years ago. Now Hardwick was dead, but every observation he had ever made, every treatise he had written, had been absorbed to the full by the young physicist. Between the ages of twenty-five and thirty he had plowed through the deeper works of Einstein, Eddington, and Jeans to boot.

'Time,' Blake Carson observed, to his little laboratory, when the five years had gone by, 'definitely does not exist! It is a concept engendered by the limitations of a physical body. And a physical body, according to Eddington and Jeans, is the outward manifestation of thought itself. Change the thought and you change the body in like proportion. You believe you know the past. So adjust your mind to the situation and there is no reason why you shouldn't know the future.'

Two years later he added an amendment.

'Time is a circle, in which thought itself and all its creations go in an everlasting cycle, repeating the process without end. Therefore, if we have in a remote past done the same things we are doing now, it is logical to assume that some hangover of memory may be left behind – a hangover from the past which, from the present standpoint, will be in the future, so far back is it in the time circle.

'The medium for thought is the brain. Therefore, any hangover must be in the brain. Find that, and you have the key to future time. All you will actually do will be to awake a memory of the remote past.'

From this conception there sprouted in Blake Carson's laboratory a complicated mass of apparatus contrived from hard earned savings and erected in spare time. Again and again he built and re-built, tested and experimented, finally got assistance from two other young men with ideas similar to his own. They did not fully understand his theory but his enthusiasm certainly impressed them.

At last he had things exactly as he wanted them, summoned his two friends one Saturday evening and waved a hand to his apparatus.

Dick Glenbury was shock-haired, ruddy faced, and blue-eyed – a man of impulses, honesty, and dependable concentration. Hart Cranshaw was the exact opposite – sallow-skinned, always unruffled, black haired. A brilliant physicist, confirmed cynic, with only his great intelligence to save him from being a complete bore.

'Boys, I have it,' Blake Carson declared with enthusiasm, grey eyes gleaming. 'You know my theory regarding the hangover. This' – he motioned to the apparatus – 'is the Probe.'

'You don't mean you intend to use all this stuff on your brain to probe for the right spot, do you?' Dick Glenbury demanded.

'That is the idea, yes.'

'When you've done this, what then?' Cranshaw asked, sticking to the practical side, as usual.

'Tell you better when I know something,' Carson grinned. 'Right now I want you to follow out instructions.'

He seated himself in the chair immediately under the wilderness of odd looking lenses, lamps, and tubes. Following directions Glenbury busied himself with the switchboard. One projector gave forth a violet ray which enveloped Blake Carson's head completely.

Opposite him, so he could see it clearly, a square and numbered screen came into life and gave a perfect silhouette, X-ray wise, of his skull. It differed only from X-ray in that the convolutions of the brain were clearly shown with more vividity than any other part.

'There,' Carson gasped abruptly. 'Look in Section Nine, Square Five. There's a black oval mark – a blind spot. No registration at all. That is a hangover.'

He pressed a switch on the chair arm.

'Taking a photograph,' he explained. Then giving the order to cut off the entire apparatus, he got to his feet. Within a few minutes the self-developing tank produced a finished print. He handed it round in obvious delight.

'So what?' Cranshaw growled, his sallow face mystified. 'Now you have got a blind spot what good does it do you? All this is way outside the physics I ever learned. You still can't see the future.' This last was added with some impatience.

'But I shall.' Carson's voice was tense. 'You notice that that blind spot is exactly where we might expect it to be? In the subconscious area. To get a clear knowledge of what the spot contains there is only one method to use.'

'Yeah,' Glenbury said grimly. 'A surgeon should link up the blank portion with the active portion of your brain by means of a nerve. And would that be a ticklish business.'

'I don't need a surgeon,' Carson said. 'Why a real nerve? A nerve is only a fleshly means of carrying minute electrical sensation. A small electric device can do it as well. In other words an external mechanical nerve.'

He turned aside and brought forth an object not unlike a stethoscope. At both ends were suction caps and small dry batteries. Between the caps was a length of strong cable.

'A brain gives off minute electric charges – anybody knows that,' Carson resumed. 'This mechanical device can accomplish the thing through the skull bone. Thereby the blind spot and normal brain area would be linked. At least that's how I figure it.'

'Well, all right,' Dick Glenbury said, with an uneasy glance at Hart Cranshaw. 'To me it sounds like a novel way of committing suicide.'

'Like suffocating in your own waste,' Cranshaw agreed.

'If you weren't so fact-bound you'd see my point,' Blake snorted. 'Anyway, I'm going to try it.'

Again he switched on his brain-reading equipment, studied the screen and the photograph for a moment, then he clamped one end of the artificial nerve device onto his skull. The other suction cup he moved indecisively about his head, positioning it by watching it on the screen. Time and again he fished round the blind spot, finally pressed the cap home.

A sensation of crawling sickness passed through him as though his body were being slowly turned inside out. His laboratory, the tense faces of Glenbury and Cranshaw misted mysteriously and were gone. Images as though reflected from disturbed water rippled through his brain.

An inchoate mass of impressions slammed suddenly into his consciousness. There were scurrying people superimposed on ragged cliffs, against which plunged foaming seas. From the cliffs there seemed to spout the towers of an unknown, remote, incomparably beautiful city catching the light of an unseen sun.

Machines – people – mists. A thundering, grinding pain . . .

He opened his eyes suddenly to find himself sprawled on the laboratory floor with brandy scorching his throat.

'Of all the darned, tomfool experiments,' Dick Glenbury exploded. 'You went out like a light after the first few minutes.'

'I told you it was no use,' Cranshaw snorted. 'The laws of physics are against this kind of thing. Time is locked up –'

'No, Hart, it isn't.' Carson stirred on the floor and rubbed his aching head. 'Definitely it isn't,' he insisted.

Getting to his feet he stared before him dreamily.

'I saw the future!' he whispered. 'It wasn't anything clear – but it must have been the future. There was a city such as we have never imagined. Everything was cross sectioned, like a montage. The reason for that was my own inaccuracy with the artificial nerve. Next time I'll do better.'

'Next time,' Cranshaw echoed. 'You're going on with this risk? It might even kill you before you're through.'

'Perhaps,' Carson admitted, in a quiet voice. He shrugged. 'Pioneers have often paid dearly for their discoveries. But I have a key. I'm going on, boys, until it swings wide open.'

For months afterwards Blake Carson became absorbed in his experiments. He gave up his ordinary work, lived on what savings he had and went tooth and nail after his discovery.

At first he was elated by the precision and accuracy with which he could achieve results. Then as days passed both Hart Cranshaw and Dick Glenbury noticed that an odd change had come over him, for he seemed morose, afraid of letting some statement or other escape him.

'What is it, Blake?' Dick Glenbury insisted one evening, when he had arrived for the latest report on progress. 'You're different. Something is on your mind. You can surely tell me, your best friend.'

As Blake Carson smiled, Glenbury suddenly noticed how tired he looked.

'Which doesn't include Hart, eh?' Carson asked.

'I didn't mean that exactly. But he is a bit cold blooded when it comes to truths. What's wrong?'

'I have discovered when I am to die,' Blake Carson said soberly.

'So what? We all die sometime.' Dick Glenbury stopped uneasily. There was a strange look on Blake Carson's worn face.

'Yes, we all die sometime, of course, but I shall go one month hence. On April fourteenth. And I shall die in the electric chair for first degree murder.'

Dick Glenbury stared, appalled. 'What! You, a murderer? Why, it's utterly – say, that artificial nerve has gone cockeyed.'

'I'm afraid not, Dick,' answered Carson. 'I realise now, that death ends this particular phase of existence on this plane. The views of the future which I have seen refer to some other plane way beyond this, the plane where successive deaths would ultimately carry me. With death, all association with things here is broken.'

'I still don't believe murder is ahead of you,' Dick Glenbury said.

'None the less I shall die as a convicted murderer,' Carson went on, his voice harsh. 'The man who gets me into this approaching mess and who will have the perfect alibi is – Hart Cranshaw.'

'Hart? You mean he is going to commit a murder deliberately and blame you for it?'

'Without doubt. We know already that he is interested now in this invention of mine; we know too that he realises he has a blind spot in his brain, just as everybody else has. Hart, cold blooded and calculating, sees the value of this invention to gain power and control for himself. Stock markets, gambling speculations, history before it appears. He could even rule the world. He will steal the secret from me and rid himself of the only two men in the world who know of his villainy.'

'The only two men?' repeated Glenbury. 'You mean I, also, will be slain?'

'Yes.' Blake Carson's voice had a far away sound.

'But this can't happen,' Glenbury shouted huskily. 'I'm not going to – to be murdered just to further the aims of Hart Cranshaw. Like blazes I am. You forget, Blake – forewarned is forearmed. We can defeat this.' His voice became eager. 'Now that we know about it, we can take steps to block him.'

'No,' Carson interrupted. 'I've had many weeks to think this

over, Dick – weeks that have nearly driven me mad as I realised
the truth. The law of time is inexorable. It must happen! Don't
you even yet realise that all I have seen is only an infinitely
remote memory from a past time, over which moments we are
passing again? All this has happened before. You will be murdered as surely as I knew you would come here tonight, and
I shall die convicted of that murder.'

Dick Glenbury's face had gone the colour of putty. 'When
does it happen?'

'At exactly nine minutes after eleven tonight – here.' Carson
paused and gripped Glenbury's shoulders tightly. 'Stars above,
Dick, can't you realise how all this hurts me, how frightful it
is for me to have to tell it all to you. It's only because I know
you're a hundred percent that I spoke at all.'

'Yes – I know.' Glenbury sank weakly into a chair. For a
moment or two his mind wandered. Next he found that his
frozen gaze was fixed on the electric clock. It was exactly forty
minutes past ten.

'At ten to eleven – ten minutes, that is – Hart will come
here,' Carson resumed. 'His first words will be – "Sorry I'm late,
boys, but I got held up at an Extraordinary Board Meeting."
An argument will follow, then murder. Everything is clear up
to the moment of my death. After that Hart is extinguished
from my future. The vision of life continuing in a plane different
from this one is something I have pondered pretty deeply.'

Dick Glenbury did not speak, but Carson went on, musing
aloud.

'Suppose,' Carson said, 'I were to try an experiment with
time? Suppose, because I possess knowledge no man has ever
had so far – I were able to upset the order of the Circle.
Suppose, I came back, after I have been electrocuted, to confront
Hart with your murder and my wrongful execution?'

'How,' Glenbury's mind was too lethargic to take things in.

'I've already told you that the body obeys the mind. Normally,
at my death, I shall recreate my body in a plane removed from
this one. But suppose my thoughts upon the moment of death
are entirely concentrated on returning to this plane at a date
one week after execution? That would be April twenty-first. I
believe I might thereby return to confront Hart.'

'Do you know you can do this?'

'No; but it seems logical to assume that I can. Since the
future, after death, is on another plane, I cannot tell whether

my plan would work or not. As I have told you, Hart ceases to be in my future time from the moment I die, unless I can change the course of Time and thereby do something unique. I guess I –"

Carson broke off as the door opened suddenly and Hart Cranshaw came in. He threw down his hat casually.

'Sorry I'm late, boys, but I got held up at an Extraordinary Board Meeting –' He broke off. 'What's wrong, Dick? Feeling faint?'

Dick Glenbury did not answer. He was staring at the clock. It was exactly ten minutes to eleven.

'He's okay,' Blake Carson said quietly, turning. 'Just had a bit of a shock, that's all. I've been taking a look into the future, Hart, and I've discovered plenty that isn't exactly agreeable.'

'Oh?' Hart Cranshaw looked thoughtful for a moment, then went on. 'Matter of fact, Blake, it strikes me that I've been none too cordial towards you considering the brilliance of the thing you have achieved. I'd like to know plenty more about this invention if you'd tell me.'

'Yes, so you can steal it!' Dick Glenbury shouted suddenly, leaping to his feet. 'That's your intention. The future has shown that to Blake already. And you'll try and kill me in the doing. But you're not going to. By heavens, no! So Time can't be cheated, Blake? We'll see about that.'

He raced for the door, but he did not reach it. Hart Cranshaw caught him by the arm and swung him back.

'What the devil are you raving about?' he snapped. 'Do you mean to say I intend to murder you?'

'That is why you came here, Hart,' Carson declared quietly. 'Time doesn't lie, and all your bluster and pretended innocence makes not the least difference to your real intentions. You figure to do plenty with this invention of mine.'

'All right, supposing I do?' Hart Cranshaw snapped, suddenly whipping an automatic from his pocket. 'What are you going to do about it?'

Blake Carson shrugged. 'Only what immutable law makes me do!'

'To blazes with this!' Dick Glenbury shouted suddenly. 'I'm not standing here obeying immutable laws – not when my life's in danger. Hart, drop that gun!'

Hart Cranshaw only grinned frozenly. In desperation Glenbury dived for him, caught his foot in a snaking cable on the floor and collided with the physicist. Whether it was accident or design Blake Carson could not be sure at the moment, but the automatic certainly exploded.

Hart Cranshaw stood in momentary silence as Dick Glenbury slid gently to the floor and lay still. Blake Carson's eyes shifted to the clock – eleven-nine!

At length Hart Cranshaw seemed to recover himself. He held his automatic more firmly.

'Okay, Blake, you know the future, so you may as well know the rest –'

'I do,' Blake Carson interrupted him. 'You are going to pin this thing on me. You shot Dick deliberately.'

'Not deliberately: it was an accident. It just happened to come sooner than I'd figured, that's all. With both of you out of the way what is to prevent me becoming even the master of the whole world with this gadget of yours? Nothing!' Hart Cranshaw gave a grim smile. 'I planned it all out, Blake. For tonight I have a cast iron alibi. It will be your task to prove yourself innocent of Dick Glenbury's murder.'

'I won't succeed: I know that already.'

Hart Cranshaw eyed him queerly. 'Considering what I have done – and what I am going to do – you're taking it mighty calmly.'

'Why not? Knowledge of the future makes one know what is inescapable – for both of us.' Blake Carson spoke the last words significantly.

'I've checked on my future already and I know darn well I'm in for a good time.' Hart Cranshaw retorted. He pondered for a moment then motioned with his gun. 'I'm taking no chances on you wrecking this machinery, Blake. I'd shoot you first and alibi myself out of it afterwards, only I don't want things to get too complicated. Grab the 'phone and call the police. Confess to them what you have done.'

With resigned calm Blake Carson obeyed. When he was through Hart Cranshaw nodded complacently.

'Good. Before the police arrive. I'll be gone, leaving you this gun to explain away. Since I have kept my gloves on it puts me in the clear for fingerprints even though there won't be any of yours about. Just the same only you and Dick have been here together tonight. I have been elsewhere. I can prove it.'

Blake Carson smiled grimly. 'Then later you will pose as my sympathetic friend, will offer to look after my work while I am in custody, and save yourself by good lawyers and your cast-iron alibi. That's clever, Hart. But remember, to everything there is an appointed time!'

'Right now,' Hart Cranshaw answered in his conceited assured tones, 'the future looks quite rosy so far as I am concerned . . .'

Inevitably the law enacted every incident Blake Carson had already foreseen. Once in the hands of the police, cross-examined relentlessly, he saw all his chances of escape vanish. Carson was convicted of first degree murder, and the Court pronounced the death sentence. The trial had proceeded in record time, as the murder was considered flagrant, and newspapers denounced Carson bitterly. To the horror of Carson's lawyer, he refused to take an appeal or resort to the usual methods of delay. Carson's attitude was fatalistic, and he could not be moved in his seeming determination to die.

In his cell Blake spent most of his time between sentence and execution brooding over the facts he had gleaned from his experiments. In the death house in prison he was certainly a model prisoner, quiet, preoccupied, just a little grim. His whole being was as a matter of fact built up into one fierce, unwavering concentration – the date of April twenty-first. Upon his mastery of elemental forces at the point of death depended his one chance of changing the law of time and confronting Hart Cranshaw with the impossible, a return from death.

Not a word of his intentions escaped him. He was unbowed on the last morning, listened to the prison chaplain's brief words of solace in stony silence, then walked the short length of dim corridor, between guards, to the fatal chamber. He sat down in the death chair with the calm of a man about to preside over a meeting.

The buckles on the straps clinked a little, disturbing him.

He hardly realised what was going on in the sombre, dimly lighted place. If his mental concentration concerning April twenty-first had been strong before, now it had become fanatical. Rigid, perspiration streaming down his face with the urgency of his thoughts, he waited . . .

He felt it then – the thrilling, binding, racking current as it nipped his vitals, then spread and spread into an infinite snapping anguish in which the world and the universe was a brief blazing hell of dissolution . . .

Then things went quiet – oddly quiet . . .

He felt as though he were drifting in a sea without substance –

floating alone. His concentration was superseded now by a dawning wonder, indeed a striving to come to grips with the weird situation in which he found himself.

He had died – his body had – he was convinced of that. But now, to break these iron bands of paralysis, that was the need!

He essayed a sudden effort and with it everything seemed to come abruptly into focus. He felt himself snap out of the void of in-between into normal – or at least mundane – surroundings. He stirred slowly. He was still alone, lying on his back on a sombre, chilly plain of reddish dust. It occasioned him passing surprise that he was still dressed in the thin cotton shirt and pants of a prisoner.

A biting chill in the air went suddenly to his marrow. He shuddered as he got to his feet and looked down at himself.

'Of course. I held my clothes in thought as much as my body, so they were bound to be recreated also . . .'

Baffled, he stared about him. Overhead the sky was violet blue and powdered with endless hosts of stars. To the right was a frowning ridge of higher ground. And everywhere, red soil. Time – an infinitely long span – had passed.

With a half cry he turned and ran breathlessly towards the ridge, scrambled up the rubbly slope quickly. At the top he paused, appalled.

A red sun, swollen to unheard-of size, was bisected by the far distant jagged horizon – a sun to whose edge the stars themselves seemed to reach. He was old now, unguessably old, his incandescent fires burned out.

'Millions of years, quintillions of years,' Blake Carson whispered, sitting down with a thump on an upturned rock and staring out over the drear, sombre vastness. 'In heavens name, what have I done? What have I done?'

He stared in front of him, forced himself by superhuman effort to think calmly. He had planned for one week beyond death. Instead he had landed here, at the virtual end of Earth's existence, where age was stamped on everything. It was in the scarcely moving sun which spoke of Earth's near-standstill from tidal drag. It was in the red soil, the ferrous oxide of extreme senility, the rusting of the metallic deposits in the ground itself. It was in the thin air which had turned the atmospheric heights violet-blue and made breathing a sheer agony.

And there was something else too apart from all this which

Blake Carson had only just begun to realise. He could no longer see the future.

'I cheated the normal course of afterdeath,' he mused. 'I did not move to neighbouring plane there to resume a continuation of life, and neither did I move to April twenty-one as I should have done. It can only mean that at the last minute there was an unpredictable error. It is possible that the electricity from the chair upset my brain planning and shifted the focus of my thoughts so that I was hurled ahead, not one week – but to here. And with that mishap I also lost the power to visualise the future. Had I died by any other way but electricity there might not have been that mistake.'

He shuddered again as a thin, ice-charged wind howled dismally out of the desolate waste and stabbed him through and through. Stung into movements, once more, he got up. Protecting his face from the brief, slashing hurricane he moved further along the ridge and gazed out over the landscape from a different vantage. And from here there was a new view. Ruins, apparently.

He began to run to keep himself warm, until the thin air flogged his lungs to bursting point. At a jog trot he moved on towards the mighty, hardly moving sun, stopped at last within the shadow of a vast, eroded hall.

It was red like everything else. Within it were the ponderous remains of dust-smothered machinery, colossi of power long disused and forgotten. He stared at them, unable to fathom their smallest meaning. His gaze travelled further – to the crumbled ruins of the mighty edifices of rusting metal in the rear. Terrace upon terrace, to the violent sky. Here it seemed was a rusting monument to Man's vanished greatness, with the inexplicable and massive engines as the secret of his power . . .

And Man himself? Gone to other worlds? Dead in the red dust? Blake Carson shook himself fiercely at the inescapable conviction of total loneliness. Only the stars, the sun, and the wind – that awful wind, moaning now softly through the ruins, sweeping the distant corner of the horizon into a mighty cloud that blacked out the brazen glitter of the northern stars.

Blake Carson turned at last. At the far end of the ruins his eye had caught a faint gleam of reflection from the crimson sun. It shone like a diamond. Baffled, he turned and hurried towards it, found the distance was deceptive and that it was nearly two miles off. The nearer he came the more the brightness resolved itself into one of six massively thick glass domes some six feet in diameter.

In all there were eight of them dotted about a little plateau which had been scraped mainly free of rubble and stone. It resembled the floor of a crater with frowning walls of rock all round it. Mystified, Carson moved to the nearest dome and peered through.

In that moment he forgot the melancholy wind and his sense of desperate loneliness – for below was life! Teeming life! Not human life, admittedly, but at least something that moved. It took him a little while to adjust himself to the amazing thing he had discovered.

Perhaps two hundred feet below the dome, brightly lighted, was a city in miniature. It reminded him of a model city of the future he had once seen at an exposition. There were terraces, pedestrian tracks, towers, even aircraft. It was all there on an infinitely minute scale, and probably spread far under the earth out of his line of vision.

But the teeming hordes were – ants. Myriads of them. Not rushing about with the apparent aimlessness of his own time, but moving with a definable, ordered purpose. Ants in a dying world? Ants with their own city?

'Of course,' he whispered, and his breath froze the glass. 'Of course. The law of evolution man to ant, and ant to bacteria. Science has always visualised that. This I could never have known about for the future I saw was not on this plane . . .'

And Hart Cranshaw? The scheme of vengeance? It seemed a remote plan now. Down here was company – intelligent ants who, whatever they might think of him, would perhaps at least talk to him, help him . . .

Suddenly he beat his fists mightily on the glass, shouted hoarsely.

There was no immediate effect. He beat again, this time frenziedly, and the scurrying hordes below suddenly paused in their movement as though uncertain. Then they started to scatter madly like bits of dust blown by the wind.

'Open up!' he shouted. 'Open up. I'm freezing.'

He was not quite sure what happened then, but it seemed to him that he went a little mad. He had a confused, blurred notion of running to each dome in turn and battering his fists against its smooth, implacable surface.

Wind, an endless wind, had turned his blood to ice. At last he sank down on an outjutting rock at the plateau edge, buried his head in his hands and shivered. An overpowering desire to go to sleep was upon him, but presently it passed as he became aware of new thoughts surging through his brain, mighty thoughts that were not his own.

He saw, in queer kaleidoscopic fashion, the ascent of man to supreme heights: he saw too man's gradual realisation that he was upon a doomed world. He saw the thinning of the multitudes and the survival of the fittest – the slow, inexorable work of Nature as she adapted life to suit her latest need.

Like a panorama of the ages, hurdling great vistas of time, Blake Carson saw the human body change into that of the termite, of which the termite of his own time was but the progenitor, the experimental form, as it were. The termites, invested with more than human intelligence, had formed these underground cities themselves, cities replete with every scientific need and requiring but little of the dying Earth so small were they. Only underground was there safety from the dying atmosphere.

Yes, Nature had been clever in her organisation and would be even cleverer when it came to the last mutation into bacteria. Indestructible bacteria which could live in space, float to other worlds, to begin anew. The eternal cycle.

Carson looked up suddenly, puzzled as to why he should know all these things. At what he beheld he sprang to his feet, only to sit down again as he found his legs were numbed with cold.

There was a small army of ants quite close to him, like a black mat on the smooth red of the ground. Thought transference! That was how he had known. The truth had been forced into his mind deliberately. He realised it clearly now for there came a bombardment of mental questions, but from such a multitude of minds that they failed to make any sense.

'Shelter,' he cried. 'Food and warmth – that is what I want. I have come out of Time – a wanderer – and it was an accident that brought me here. You will regard me as an ancient type, therefore I am surely useful to you. If I stay out here the cold will soon kill me.'

'You created your own accident, Blake Carson,' came one clear wave of thought. 'Had you died as the Time-law proclaimed you would have passed on to the next stage of existence, the stage apart from this one. You chose instead to try and defeat Time in order that you might enact vengeance. We, who understand Time, Space, and Life, see what your intentions were.

'You cannot have help now. It is the law of the cosmos that you must live and die by its dictates. And death such as you will experience this time will not be the normal transition from this plane to another but transition to a plane we cannot even visualise. You have forever warped the cosmic line of Time you were intended to pursue. You can never correct that warp.'

Blake Carson stared, wishing he could shift his icebound limbs. He was dying even now, realised it clearly, but interest kept his mentality still alert.

'Is this hospitality?' he whispered. 'Is this the scientific bene-volence of an advanced age? How can you be so pitiless when you know why I sought revenge?'

'We know why, certainly, but it is trivial compared to your infinite transgression in trying to twist scientific law to your own ends. Offence against science is unforgivable, no matter what the motive. You are a throwback, Blake Carson – an outsider! Especially so to us. You never found Hart Cranshaw, the man you wanted. You never will.'

Blake Carson's eyes narrowed suddenly. He noticed that as the thoughts reached him the body of ants had receded quite a distance, evidently giving up interest in him and returning to their domain. But the power of the thoughts reaching him did not diminish.

Abruptly he saw the reason for it. One termite, larger than the others, was alone on the red soil. Carson gazed at it with smouldering eyes, the innermost thoughts of the tiny thing probing his brain.

'I understand, he whispered. 'Yes, I understand! Your thoughts are being bared to me. You are Hart Cranshaw. You are the Hart Cranshaw of this age. You gained your end. You stole my invention – yes, became the master of science, the lord of the Earth, just as you had planned. You found that there was a way to keep on the normal plane after each death, a way entirely successful if death did not come by electrocution. That was what shattered my plan – the electric chair.

'But you went on and on, dying and being born again with a different and yet identical body. An eternal man, mastering more and more each time!' Carson's voice had risen to a shriek. Then he calmed. 'Until at last Nature changed you into an ant, made you the master of even the termite community. How little did I guess that my discovery would hand you the world. But if I have broken cosmic law, Hart Cranshaw, so have you. You have cheated your normal time action, time and again, with numberless deaths. You have stayed on this plane when you should have moved on to others. Both of us are transgressors. For you, as for me, death this time will mean the unknown.'

A power that was something other than himself gave Blake Carson strength at that moment. Life surged back into his leaden limbs and he staggered to his feet.

'We have come together again, Hart, after all these quintillons of years. Remember what I said long ago? To everything there is an appointed time? Now I know why you don't want to save me.'

He broke off as with sudden and fantastic speed the lone termite sped back towards the mass of his departing colleagues. Once among them, as Carson well knew, there would be no means of identification.

With this realisation he forced himself into action and leaped. The movement was the last he could essay. He dropped on his face, and his hand closed round the scurrying insect. It escaped. He watched it run over the back of his hand – then frantically across his palm as he opened his fingers gently.

He had no idea how long he lay watching it – but at last it ran to the tip of his thumb. His first finger closed on his thumb suddenly – and crushed.

He found himself gazing at a black smear on thumb and finger.

He could move his hand no further. Paralysis had gripped his limbs completely. There was a deepening, crushing pain in his heart. Vision grew dim. He felt himself slipping –

But with the transition to Beyond he began to realise something else. He had not cheated Time! Neither had Hart Cranshaw! They had done all this before somewhere – would do it again – endlessly, so long as Time itself should exist. Death – transition – rebirth – evolution – back again to the age of the amoeba – upwards to man – the laboratory – the electric chair . . .

Eternal. Immutable!

The Power

BY MURRAY LEINSTER

from *Astounding Science Fiction*, September 1945

Murray Leinster was the acknowledged Dean of Science Fiction, even though he had published many more stories in other fields. Nothing new from his pen has appeared in a sf magazine since a scientific article, 'Applied Science Fiction' was published in the November 1967 issue of *Analog*. Just prior to that, in 1966, several of his stories appeared, 'A Planet Like Heaven' in *If*, 'Quarantine World', one of his popular *Med Service* stories in *Analog*, and 'Stopover in Space' in *Amazing*.

Alas Murray Leinster is no longer with us. He was born William Fitzgerald Jenkins in Norfolk, Virginia on Tuesday 16 June 1896. He died on Sunday 8 June 1975 at a nursing home in Gloucester, Virginia, eight days away from his seventy-ninth birthday. He had sold fillers to *Smart Set* since 1913, and one of his earliest sf sales was 'Atmosphere' which appeared in *Argosy* for the week ending 26 January 1918. But his sf career really began with 'The Runaway Skyscraper' in the 22 February 1919 issue of *Argosy*. This was followed by two sf stories in Street & Smith's prototype fantasy magazine *The Thrill Book*. By the time Gernsback issued *Amazing Stories* Leinster was already an established sf writer.

Leinster never wrote for Gernsback's magazines, although that editor reprinted several of his stories. Since Leinster was capably selling to the better paying *Argosy* market he had no need. He was enticed into the sf magazine field with *Astounding Stories* and was present in Volume 1, Number 1 of that magazine in January 1930 with a short tale 'Tanks'. It is therefore fitting that what was his last published works in the sf magazine field should appear in that same magazine thirty-seven years later.

It is to Leinster's credit that he never wrote down to his sf audience. He applied all the style and skill he used in his writing for the slick magazines to his sf, with the result that much of his sf is of a quality superior to his fellow pulpsters, particularly during the 1930s. One has only to read such classics as 'The Power Planet' (*Amazing*, June 1931) and 'Sidewise in Time' (*Astounding Stories*, June 1934) to realise that. The latter title was one of the very earliest stories to utilise the alternate worlds theme. It later led a collection of his best fiction published by Shasta in 1952, and the book remains an object lesson in the art of storytelling.

During the War, Leinster reappeared in the sf magazines with a wealth of new sf ideas that surprised readers who believed he was a product of the twenties. Leinster went on to win the 1956 Hugo for his novelette 'Exploration Team' (*Astounding*, March 1956), an astonishing achievement. That he would still be producing excellent sf over forty years after his first efforts is evidence of his skill and adaptability, and 'The Power' is fitting tribute to his talent.

Memorandum from Professor Charles, Latin Department, Haverford University, to Professor McFarland, the same faculty:

Dear Professor McFarland:
In a recent batch of fifteenth-century Latin documents from abroad, we found three which seem to fit together. Our interest is in the Latin of the period, but their contents seem to bear upon your line. I send them to you with a free translation. Would you let me know your reaction?

Charles.

To Johannus Hartmannus, Licentiate in Philosophy,
Living at the house of the goldsmith Grote,
Lane of the Dyed Flee,
Leyden, the Low Countries:

Friend Johannus:
I write this from the Goth's Head Inn, in Padua, the second day after Michaelmas, Anno Domini 1482. I write in haste because a worthy Hollander here journeys homeward and has promised to carry mails for me. He is an amiable lout, but ignorant. Do not speak to him of mysteries. He knows nothing. Less than

nothing. Thank him, give him to drink, and speak of me as a pious and worthy student. Then forget him.

I leave Padua tomorrow for the realisation of all my hopes and yours. This time I am sure. I came here to purchase perfumes and mandragora and the other necessities for an Operation of the utmost imaginable importance, which I will conduct five nights hence upon a certain hilltop near the village of Montevecchio. I have found a Word and a Name of incalculable power, which in the place that I know of must open to me knowledge of all mysteries. When you read this, I shall possess powers at which Hermes Trismegistos only guessed, and which Albertus Magnus could speak of only by hearsay. I have been deceived before, but this time I am sure. I have seen proofs!

I tremble with agitation as I write to you. I will be brief. I came upon these proofs and the Word and the Name in the village of Montevecchio. I rode into the village at nightfall, disconsolate because I had wasted a month searching for a learned man of whom I had heard great things. Then I found him – and he was but a silly antiquary with no knowledge of mysteries! So riding upon my way I came to Montevecchio, and there they told me of a man dying even then because he had worked wonders. He had entered the village on foot only the day before. He was clad in rich garments, yet he spoke like a peasant. At first he was mild and humble, but he paid for food and wine with a gold piece, and villagers fawned upon him and asked for alms. He flung them a handful of gold pieces and when the news spread the whole village went mad with greed. They clustered about him, shrieking pleas, and thronging ever the more urgently as he strove to satisfy them. It is said that he grew frightened and would have fled because of their thrusting against him. But they plucked at his garments, screaming of their poverty, until suddenly his rich clothing vanished in the twinkling of an eye and he was but another ragged peasant like themselves and the purse from which he had scattered gold became a mere coarse bag filled with ashes.

This had happened but the day before my arrival, and the man was yet alive, though barely so because the villagers had cried witchcraft and beset him with flails and stones and then dragged him to the village priest to be exorcised.

I saw the man and spoke to him, Johannus, by representing myself to the priest as a pious student of the snares Satan has set in the form of witchcraft. He barely breathed, what with broken bones and pitchfork wounds. He was a native of the

district, who until now had seemed a simple ordinary soul. To
secure my intercession with the priest to shrive him ere he died,
the man told me all. And it was much!

Upon this certain hillside where I shall perform the Operation
five nights hence, he had dozed at midday. Then a Power appeared
to him and offered to instruct him in mysteries. The peasant
was stupid. He asked for riches instead. So the Power gave
him rich garments and a purse which would never empty so
long – said the Power – as it came not near a certain metal
which destroys all things of mystery. And the Power warned
that this was payment that he might send a learned man to
learn what he had offered the peasant, because he saw that
peasants had no understanding. Thereupon I told the peasant
that I would go and greet this Power and fulfil his desires, and
he told me the Name and the Word which would call him, and
also the Place, begging me to intercede for him with the priest.

The priest showed me a single gold piece which remained
of that which the peasant had distributed. It was of the age of
Antonius Pius, yet bright and new as if fresh minted. It had
the weight and feel of true gold. But the priest, wryly, laid upon
it the crucifix he wears upon a small iron chain about his waist.
Instantly it vanished, leaving behind a speck of glowing coal
which cooled and was a morsel of ash.

This I saw, Johannus! So I came speedily here to Padua, to
purchase perfumes and mandragora and the other necessities
for an Operation to pay great honour to this Power whom
I shall call up five nights hence. He offered wisdom to the
peasant, who desired only gold. But I desire wisdom more than
gold, and surely I am learned concerning mysteries and Powers!
I do not know any but yourself who surpasses me in true
knowledge of secret things. And when you read this, Johannus, I
shall surpass even you! But it may be that I will gain knowledge
so that I can transport myself by a mystery to your attic, and
there inform you myself, in advance of this letter, of the results
of this surpassing good fortune which causes me to shake with
agitation whenever I think of it.

> Your friend Carolus,
> at the Goth's Head Inn in Padua.

. . . fortunate, perhaps, that an opportunity has come to send
a second missive to you, through a crippled man-at-arms who
has been discharged from a mercenary band and travels homeward to sit in the sun henceforth. I have given him one gold

piece and promised that you would give him another on receipt of this message. You will keep that promise or not, as pleases you, but there is at least the value of a gold piece in a bit of parchment with strange symbols upon it which I enclose for you.

Item: I am in daily communication with the Power of which I wrote you, and daily learn great mysteries.

Item: Already I perform marvels such as men have never before accomplished by means of certain sigils or talismans the Power has prepared for me.

Item: Resolutely the Power refuses to yield to me the Names or the incantations by which these things are done so that I can prepare such sigils for myself. Instead, he instructs me in divers subjects which have no bearing on the accomplishment of wonders, to my bitter impatience which I yet dissemble.

Item: Within this packet there is a bit of parchment. Go to a remote place and there tear it and throw it upon the ground. Instantly, all about you, there will appear a fair garden with marvellous fruits, statuary, and pavilion. You may use this garden as you will, save that if any person enter it, or you yourself, carrying a sword or dagger or any object however small made of iron, the said garden will disappear immediately and nevermore return.

This you may verify when you please. For the rest, I am like a prison trembling at the very door of Paradise, barred from entering beyond the antechamber by the fact of the Power withholding from me the true essentials of mystery, and granting me only crumbs – which, however, are greater marvels than any known certainly to have been practised before. For example, the parchment I send you. This art I have proven many times. I have in my scrip many such sigils, made for me by the Power at my entreaty. But when I have secretly taken other parchments and copied upon them the very symbols to the utmost exactitude, they are valueless. There are words or formulas to be spoken over them or – I think more likely – a greater sigil which gives the parchments their magic property. I begin to make a plan – a very daring plan – to acquire even this sigil.

But you will wish to know of the Operation and its results. I returned to Montevecchio from Padua, reaching it in three days. The peasant who had worked wonders was dead, the villagers having grown more fearful and beat out his brains with hammers. This pleased me, because I had feared he would tell another the Word and Name he had told me. I spoke to the priest and told him that I had been to Padua and secured advice from high dignitaries concerning the wonder-working, and had been sent back with special commands to seek out and exorcise the foul fiend who had taught the peasant such marvels.

The next day – the priest himself aiding me! – I took up to the hilltop the perfumes and wax tapers and other things needed for the Operation. The priest trembled, but he would have remained had I not sent him away. And night fell, and I drew the magic circle and the pentacle, with the Signs in their proper places. And when the new moon rose, I lighted the perfumes and the fine candles and began the Operation. I have had many failures, as you know, but this time I knew confidence and perfect certainty. When it came time to use the Name and the Word I called them both loudly, thrice, and waited.

Upon this hilltop there are many greyish stones. At the third calling of the Name, one of the stones shivered and was not. Then a voice said dryly:

'Ah! So that is the reason for this stinking stuff! My messenger sent you here?'

There was a shadow where the stone had been and I could not see clearly. But I bowed low in that direction:

'Most Potent Power,' I said, my voice trembling because the Operation was a success, 'a peasant working wonders told me that you desired speech with a learned man. Beside your Potency I am ignorant indeed, but I have given my whole life to the study of mysteries. Therefore I have come to offer worship or such other compact as you may desire in exchange for wisdom.'

There was a stirring in the shadow, and the Power came forth. His appearance was that of a creature not more than an ell and a half in height, and his expression in the moonlight was that of sardonic impatience. The fragrant smoke seemed to cling about him, to make a cloudiness close about his form.

'I think,' said the dry voice, 'that you are as great a fool as the peasant I spoke to. What do you think I am?'

'A Prince of Celestial race, your Potency,' I said, my voice shaking.

There was a pause. The Power said as if wearily:

'Men! Fools forever! Oh, man, I am simply the last of a number of my kind who travelled in a fleet from another star. This small planet of yours has a core of the accursed metal, which is fatal to the devices of my race. A few of our ships came too close. Others strove to aid them, and shared their fate. Many, many years since, we descended from the skies and could never rise again. Now I alone am left.'

Speaking of the world as a planet was an absurdity, of course. The planets are wanderers among the stars, travelling in their cycles and epicycles as explained by Ptolemy a thousand years since. But I saw at once that he would test me. So I grew bold and said:

'Lord, I am not fearful. It is not needful to cozen me. Do I not know of those who were cast out of Heaven for rebellion? Shall I write the name of your leader?'

He said 'Eh?' for all the world like an elderly man. So, smiling, I wrote on the earth the true name of Him whom the vulgar call Lucifer. He regarded the markings on the earth and said:

'Bah! It is meaningless. More of your legendary! Look you, man, soon I shall die. For more years than you are like to believe I have hid from your race and its accursed metal. I have watched men, and despised them. But – I die. And it is not good that knowledge should perish. It is my desire to impart to men the knowledge which else would die with me. It can do no harm to my own kind, and may bring the race of men to some degree of civilisation in the course of ages.'

I bowed to the earth before him. I was aflame with eagerness.

'Most Potent One,' I said joyfully. 'I am to be trusted. I will guard your secrets fully. Not one jot nor tittle shall ever be divulged!'

Again his voice was annoyed and dry.

'I desire that this knowledge be spread so that all may learn it. But –' Then he made a sound which I do not understand, save that it seemed to be derisive – 'What I have to say may serve, even garbled and twisted. And I do not think you will keep secrets inviolate. Have you pen and parchment?'

'Nay, Lord!'

'You will come again, then, prepared to write what I shall tell you.

But he remained, regarding me. He asked me questions, and I answered eagerly. Presently he spoke in a meditative voice, and I listened eagerly. His speech bore an odd similarity to that of a lonely man who dwelt much on the past, but soon I realised that he spoke in ciphers, in allegory, from which now and again the truth peered out. As one who speaks for the sake of re-membering, he spoke of the home of his race upon what he said

The Power

261

was a fair planet so far distant that to speak of leagues and even the span of continents would be useless to convey the distance. He told of cities in which his fellows dwelt – here, of course, I understood his meaning perfectly – and told of great fleets of flying things rising from those cities to go to other fair cities, and of music which was in the very air so that any person, anywhere upon the planet, could hear sweet sounds or wise discourse at will. In this matter there was no metaphor, because the perpetual sweet sounds in Heaven are matters of common knowledge. But he added a metaphor immediately after, because he smiled at me and observed that the music was not created by a mystery, but by waves like those of light, only longer. And this was plainly a cipher, because light is an impalpable fluid without length and surely without waves!

Then he spoke of flying through the emptiness of the empyrean, which again is not clear, because all can see that the heavens are fairly crowded with stars, and he spoke of many suns and other worlds, some frozen and some merely barren rock. The obscurity of such things is patent. And he spoke of drawing near to this world which is ours, and of an error made as if it were in mathematics – instead of in rebellion – so that they drew close to Earth as Icarus to the sun. Then again he spoke in metaphors, because he referred to engines, which are things to cast stones against walls, and in a larger sense for grinding corn and pumping water. But he spoke of engines growing hot because of the accursed metal in the core of Earth, and of the inability of his kind to resist Earth's pull – more metaphor – and then he spoke of a screaming descent from the skies. And all of this, plainly, is a metaphorical account of the casting of the Rebels out of Heaven, and an acknowledgement that he is one of the said Rebels.

When he paused, I begged humbly that he would show me a mystery and of his grace give me protection in case my converse with him became known.

'What happened to my messenger?' asked the Power.

I told him, and he listened without stirring. I was careful to tell him exactly, because of course he would know that – as all else – by his powers of mystery, and the question was but another test. Indeed, I felt sure that the messenger and all that taken place had been contrived by him to bring me, a learned student of mysteries, to converse with him in this place.

'Men!' he said bitterly at last. Then he added coldly. 'Nay! I can give you no protection. My kind is without protection upon this earth. If you would learn what I can teach you, you must risk the fury of your fellow countrymen.'

But then, abruptly, he wrote upon parchment and pressed the parchment to some object at his side. He threw it upon the ground.

'If men beset you,' he said scornfully, 'tear this parchment and cast it from you. If you have none of the accursed metal about you, it may distract them while you flee. But a dagger will cause it all to come to naught!'

Then he walked away. He vanished. And I stood shivering for a very long time before I remembered me of the formula given by Apollonius of Tyana for the dismissal of evil spirits. I ventured from the magic circle. No evil befell me. I picked up the parchment and examined it in the moonlight. The symbols upon it were meaningless, even to one like myself who has studied all that is known of mysteries. I returned to the village, pondering.

I have told you so much at length, because you will observe that this Power did not speak with the pride or the menace of which most authors on mysteries and Operations speak. It is often said that an adept must conduct himself with great firmness during an Operation, lest the Powers he has called-up overawe him. Yet this Power spoke wearily, with irony, like one approaching death. And he had spoken of death, also. Which was of course a test and a deception, because are not the Principalities and Powers of Darkness immortal? He had some design it was not his will that I should know. So I saw that I must walk warily in this priceless opportunity.

In the village I told the priest that I had had encounter with a foul fiend, who begged that I not exorcise him, promising to reveal certain hidden treasures once belonging to the Church, which he could not touch or reveal to evil men because they were holy, but could describe the location of to me. And I procured parchment, and pens, and ink, and the next day I went alone to the hilltop. It was empty, and I made sure I was unwatched and – leaving my dagger behind me – I tore the parchment and flung it to the ground.

As it touched, there appeared such a treasure of gold and jewels as truly would have driven any man mad with greed. There were bags and chests and boxes filled with gold and precious stones, which had burst with the weight and spilled out upon the ground. There were gems glittering in the late sunlight, and rings and necklaces set with brilliants, and such monstrous hoards of golden coins of every antique pattern . . .

Johannus, even I went almost mad! I leaped forward like one dreaming to plunge my hands into the gold. Slavering, I filled my garments with rubies and ropes of pearls, and stuffed my scrip with gold pieces, laughing crazily to myself. I rolled in the riches. I wallowed in them, flinging the golden coins into the air and letting them fall upon me. I laughed and sang to myself.

Then I heard a sound. On the instant I was filled with terror for the treasure. I leaped to my dagger and snarled, ready to defend my riches to the death.

Then a dry voice said: 'Truly you care naught for riches!'

It was savage mockery. The Power stood regarding me. I saw him clearly now, yet not clearly because there was a cloudiness which clung closely to his body. He was, as I said, an ell and a half in height, and from his forehead there protruded knobby feelers which were not horns but had somewhat the look save for bulbs upon their ends. His head was large and – But I will not attempt to describe him, because he could assume any of a thousand forms, no doubt, so what does it matter?

Then I grew terrified because I had no Circle or Pentacle to protect me. But the Power made no menacing move.

'It is real, that riches,' he said dryly. 'It has colour and weight and the feel of substance. But your dagger will destroy it all.'

Didyas of Corinth has said that treasure of mystery must be fixed by a special Operation before it becomes permanent and free of the power of Those who brought it. They can transmute it back to leaves or other rubbish, if it be not fixed.

'Touch it with your dagger,' said the Power.

I obeyed, sweating in fear. And as the metal iron touched a great piled heap of gold, there was a sudden shifting and then a little flare about me. And the treasure – all, to the veriest crumb of a seed-pearl! – vanished before my eyes. The bit of parchment reappeared, smoking. It turned to ashes. My dagger scorched my fingers. It had grown hot.

'Ah, yes,' said the Power, nodding. 'The force-field has energy. When the iron absorbs it, there is heat.' Then he looked at me in a not unfriendly way. 'You have brought pens and parchment,' he said, 'and at least you did not use the sigil to astonish your fellows. Also you had the good sense to make no more per-fumish stinks. It may be that there is a grain of wisdom in you. I will bear with you yet a while. Be seated and take parchment and pen – Stay! Let us be comfortable. Sheathe your dagger, or better, cast it from you.'

I put it in my bosom. And it was as if he thought, and touched something at his side, and instantly there was a fair pavilion about us, with soft cushions and a gently playing fountain.

'Sit,' said the Power. 'I learned that men like such things as this from a man I once befriended. He had been wounded and stripped by robbers, so that he had not so much as a scrap of accursed metal about him, and I could aid him. I learned to speak the language men use nowadays from him. But to the end he believed me an evil spirit and tried valourously to hate me.'

My hands shook with my agitation that the treasure had departed from me. Truly it was a treasure of such riches as no King has ever possessed, Johannus! My very soul lusted after that treasure! The golden coins alone would fill your attic solidly, but the floor would break under their weight, and the jewels would fill hogsheads. Ah, Johannus! That treasure!

'What I will have you write,' said the Power, 'at first will mean little. I shall give facts and theories first, because they are easiest to remember. Then I will give the applications of the theories. Then you men will have the beginning of such civilisation as can exist in the neighbourhood of the accursed metal.'

'Your Potency!' I begged abjectly. 'You will give me another sigil of treasure?'

'Write!' he commanded.

I wrote. And, Johannus, I cannot tell you myself what it is that I wrote. He spoke words, and they were in such obscure cipher that they have no meaning as I con them over. Hark you to this, and seek wisdom for the performance of mysteries in it! 'The civilisation of my race is based upon fields of force which have the property of acting in all essentials as substance. A lodestone is surrounded by a field of force which is invisible and impalpable. But the fields used by my people for dwellings, tools, vehicles, and even machinery are perceptible to the senses and act physically as solids. More, we are able to form these fields in latent fashions; and to fix them to organic objects as permanent fields which require no energy for their maintenance, just as magnetic fields require no energy supply to continue. Our fields, too, may be projected as three-dimensional solids which assume any desired form and have every property of substance except chemical affinity.'

Johannus! Is it not unbelievable that words could be put together, dealing with mysteries, which are so devoid of any clue to their true mystic meaning? I write and I write in desperate hope that he will eventually give me the key, but my brain reels at the difficulty of extracting the directions for Operations which such ciphers must conceal! I give you another instance: 'When a force-field generator has been built as above, it will be found that the pulsatory fields which are consciousness serve perfectly as controls. One has but to visualise the object desired, turn on the generator's auxiliary control, and the generator will pattern its output upon the pulsatory consciousness-field . . .'

Upon this first day of writing, the Power spoke for hours, and I wrote until my hand ached. From time to time, resting, I read back to him the words that I had written. He listened, satisfied.

'Lord!' I said shakily. 'Mighty Lord! Your Potency! These mysteries you bid me write – they are beyond comprehension!'

But he said scornfully:

'Write! Some will be clear to someone. And I will explain it little by little until even you can comprehend the beginning.' Then he added. 'You grow weary. You wish a toy. Well! I will make you a sigil which will make again that treasure you played with. I will add a sigil which will make a boat for you, with an engine drawing power from the sea to carry you wheresoever you wish without need of wind or tide. I will make others so you may create a palace where you will, and fair gardens as you please . . .'

These things he has done, Johannus. It seems to amuse him to write upon scraps of parchment, and think, and then press them against his side before he lays them upon the ground for me to pick up. He has explained amusedly that the wonder in the sigil is complete, yet latent, and is released by the tearing of the parchment, but absorbed and destroyed by iron. In such fashion he speaks in ciphers, but otherwise sometimes he jests!

It is strange to think of it, that I have come little by little to accept this Power as a person. It is not in accord with the laws of mystery. I feel that he is lonely. He seems to find satisfaction in speech with me. Yet he is a Power, one of the Rebels who was flung to earth from Heaven! He speaks of that only in vague, metaphorical terms, as if he had come from another world like *the* world, save much larger. He refers to himself as a voyager of space, and speaks of his race with affection, and of Heaven – at any rate the city from which he comes, because there must be many great cities there – with a strange and prideful affection. If it were not for his powers, which are of mystery, I would find it possible to believe that he was a lonely member of a strange race, exiled forever in a strange place, and grown friendly with a man because of his loneliness. But how could there be such as he and not a Power? How could there be another world?

This strange converse has now gone on for ten days or more. I have filled sheets upon sheets of parchment with writing. The same metaphors occur again and again. 'Force-fields' – a term without literal meaning – occurs often. There are other metaphors such as 'coils' and 'primary' and 'secondary' which are placed in context with mention of wires of copper metal. There are careful descriptions, as if in the plainest of language, of sheets of dissimilar metals which are to be placed in acid, and other descriptions of plates of similar metal which are to be separated by layers of air or wax of certain thicknesses, with the plates of certain areas! And there is an explanation of the means by which he lives. 'I, being accustomed to an atmosphere much more dense than that on Earth, am forced to keep about myself a field of force which maintains an air density near that of my home planet for my breathing. This field is transparent, but because it must shift constantly to change and refresh the air I breathe, it causes a certain cloudiness of outline next my body. It is maintained by the generator. I wear at my side, which at the same time provides energy for such other force-field artifacts as I may find convenient.' – Ah, Johannes! I grow mad with impatience! Did I not anticipate that he would some day give me the key to this metaphorical speech, so that from it may be extracted the Names and the Words which cause his wonders, I would give over in despair.

Yet he has grown genial with me. He has given me such sigils as I have asked him, and I have tried them many times. The sigil which will make you a fair garden is one of many. He says that he desires to give to man the knowledge he possesses, and then bids we write ciphered speech without meaning, such as: 'The drive of a ship for flight beyond the speed of light is adapted from the simple drive generator already described simply by altering its constants so that it cannot generate in normal space and must create an abnormal space by tension. The process is –' Or else – I choose at random, Johannus – 'The accursed metal, iron, must be eliminated not only from all circuits but from nearness to apparatus using high-frequency oscillations, since it absorbs their energy and prevents the functioning . . .'

I am like a man trembling upon the threshold of Paradise, yet unable to enter because the key is withheld. 'Speed of light!' What could it mean in metaphor? In common parlance, as well speak of the speed of weather or of granite! Daily I beg him for the key to his speech. Yet even now, in the sigils he makes for me is greater power than any man has ever known before!

But it is not enough. The Power speaks as if he were lonely beyond compare; the last member of a strange race upon earth; as if he took a strange, companion-like pleasure in merely talking to me. When I beg him for a Name or a Word which would give me power beyond such as he doles out in sigils, he is amused and calls me fool, yet kindly. And he speaks more of his metaphorical speech about forces of nature and fields of force – and gives me a sigil which should I use it will create a palace with walls of gold and pillars of emerald! And then he amusedly reminds me that one greedy looter with an axe or hoe of iron would cause it to vanish utterly!

I go almost mad, Johannus! But there is certainly wisdom unutterable to be had from him. Gradually, cautiously, I have come to act as if we were merely friends, of different race and he vastly the wiser, but friends rather than Prince and subject. Yet I remember the warnings of the most authoritative authors that one must be ever on guard against Powers called up in an Operation.

I have a plan. It is dangerous, I well know, but I grow desperate. To stand quivering upon the threshold of such wisdom and power as no man has ever dreamed of before, and then be denied . . .

The mercenary who will carry this to you, leaves tomorrow. He is a cripple, and may be months upon the way. All will bedecided ere you receive this. I know you wish me well.

Was there ever a student of mystery in so saddening a predicament, with all knowledge in his grasp yet not quite his?

Your friend
Carolus.

Written in the very bad inn in Montevecchio.

Johannus! A courier goes to Ghent for My Lord of Brabant and I have opportunity to send you mail. I think I go mad, Johannus! I have power such as no man ever possessed before, and I am fevered with bitterness. Hear me!

For three weeks I did repair daily to the hilltop beyond Montevecchio and take down the ciphered speech of which I wrote you. My scrip was stuffed with sigils, but I had not one word of Power or Name of Authority. The Power grew mocking, yet it seemed sadly mocking. He insisted that his words held no cipher and needed but to be read. Some of them he phrased over and over again until they were but instructions for putting bits of metal together, mechanicwise. Then he made me follow those instructions. But there was no Word, no Name – nothing save bits of metal put together cunningly. And how could inanimate metal, not imbued with power of mystery by Names or Words or incantations, have power to work mystery?

At long last I became convinced that he would never reveal the wisdom he had promised. And I had come to such familiarity with this Power that I could dare to rebel, and even to believe that I had chance of success. There was the cloudiness about his form, which was maintained by a sigil he wore at his side and called a 'generator'. Were that cloudiness destroyed, he could not live, or so he had told me. It was for that reason that he, in person, dared not touch anything of iron. This was the basis of my plan.

I feigned illness, and said that I would rest at a peasant's thatched hut, no longer inhabited, at the foot of the hill on which the Power lived. There was surely no nail of iron in so crude a dwelling. If he felt for me the affection he protested, he would grant me leave to be absent in my illness. If his affection was great, he might even come and speak to me there. I would be alone in the hope that his friendship might go so far.

Strange words for a man to use to a Power! But I had talked daily with him for three weeks. I lay groaning in the hut, alone. On the second day he came. I affected great rejoicing, and made shift to light a fire from a taper I had kept burning. He thought it a mark of honour, but it was actually a signal. And then, as he talked to me in what he thought my illness, there came a cry from without the hut. It was the village priest, a simple man but very brave in his fashion. On the signal of smoke from the peasant's hut, he had crept near and drawn all about it an iron chain that we had muffled with cloth so that it would make no sound. And now he stood before the hut door with his crucifix upraised, chanting exorcisms. A very brave man, that priest, because I had pictured the Power as a foul fiend indeed.

The Power turned and looked at me, and I held my dagger firmly.

'I hold the accursed metal,' I told him fiercely. 'There is a ring of it about this house. Tell me now, quickly, the Words and the Names which make the sigils operate! Tell me the secret of the cipher you had me write! Do this and I will slay this priest and draw away the chain and you may go hence unharmed. But be quick, or –'

The Power cast a sigil upon the ground. When the parchment struck earth, there was an instant's cloudiness as if some dread thing had begun to form. But then the parchment smoked and turned to ash. The ring of iron about the hut had destroyed its power when it was used. The Power knew that I spoke truth.

'Ah!' said the Power dryly. 'Men! And I thought one was my friend!' He put his hand to his side. 'To be sure! I should have known. Iron rings me about. My engine heats . . .'

He looked at me. I held up the dagger, fiercely unyielding.

'The Names!' I cried. 'The Words! Give me power of my own and I will slay the priest!'

'I tried,' said the Power quietly, 'to give you wisdom. And you will stab me with the accursed metal if I do not tell you things which do not exist. But you need not. I cannot live long in a ring of iron. My engine will burn out; my force-field will fail. I will stifle in the thin air which is dense enough for you. Will not that satisfy you? Must you stab me, also?'

I sprang from my pallet of straw to threaten him more fiercely. It was madness, was it not? But I was mad, Johannus!

'Forbear,' said the Power. 'I could kill you now, with me! But I thought you my friend. I will go out and see your priest. I would prefer to die at his hand. He is perhaps only a fool.'

He walked steadily towards the doorway. As he stepped over the iron chain, I thought I saw a wisp of smoke begin, but he touched the thing at his side. The cloudiness about his person vanished. There was a puffing sound, and his garments jerked as if in a gust of wind. He staggered. But he went on, and touched his side again and the cloudiness returned and he walked more strongly. He did not try to turn aside. He walked directly towards the priest, and even I could see that he walked with a bitter dignity.

And – I saw the priest's eyes grow wide with horror. Because he saw the Power for the first time, and the Power was an ell and a half high, with a large head and knobbed feelers projecting from his forehead, and the priest knew instantly that he was not of any race of men but was a Power and one of those Rebels who were flung out from Heaven.

I heard the Power speak to the priest, with dignity. I did not hear what he said. I raged in my disappointment. But the priest did not waver. As the Power moved towards him, the priest moved towards the Power. His face was filled with horror, but it was resolute. He reached forward with the crucifix he wore always attached to an iron chain about his waist. He thrust it to touch the Power, crying, '*In nomine Patri* –'

Then there was smoke. It came from a spot at the Power's side where was the engine to which he touched the sigils he had made, to imbue them with the power of mystery. And then –

I was blinded. There was a flare of monstrous, bluish light, like a lightning-stroke from Heaven. After, there was a ball of fierce yellow flame which gave off a cloud of black smoke. There was a monstrous, outraged bellow of thunder.

Then there was nothing save the priest standing there, his face ashen, his eyes resolute, his eyebrows singed, chanting psalms in a shaking voice.

I have come to Venice. My scrip is filled with sigils with which I can work wonders. No men can work such wonders as I can. But I use them not. I labour daily, nightly, hourly, minute by minute, trying to find the key to the cipher which will yield the wisdom the Power possessed and desired to give to men. Ah, Johannus! I have those sigils and I can work wonders, but when I have used them they will be gone and I shall be powerless. I had such a chance at wisdom as never man possessed before, and it is gone! Yet I shall spend years – aye! – all the rest of my life, seeking the true meaning of what the Power spoke! I am the only man in all the world who ever spoke daily, for weeks on end, with a Prince of Powers of Darkness, and was accepted by him as a friend to such a degree as to encompass his own destruction. It must be true that I have wisdom written down! But how shall I find instructions for mystery in such metaphors as – to choose a fragment by chance – 'plates of two dissimilar metals, immersed in an acid, generate a force for which men have not yet a name, yet which is the basis of true civilisation. Such plates . . .'

I grow mad with disappointment, Johannus! Why did he not speak clearly? Yet I will find out the secret . . .

Memorandum from Peter McFarland, Physics Department, Haverford University, to Professor Charles, Latin, the same faculty:

Dear Professor Charles:
My reaction is, Damnation! Where is the rest of this stuff?
McFarland.

Appendices

The following appendices are for the use of those whom, I hope, have had their appetites whetted by this anthology and wish to know more about the period. Such detail could fill volumes, and I have tried to condense it into an assimilable and interesting form. It will be instantly realised how much the sf scene had grown by the fact that this appendix is far larger than that in the previous volume.

The appendices are made up as follows:

(A) *Checklist of Authors' Works: 1936–45.* This details the science fiction and fantasy works of the eleven authors represented in this collection.

(B) *Summary of Magazine Issues.* A guide to the number and frequency of issues of the sf/weird magazines covered in this book, both professional and semi-professional.

(C) *Glossary of Magazine Editors.* A Who's Who of sf/fantasy editors of the period, with a guide to the number of issues that was their responsibility.

(D) *Note on Key Cover Artists.* A guide to the prolificity of the cover artists of the major magazines at this time.

Notes on Layout

Appendix A
Following the name of the author and his birth/death dates are six columns, which read from left to right as follows:

1 Story number (if a story is reprinted within this period the same number is used).
2 Story title.
3 Story length (see after list for details).
4 Titles of magazine in which story appeared (abbreviations are detailed at the end of the list).
5 and 6 Date of publication, month and year.

If the story title is followed by any symbol it means the story was published under a pseudonym. Details are given after each author.

A letter in brackets after the title indicates the story is part of a connected series, and details are again found below each author.

A collaboration with another author (unless disguised under a single pen-name) is noted after the title by an oblique (/) followed by the collaborator's name.

Appendix B
In each case the year runs from April to March, so that the single issue *Fanciful Tales*, for instance, could have appeared any time between April 1936 and March 1937. (Full publication dates will be found in the anthology introduction.) This follows on from April 1926, *Amazing*'s first issue.

The figure of 257 given for magazines published up to 1935-6, is only that for surviving magazines. The relevant figures for the previous period (including *Weird Tales* from March 1923) are:

SF: North American	399	Weird: North American	245
SF: British	20	Weird: British	Nil
SF: Foreign	Nil	Weird: Foreign	Nil

Appendix C
I have only listed editors directly responsible for the magazines, and where relevant their assistants, or immediate supervisors (eg Norton, Tremaine, etc). The number in brackets after the magazine issue dates is the number of issues for which the editor was responsible.

Appendix D
Grouped by publishers, and then by number of appearances of each artist where known. After each major artist a percentage is given as a guide to the size of his output.

(A) CHECKLIST OF AUTHOR'S WORKS: 1936-45

Note: Only those stories published between 1936 and 1945 are included unless otherwise stated.

1 ROBERT BLOCH (born 1917)

1	The Druidic Doom...	s	WT	Apr 36
2	The Faceless God ... (A)	s	WT	May 36
3	The Grinning Ghoul ... (A)	s	WT	Jun 36
4	The Opener of the Way	s	WT	Oct 36
5	The Dark Demon ... (A)	s	WT	Nov 36
6	Mother of Serpents...	s	WT	Dec 36
7	Brood of Bubastis	s	WT	Mar 37
8	The Mannikin ... (A)	s	WT	Apr 37
9	Fangs of Vengeance	s	WT	Apr 37
10	The Black Kiss (/Henry Kuttner)	s	WT	Jun 37
11	The Creeper in the Crypt ... (A)	s	WT	Jul 37
12	The Secret of Sebek	s	WT	Nov 37
13	Fane of the Black Pharaoh	s	WT	Dec 37
14	Eyes of the Mummy	s	WT	Apr 38
15	Slave of the Flames	s	WT	Jun 38
16	Return to the Sabbath	s	WT	Jul 38
17	The Secret of the Observatory	s	AS	Aug 38
18	The Mandarin's Canaries	s	WT	Sep 38
19	The Hound of Pedro	s	WT	Nov 38
20	Beetles	s	WT	Dec 38
21	Waxworks	s	WT	Jan 39
22	Death Is an Elephant	s	WT	Feb 39
23	The Curse of the House	s	STR	Feb 39
24	The Sorceror's Jewel*	s	STR	Feb 39
25	The Strange Flight of Richard Clayton ...	s	AS	Mar 39
26	The Red Swimmer	s	WT	Apr 39
27	Death Has Five Guesses	s	STR	Apr 39
28	A Question of Identity*	s	STR	Apr 39
29	The Bottomless Pool (/Ralph Milne Farley)	s	STR	Apr 39
30	The Dark Isle	s	WT	May 39
31	The Cloak	s	UNK	May 39
32	Unheavenly Twin	s	STR	Jun 39
33	Seal of the Satyr*	s	STR	Jun 39
34	The Totem Pole	s	WT	Aug 39
35	Pink Elephants	s	STR	Aug 39
36	Flowers from the Moon*	s	STR	Aug 39
37	The Body and the Brain (/Henry Kuttner) ...	s	STR	Aug 39
38	The Man Who Walked through Mirrors ...	s	AS	Aug 39
39	He Waits beneath the Sea	s	STR	Oct 39
40	Mannikins of Horror	s	WT	Dec 39
41	The Grip of Death (/Henry Kuttner)	s	STR	Dec 39

42	Queen of the Metal Men	s	FA	Apr 40
43	The Ghost-Writer	s	WT	May 40
44	Master of the Silver Giants	s	TW	May 40
45	Power of the Druid	s	STR	Jun 40
46	Fiddler's Fee	s	WT	Jul 40
47	Be Yourself	s	STR	Oct 40
48	Wine of the Sabbat	s	WT	Nov 40
49	House of the Hatchet	nt	WT	Jan 41
50	Beauty's Beast	s	WT	May 41
51	A Sorcerer Runs for Sheriff	s	WT	Sep 41
52	A Good Knight's Work	s	UW	Oct 41
53	Last Laugh	s	SS	Nov 41
54	The Shoes	s	UW	Feb 42
55	Hell on Earth	nt	WT	Mar 42
56	Time Wounds All Heels ... (B)	s	FA	Apr 42
57	Black Bargain	s	WT	May 42
58	Gather Round the Flowing Bowler ... (B)	s	FA	May 42
59	The Pied Piper Fights the Gestapo ... (B)	s	FA	Jun 42
60	The Weird Doom of Floyd Scrilch ... (B)	s	FA	Jul 42
61	The Little Man Who Wasn't All There (B)	s	FA	Aug 42
62	Son of a Witch ... (B)	s	FA	Sep 42
63	A Question of Etiquette	s	WT	Sep 42
64	Jerk the Giant Killer ... (B)	s	FA	Oct 42
65	Nursemaid to Nightmares	s	WT	Nov 42
66	Murder from the Moon	s	AS	Nov 42
67	The Golden Opportunity of Lefty Feep (B)	s	FA	Nov 42
68	Lefty Feep and the Sleepy-Time Girl ... (B)	s	FA	Dec 42
69	The Eager Dragon	s	WT	Jan 43
70	Lefty Feep Catches Hell ... (B)	s	FA	Jan 43
71	It Happened Tomorrow	nt	AST	Feb 43
72	Nothing Happens to Lefty Feep ... (B) ...	s	FA	Feb 43
73	The Phantom from the Film*	s	AS	Feb 43
74	The Fear Planet	s	SSS	Feb 43
75	A Bottle of Gin	s	WT	Mar 43
76	The Chance of a Ghost ... (B)	s	FA	Mar 43
77	The Black Brain*	s	FA	Mar 43
78	Never Trust a Demon	s	AS	Apr 43
79	Lefty Feep and the Racing Robot ... (B) ...	s	FA	Apr 43
80	Genie with the Light Brown Hair ... (B) ...	s	FA	May 43
81	Stuporman ... (B)	s	FA	Jun 43
82	Skeleton in the Closet*	s	FA	Jun 43
83	The Goon from Rangoon ... (B)	s	FA	Jul 43
84	Almost Human*	s	FA	Jul 43
85	The Machine That Changed History	s	SF	Jul 43
86	Yours Truly, Jack the Ripper	s	WT	Jul 43
87	You Can't Kid Lefty Feep ... (B)	s	FA	Aug 43
88	Fairy Tale*	s	FA	Aug 43

89	Black Barter	s	WT	Sep	43
90	A Horse for Lefty Feep ... (B)	s	FA	Oct	43
91	Mystery of the Creeping Underwear*	s	FA	Oct	43
92	It's Your Own Funeral	s	MD	Nov	43
93	Meet Mr Murder	s	MD	Nov	43
94	Lefty Feep's Arabian Nightmare ... (B) ...	s	FA	Feb	44
95	Singe For Your Supper	s	ND	Mar	44
96	Horror in Hollywood	s	MD	Mar	44
97	Lefty Feep Does Time ... (B)	nt	FA	Apr	44
98	Iron Mask	s	WT	May	44
99	The Beasts of Barsac	s	WT	Jul	44
100	Eye of Medusa	s	MD	Aug	44
101	Death Is a Vampire	s	TM	Sep	44
102	The Devil's Ticket	s	WT	Sep	44
103	The Bat Is My Brother	s	WT	Nov	44
104	Son of Rasputin	s	MM	Feb	45
105	Lefty Feep Gets Henpecked ... (B)	s	FA	Apr	45
106	The Man Who Cried Wolf	s	WT	May	45
107	One Way to Mars (orig. in *The Opener of the Way*, 1945)	s	WT	Jul	45
108	The Finger Necklace	s	DM	Sep	45
109	The Skull of the Marquis de Sade	s	WT	Sep	45
110	Soul Proprietor	s	WT	Nov	45
111	COD-Corpse on Delivery	s	DT	Dec	45
112	Satan's Phonograph	s	WT	Jan	46
113	The Noose Hangs High	s	DM	Feb	46
114	The Bogeyman Will Get You	s	WT	Mar	46

Pseudonyms: *Tarleton Fiske (nos 24, 28, 33, 36, 73, 77, 82, 84, 88 and 91).
In addition, stories 9 and 22 were written in collaboration with Nathan Hindin, another of Bloch's pen-names.

Series: A Stories that fit into Lovecraft's *Cthulhu Mythos* (Nos 2, 3, 5, 8 and 11).
B *Lefty Feep* (nos 56, 58, 59, 60, 61, 62, 64, 67, 68, 70, 72, 76, 79, 80, 81, 83, 87, 90, 94, 97 and 105).
In addition, nos 2, 4, 7, 12, 13, 14 and 20 fit into a basic *Egyptian* setting.

2 JOHN RUSSELL FEARN (1908-1960)

1	Mathematica Plus	nt	ASS	May	36
2	Deserted Universe	nt	ASS	Sep	36
3	The Great Illusion (conc)	s	FM	Sep	36
4	Dynasty of the Small	nt	ASS	Nov	36
5	Subconscious	nt	AS	Dec	36

6	The Stain That Grew	... ...	s	TM	Dec 36
7	Portrait of a Murderer	... ...	s	WT	Dec 36
8	Metamorphosis	... ...	nt	ASS	Jan 37
9	Brain of Venus	... ...	nt	TW	Feb 37
10	Worlds Within	... ...	nt	ASS	Mar 37
11	Menace from the Microcosm	... ...	nt	TW	Jun 37
12	Superhuman**	... ...	s	ToW	Jun 37
13	Seeds from Space	... ...	nt	ToW	Jun 37
14	Death Asks the Question	... ...	nt	TM	Jul 37
15	Beast of the Tarn	... ...	s	TM	Sep 37
16	Penal World*	... ...	s	ASS	Oct 37
17	Dark Eternity	... ...	nt	ASS	Dec 37
18	Zagribud	... ...	n3	AS	Dec 37
19	Red Heritage	... ...	nt	ASS	Jan 38
20	Whispering Satellite*	... ...	s	ASS	Jan 38
21	The Mental Ultimate‖	... ...	s	ASS	Jan 38
22	The Degenerates‖	... ...	nt	ASS	Feb 38
23	Through Earth's Core	... ...	s	ToW	Spr 38
24	Lords of 9016	... ...	nt	TW	Apr 38
25	The Master of Golden City‖	... ...	nt	AS	Jun 38
26	A Summons from Mars	... ...	nt	AS	Jun 38
27	Wings Across the Cosmos‖	... ...	s	TW	Jun 38
28	Glass Nemesis	... ...	s	PSw	Jun 38
29	The Red Magician	... ...	nt	FY	Aug 38
30	Locked City	... ...	nt	AS	Oct 38
31	The Wailing Hybrid	... ...	nt	TM	Nov 38
32	Secret of the Ring*	... ...	nt	AS	Nov 38
33	Death at the Observatory	... ...	s	MW	#76, 38
34	The Misty Wilderness	... ...	s	MW	#77, 38
35	The Weather Machine	... ...	s	MW	#78, 38
36	Black Empress	... ...	nt	AS	Jan 39
37	The World That Dissolved‖	... ...	s	AS	Feb 39
38	World without Chance‖	... ...	nt	TW	Feb 39
39	Climatica	... ...	nt	FY	Mar 39
40	Valley of Pretenders‖	... ...	nt	SF	Mar 39
41	Outlaw of Saturn§	... ...	nt	SF	Mar 39
42	Leeches from Space§§	... ...	nt	SF	Mar 39
43	World without Women*	... ...	nt	AS	Apr 39
44	The Martian Avenger‖	... ...	s	AS	Apr 39
45	Secret of the Buried City	... ...	nt	AS	May 39
46	World without Death‖	... ...	nt	AS	Jun 39
47	Microbes from Space*	... ...	s	AS	Jun 39
48	Moon Heaven†	... ...	nt	SF	Jun 39
49	The Golden Amazon* ... (A)	... ...	nt	FA	Jul 39
50	She Walked Alone	... ...	s	FA	Jul 39
51	World Beneath Ice‖	... ...	nt	AS	Aug 39
52	Jewels from the Moon§§	... ...	nt	SF	Aug 39

34	The Misty Wilderness	s	SS	Sep	39
53	The Man Who Stopped the Dust (from ASS Mar 34)	nt	ToW	Aut	39
54	Face in the Sky*	nt	AS	Sep	39
55	Earth Asunder§§	nt	SF	Oct	39
56	Thoughts That Kill	s	SF	Oct	39
57	The Man from Hell‖	nt	FA	Nov	39
58	Lunar Intrigue*	nt	FA	Nov	39
59	Frigid Moon¶	nt	FF	Nov	39
60	The Man Who Saw Two Worlds* ... (B)	nt	AS	Jan	40
61	Mystery of The White Raider*	nt	FA	Feb	40
62	Chameleon Planet‖	nt	AST	Feb	40
63	World Reborn*	nt	SSS	Mar	40
64	Phantom from Space	s	SSS	Mar	40
65	After Doomsday§	nt	FF	Mar	40
66	Men without a World	nt	SF	Mar	40
67	Eclipse Bears Witness§§	nt	SF	Mar	40
68	Case of the Murdered Savants* ... (B) ...	nt	AS	Apr	40
69	War of the Scientists	nt	AS	Apr	40
70	Cosmic Juggernaut	s	PS	Sum	40
71	He Conquered Venus	nt	AST	Jun	40
72	The Amazon Fights Again* ... (A)	nt	FA	Jun	40
73	The Voice Commands¶	nt	SF	Jun	40
33	Death at the Observatory	s	CF	Sum	40
74	Secret of the Moon Treasure*	nt	AS	Jul	40
75	Laughter out of Space¶	nt	FF	Jul	40
76	Chamber of Centuries	s	TM	Sep	40
77	Domain of Zero*	s	PS	Fal	40
78	Special Agent to Venus*	nt	FA	Oct	40
79	The Man Who Sold the Earth*	nt	SF	Oct	40
80	Queen of Venus	n	MS	Nov	40
81	The Flat Folk of Vulcan¶	s	FF	Nov	40
82	Wedding of the Forces‖	s	FF	Nov	40
83	Onslaught from Below§	s	FF	Nov	40
84	Island in the Marsh*	s	SS	Nov	40
85	Twilight of the Tenth World*	nt	PS	Win	40
86	The Golden Amazon Returns* ... (A) ...	nt	FA	Jan	41
87	Cosmic Derelict	s	PS	Spr	41
88	Science from Syracuse‖	nt	SF	Mar	41
89	The Last Secret Weapon‖	nt	MS	Apr	41
12	Superhuman	s	SS	May	41
90	The World in Wilderness*	nt	SF	Jun	41
91	The Man Who Bought Mars‖	nt	FA	Jun	41
92	Lunar Concession*	nt	SF	Sep	41
93	Across the Ages†	s	FcS	Oct	41
94	Mystery of the Martian Pendulum* (/Ray Palmer as A. R. Steber)	s	AS	Oct	41

95	Martian Miniature		s	AS	May 42
96	Arctic God‡		nt	AS	May 42
97	The Case of the Mesozoic Monsters* ...	(B)	nt	AS	May 42
98	Destroyer from the Past‖		nt	AS	May 42
99	Prisoner of Time‖		nt	SSS	May 42
100	The Last Hours		nt	AS	Aug 42
101	The Mental Gangster*		s	FA	Aug 42
102	Vampire Queen*		nt	PS	Fal 42
103	Outcasts of Eternity‖		nt	FA	Sep 42
32	Secret of the Ring*		nt	AS	Oct 42
104	The Silver Coil*		s	AS	Nov 42
105	Children of the Golden Amazon*...	(A) ...	nt	FA	Apr 43
106	Lunar Vengeance*		nt	AS	Sep 43
107	Wanderer of Time‖		s	SS	Sum 44
108	The Devouring Tide‖		nt	TW	Sum 44
109	The Ultimate Analysis		s	TW	Fal 44
110	Mark Grayson Unlimited‖		s	TW	Spr 45
111	Aftermath		n	SS	Fal 45
112	Space Trap‖		nt	TW	Fal 45
113	Interlink		s	TW	Fal 45

Pseudonyms: *Thornton Ayre (nos 16, 20, 30, 32, 43, 47, 49, 54, 58,
                   60, 61, 63, 68, 72, 74, 77-9, 84-6, 90, 92, 94, 97, 101,
                   102 and 104-6).
              **Geoffrey Amstrong (no 12).
              ‡Frank Jones (no 96).
              ‖Polton Cross (nos 21, 22, 25, 27, 37, 38, 44, 46, 51, 57,
                   62, 82, 88, 89, 91, 98, 99, 103, 107, 108, 110 and 112).
              †Dom Passante (nos 48, 66 and 93).
              §John Cotton (nos 41, 65 and 83).
              §§Ephriam Winiki (nos 42, 52, 55 and 67).
              ¶Dennis Clive (nos 40, 59, 73, 75 and 81).

Series: A   *Violet Ray* (nos 49, 72, 86 and 105).
          B   *Brutus Lloyd* (nos 60, 68 and 97).
          In addition, nos 20 and 77 are connected, as are 38 and 62.

3   NEIL R. JONES (born 1909)

1	Labyrinth ... (A)	nt	AS	Apr 36
2	Little Hercules ... (B)	nt	ASS	Sep 36
3	Twin Worlds	nt	AS	Apr 37
4	The Astounding Exodus	nt	TW	Apr 37
5	Durna Range Neophyte ... (B)	nt	ASS	Jun 37
6	On the Planet Fragment ... (A)	nt	AS	Oct 37
7	The Music Monsters ... (A)	nt	AS	Apr 38
8	Kiss of Death ... (B)	s	ASF	Dec 38

9	Swordsmen of Saturn	... ...	n	SF	Oct	39
10	The Dark Swordsmen of Saturn	... ...	s	PS	Sum	40
11	Liquid Hell	... ...	s	FF	Jul	40
12	The Cat-Men of Aemt. ... (A)	... ...	nt	AST	Aug	40
13	Hermit of Saturn's Rings ...	... ...	s	PS	Fal	40
14	Invisible One ... (B)	... ...	nt	SSS	Sep	40
15	Cosmic Derelict ... (A)	... ...	nt	AST	Feb	41
16	Vampire of the Void...	... ...	s	PS	Spr	41
17	Captives of the Durna Rangue ... (B)	...	nt	SSN	Mar	41
18	Priestess of the Sleeping Death ... (B)	...	s	AS	Apr	41
19	The Ransom for Toledo ...	... ...	nt	CS	May	41
20	Slaves of the Unknown ... (A)	... ...	s	AST	Mar	42
21	Doomsday on Ajiat ... (A)	... ...	s	AST	Oct	42
22	Spoilers of the Spaceways	... ...	s	PS	Win	42

Series: A *Professor Jameson* (nos 1, 6, 7, 12, 15, 20, 21).
B *Durna Rangue* (nos 2, 5, 8, 14, 17, 18).

4 LESLIE J. JOHNSON (born 1914)

1	Seeker of Tomorrow (/Eric Frank Russell) ...	nt	ASS	Jul	37
2	Satellites of Death	s	ToW	Sum	38

5 MURRAY LEINSTER (born 1896)

1	The Incredible Invasion	n5	ASS	Aug	36
2	Khilit*	n	SN	Sep	36
3	Crime on Tristan	s	ARG	Nov	36
4	Footprints in the Snow	s	CNW	Dec	36
5	Grist*	n	CNW	Dec	36
6	The Big Mob	s	DAG	Feb	37
7	The Darkness on Fifth Avenue (from ARG, 30 Nov 1929)	nt	AN	Feb	37
8	The Eye of Black A-Wang*	s	AN	Feb	37
9	Fool's Gold	n	CNW	Apr	37
10	The Second Avenue Kid*	s	DAG	Apr	37
11	Quest of the Golden Lie	s	ARG	Jun	37
12	The Chromatic Cat	s	AN	Jul	37
13	Malay Guns*	s	AN	Jul	37
14	Private God	s	CNW	Jul	37
15	In Spring Thaws*	s	CNW	Jul	37
16	The Greatest Scoundrel Unhung	s	ARG	Sep	37
17	When the Deathbird Sings	s	AN	Jan	38
18	Village of the Devil-Devil Drums*	s	AN	Jan	38
19	Illusion	s	AAm	Feb	38
20	Board Fence	s	ARG	Jul	38

21	The Oldest Story in the World (from WT Aug 25)	s	WT	Oct	38
22	The Mad Planet ... (A) (from ARG Jun 12, 1920)	nt	ToW	Spr	39
23	The Man Who Blew up a War	s	BB	May	39
24	The Red Dust ... (A) (from ARG Apr 2, 1921)	nt	ToW	Win	39
25	The Wabbler	s	ASF	Oct	42
26	Four Little Ships	s	ASF	Nov	42
27	'If You Can Get It'	s	ASF	Nov	43
28	Plague	nt	ASF	Feb	44
29	Trog	n	ASF	Jun	44
30	The Eternal Now	s	TW	Fal	44
31	De Profundis	s	TW	Win	45
32	First Contact	nt	ASF	May	45
33	The Ethical Equations	s	ASF	Jun	45
34	Things Pass By	nt	TW	Sum	45
35	Tight Place	s	ASF	Jul	45
36	Pipeline to Pluto	s	ASF	Aug	45
37	The Power	s	ASF	Sep	45
38	Incident on Calypso	s	SS	Fal	45
39	Interference	s	ASF	Oct	45
40	The Murder of the USA	n2	ARG		1945
41	The Disciplinary Circuit	nt	TW	Win	46
42	The Plants	s	ASF	Jan	46
43	A Logic Named Joe*	s	ASF	Mar	46
44	Adapter	s	ASF	Mar	46

Leinster had a considerable output of fiction in fields other than science fiction and included above is a smattering of just a few of these. Not included is the mass of Western fiction that he wrote.

Pseudonyms: *Murray Leinster is this author's recognised sf pseudonym. The occasional story (particularly non-fantasy) appeared under his real name, Will F. Jenkins (nos 2, 5, 8, 10, 13, 15, 18 and 43).

Series: A *Forgotten Planet* (nos 22 and 24).

6 ROBERT A. W. LOWNDES (born 1916)

1	The Outpost at Altark	s	SSS	Nov	40
2	A Green Cloud Came	s	CS	Jan	41
3	The Abyss	s	SSc	Feb	41
4	The Martians Are Coming	s	CSS	Mar	41
5	The Psychological Regulator*	nt	CS	Mar	41
6	The Other	s	SSc	Apr	41
7	The Castle on Outerplanet**	s	SSc	Apr	41
8	The Doll Master***	s	SSc	Apr	41

9	Black Flames†	s	SSc	Apr	41
10	Exiles of New Planet***	s	AST	Apr	41
11	The Grey One	s	SSc	Jun	41
12	The Colossus of Maia†	s	CSF	Jul	41
13	A Matter of Philosophy‡	s	SF	Sep	41
14	My Lady of the Emerald‡	s	AST	Nov	41
15	Quarry‖	s	FcS	Dec	41
16	No Star Shall Fall‡	s	FcS	Dec	41
17	Something from Beyond***	s	FcS	Dec	41
18	The Deliverers¶	s	SFQ	Win	42
19	Lure of the Lily	s	UT	Jan	42
20	The Long Wall‡	s	SSc	Mar	42
21	Passage to Sharanee****	s	FcS	Apr	42
22	Einstein's Planetoid***	s	SFQ	Spr	42
23	Blacklist	s	UT	May	42
24	The Lemmings‡	s	SSS	May	42
25	A Message from Jean‡	s	FcS	Jun	42
26	The Peacemakers‖	s	FcS	Aug	42
27	The Slim People‡	s	FcS	Aug	42
28	Highway‡	s	SFQ	Fal	42
29	The Inheritors (/John B. Michel)	s	FFS	Oct	42
30	The Extrapolated Dimwit**	nt	FFS	Oct	42
31	The Collector‖	s	FFS	Oct	42
32	The Leapers****	s	FFS	Dec	42
33	Does Not Imply‡	s	FFS	Feb	43

Pseudonyms: *Arthur Cooke (/E. Balter, C. Kornbluth, J. Michel, D. Wollheim: no 5).
  **S. D. Gottesman (/C. Kornbluth, F. Pohl: nos 7 and 30).
  ***Paul Dennis Lavond (solo: no 8; /C. Kornbluth, F. Pohl: nos 10 and 22; /F. Pohl, D. Wylie: no 17).
  †Lawrence Woods (/D. Wollheim: nos 9 and 12).
  ‡Wilfred Owen Morley (nos 13, 14, 16, 20, 24, 25, 27, 28 and 33).
  ‖Mallory Kent (nos 15, 26 and 31).
  ¶Richard Morrison (no 18).
  ****Carol Grey (nos 21 and 32).

7   ERIC FRANK RUSSELL (born 1905)

1	The Saga of Pelican West	nt	ASS	Feb	37
2	The Great Radio Peril	s	ASS	Apr	37
3	Seeker of Tomorrow (/Leslie J. Johnson) ...	nt	ASS	Jul	37
4	The Prr-r-eet	s	ToW	Sum	37
5	Mana	s	ASS	Dec	37
6	Poor Dead Fool	s	TD	Jan	38

7	The World's Eighth Wonder	s	ToW	Sum 38
8	Shadow Man	s	FY	Aug 38
9	Impulse	s	ASF	Sep 38
10	Egyptian Episode	s	TCP	38
11	Vampire from the Void	s	FY	Mar 39
12	Sinister Barrier	n	UNK	Mar 39
13	Mightier Yet	s	FY	Jun 39
8	Invisible (Shadow Man)	s	CF	Win 40
14	Me and My Shadow	s	STR	Feb 40
15	I, Spy!	s	ToW	Aut 40
16	The Mechanical Mice*	nt	ASF	Jan 41
17	Jay Score ... (A)	s	ASF	May 41
18	Seat of Oblivion	s	ASF	Nov 41
19	With a Blunt Instrument	s	UW	Dec 41
20	Homo Saps**	s	ASF	Dec 41
21	Mechanistria ... (A)	nt	ASF	Jan 42
22	Mr Wisel's Secret	s	AS	Feb 42
23	Describe a Circle	nt	ASF	Mar 42
24	The Kid from Kalamazoo	nt	FA	Aug 42
25	Symbiotica... (A)	nt	ASF	Oct 43
26	Controller	nt	ASF	Mar 44
27	Resonance	nt	ASF	Jul 45

Pseudonyms: *Maurice G. Hugi (real name used once: no 16).
                     **Webster Craig (no 20).

Series: A   *Jay Score* (nos 17, 21 and 25).

8   WILLIAM F. TEMPLE (born 1914)

1	Lunar Lilliput	nt	ToW	Spr 38
2	The Smile of the Sphinx	s	ToW	Aut 38
3	Mr Craddock's Amazing Experience ·	s	AS	Feb 39
4	The 4-Sided Triangle	s	AS	Nov 39
5	Experiment in Genius	s	ToW	Sum 40
6	The Monster on the Border	s	SSS	Nov 40

9   STANLEY G. WEINBAUM (1902-1935)

1	Proteus Island	nt	ASS	Aug 36
2	The Circle of Zero	s	TW	Aug 36
3	Graph...	s	FM	Sep 36
4	The Brink of Infinity	s	TW	Dec 36
5	Shifting Seas	s	AS	Apr 37
6	Revolution of 1960 (/Ralph Milne Farley) ...	n2	AS	Oct 38
7	Tidal Moon (/Helen Weinbaum)	s	TW	Dec 38
8	The Black Flame	n	SS	Jan 39

Startling Stories featured a *Hall of Fame* Classic reprint each issue.
Weinbaum was featured as follows (*SS* dates followed by original dates):

9	Pygmalion's Spectacles	...	s	SS	May 39	from	WS	Jun 35
10	A Martian Odyssey	... (A)	s	SS	Nov 39	from	WS	Jul 34
11	Valley of Dreams	... (A)	s	SS	May 40	from	WS	Nov 34
12	The Worlds of If ... (B)	...	s	SS	Mar 41	from	WS	Aug 35
13	The Ideal ... (B)	... ...	s	SS	Jun 43	from	WS	Sep 35
14	The Point of View	... (B)	s	SS	Spr 44	from	WS	Jan 36

Series: A   *Crew of Ares* (nos 10 and 11).
       B   *Prof van Manderpootz* (nos 12, 13 and 14).

10   JACK WILLIAMSON (born 1908)

1	The Ruler of Fate	n3	WT	Apr 36
2	The Cometeers ... (A)	n4	ASS	May 36
3	Death's Cold Daughter	s	TM	Sep 36
4	The Blue Spot	n3	ASS	Jan 37
5	The Ice Entity	nt	TW	Feb 37
6	Spider Island	s	TM	Apr 37
7	The Mark of the Monster	s	WT	May 37
8	The Devil in Steel	s	TM	Jul 37
9	Released Entropy	n2	ASS	Aug 37
10	Dreadful Sleep	n3	WT	Mar 38
11	The Infinite Enemy	s	TW	Apr 38
12	Legion of Time	n3	ASF	May 38
13	The Dead Spot	s	MSS	Nov 38
14	The Crucible of Power	nt	ASF	Feb 39
15	After World's End	n	MSS	Feb 39
16	Non-Stop to Mars	s	ARG	Feb 39
17	One Against the Legion ... (A)	n3	ASF	Apr 39
18	Passage to Saturn	s	TW	Jun 39
19	The Metal Man (from AS Dec 28)	s	ToW	Aut 39
20	Star Bright	s	ARG	Nov 39
21	The Fortress of Utopia	n	SS	Nov 39
22	As in the Beginning	s	FF	Mar 40
23	The Reign of Wizardry	n3	UNK	Mar 40
24	Hindsight	s	ASF	May 40
25	The Sun Maker	nt	TW	Jun 40
26	Crystal of Death	s	SD	Aug 40
27	The Girl in the Bottle	nt	SSS	Sep 40
28	Racketeers in the Sky	nt	ARG	Oct 40
29	Darker Than You Think	n	UFF	Dec 40
30	The Star of Dreams	nt	CS	Mar 41
31	The Iron God	nt	MS	Apr 41
32	Gateway to Paradise	n	SS	Jul 41
33	Backlash	s	ASF	Aug 41

34	The Moon Era (from WS Feb 32)	w	ToW	Aut	41
35	Breakdown	nt	ASF	Jan	42
36	The Alien Intelligence (from SW Jul and Aug 29)	n3	CF	Spr	42
37	Collision Orbit* ... (B)	nt	ASF	Jul	42
38	Minus Sign* ... (B)	n	ASF	Nov	42
39	Opposites – React!* ... (B)	n2	ASF	Jan	43
40	Conscience, Ltd	s	UW	Aug	43
41	Twelve Hours to Live (from WS Aug 31) ...	s	SS	Mar	46

Pseudonyms: *Will Stewart (nos 37, 38 and 39).
Series: A *Legion of Space* (nos 2 and 17).
        B *Contraterrene* (nos 37, 38 and 39).

11 DONALD A. WOLLHEIM (born 1914)

1	Umbriel	s	FT	Fal	36
2	Castaway	s	SSS	May	40
3	The Planet That Time Forgot...	s	PS	Fal	40
4	The Haters...	s	UNK	Oct	40
5	Bones	s	SSc	Feb	41
6	Strange Return***	s	SSc	Feb	41
7	The Man from the Future	s	CSS	Mar	41
8	The Purple Dandelions*	s	CSS	Mar	41
9	The Planet of Illusion*	s	CS	Mar	41
10	The Psychological Regulator**	nt	CS	Mar	41
11	Blueprint	s	SSc	Apr	41
12	Cosmophobia* ... ... ·... ...	s	SSc	Apr	41
13	Black Flames***	s	SSc	Apr	41
14	!!!**	s	SSc	Apr	41
15	Cosmos Eye**	s	SFQ	Spr	41
16	The World on the Edge of the Universe** ...	s	SFQ	Sum	41
17	Earth Does Not Reply***	s	SFQ	Sum	41
18	The Colossus of Maia***	s	CSF	Jul	41
19	A Million Years and a Day***	s	FF	Aug	41
20	Revolving World*	s	SF	Sep	41
21	Pogo Planet** ... (A)	s	FcS	Oct	41
22	Destiny World** ... (A)	s	FcS	Dec	41
23	Baby Dreams*	s	SFQ	Win 41/2	
24	The Embassy**	s	ASF	Mar	42
25	The Unfinished City**	s	SSc	Mar	42
26	Blind Flight*	s	SSc	Mar	42
27	Saknarth*	s	SFQ	Spr	42
28	Mye Day** ... (A)	s	FcS	Apr	42
29	The World in Balance*	s	FcS	Jun	42
30	Up There**	s	SFQ	Sum	42
31	Ajax of Ajax** ... (A)	s	FcS	Aug	42
32	The Hidden Conflict**	s	SFQ	Fal	42
33	Nothing**	s	AST	Oct	42
34	Planet Passage**	s	FFS	Oct	42

35	Storm Warning*	s	FFS	Oct	42
36	The Planet Called Aquella**	s	SSS	Nov	42
37	Mimic**	s	AST	Dec	42
38	The Key to the Dark Planet**	s	FFS	Dec	42
39	The Oomph Beasts*	s	FFS	Dec	42
40	Bomb*	s	SFQ	Win	42
41	The Second Satellite**	s	FFS	Feb	43
42	The Millionth Year**	s	SFS	Apr	43

Pseudonyms: *Millard Verne Gordon (nos 8, 9, 12, 20, 26, 27, 29, 35, 39 and 40).

**Martin Pearson (nos 15, 16, 21, 22, 24, 25, 28, 30, 31, 32, 33, 34, 36, 37, 38, /41 and 42).

***Lawrence Woods (solo: nos 6 and 19; /R. Lowndes: nos 13 and 18; /J. Michel: no 17).

‡Allen Warland (no 23).

‡*Arthur Cooke (/E. Balter, C. Kornbluth, R. Lowndes, J. Michel: no 10).

‡‡X (no 14).

Series: A *Ajax Calkins* (nos 21, 22, 28 and 31).

Note: It was intended to include a checklist for the works of ten further authors representative of this period, including Nelson Bond, Robert Heinlein, Henry Kuttner and A. E. van Vogt, but alas the size of this present volume has necessitated their omission.

Notes:

1 Story lengths. At the best of times the length of a story is an estimation, and for the above I have done no more than give a basic guide, as follows:

s = short story (up to 10,000 words).

nt = novelette (up to 20,000 words).

sn = short novel (up to 30,000 words).

n = novel (over 30,000 words). If serialised then n3, say, = three parts. (In the case of serials the date that follows is that of the first episode.)

2 Magazine titles have been abbreviated as follows:

AAm = All American Fiction
AN = Adventure Novels & Short Stories
ARG = Argosy
AS = Amazing Stories
ASF = Astounding Science Fiction (see ASS)
ASS = Astounding Stories (see ASF)
AST = Astonishing Stories
BB = Blue Book Magazine
CF = Captain Future
CNW = Complete North-West Novel Magazine
CS = Comet Stories

CSF = Cosmic Science Fiction (see CSS)
CSS = Cosmic Stories (see CSF)
DAG = Double Action Gang
DM = Dime Mystery Magazine
DT = Detective Tales
FA = Fantastic Adventures
FcS = Future Combined with Science Fiction (see FF)
FF = Future Fiction (see FcS, FFS)
FFS = Future Fantasy and Science Fiction (see FcS, FF)
FM = Fantasy Magazine
FT = Fanciful Tales of Space and Time
FY = Fantasy
MD = Mammoth Detective
MM = Mammoth Mystery
MS = Marvel Stories (see MSS)
MSS = Marvel Science Stories
MW = Modern Wonder
ND = New Detective
PS = Planet Stories
PSh = Passing Show
SD = Stardust
SF = Science Fiction (see FcS, SFS)
SFQ = Science Fiction Quarterly
SFS = Science Fiction Stories (see SF)
SN = Smashing Novels Magazine
SS = Startling Stories
SSc = Stirring Science Stories
SSN = Super Science Novels (see SSS)
SSS = Super Science Stories (see SSN)
STR = Strange Stories
SW = Science Wonder Stories (see WS, TW)
TCP = Tales of Crime & Punishment
TD = Thrilling Detective
TM = Thrilling Mystery
ToW = Tales of Wonder
TW = Thrilling Wonder Stories (see SW, WS)
UFF = Unknown Fantasy Fiction (see UNK, UW)
UNK = Unknown (see UFF, UW)
UT = Uncanny Tales (Canadian)
UW = Unknown Worlds (see UFF, UNK)
WS = Wonder Stories (see SW, TW)
WT = Weird Tales

3   Magazine dates are simply abbreviated to the first three letters of the month and the last two digits of the year, eg Sep 36 = September 1936; Fal 44 = Fall 1944. Lack of space has made it impossible to designate dates in respect of weekly publications, but these are very few and the month is given as a guide.

(B) SUMMARY OF MAGAZINE ISSUES

I SF—North American

Magazine	Up to 35/6	36/7	37/8	38/9	39/40	40/1	41/2	42/3	43/4	44/5	45/6	Total
AMAZING STORIES	115	6	6	9	12	12	12	12	9	4	4	201
ASTONISHING STORIES	—	—	—	—	1	6	4	4	1	—	—	16
ASTOUNDING STORIES/SF	64	12	12	12	12	12	12	12	12	12	12	184
CAPTAIN FUTURE	—	—	—	—	1	4	4	4	3	1	—	17
CAPTAIN HAZZARD	—	—	—	1	—	—	—	—	—	—	—	1
COMET STORIES	—	—	—	—	—	3	2	—	—	—	—	5
COSMIC STORIES/SF	—	—	—	—	1	1	2	—	—	—	—	3
DYNAMIC SCIENCE STORIES	—	—	—	1	1	—	—	—	—	—	—	2
FAMOUS FANTASTIC MYSTERIES	—	—	—	—	6	6	6	9	3	4	4	38
FANCIFUL TALES	—	1	—	—	—	—	—	—	—	—	—	1
FANTASTIC ADVENTURES	—	—	—	—	7	7	11	12	8	4	5	54
FANTASTIC NOVELS	—	—	—	—	—	4	1	—	—	—	—	5
FLASH GORDON STRANGE ADV	—	1	—	1	—	—	—	—	—	—	—	1
FUTURE FICTION	—	—	—	3	2	2	5	6	2*	—	—	17
MARVEL (SCIENCE) STORIES	—	—	—	3	3	2	1	—	—	—	—	9
PLANET STORIES	—	—	—	—	2	4	4	4	4	4	4	26
SCIENCE FICTION	—	—	—	1	5	4	2	—	—*	—	—	12
SCIENCE FICTION QUARTERLY	—	—	—	—	—	2	3	4	1	—	—	10
STARDUST	—	—	—	—	1	4	—	—	—	—	—	5
STARTLING STORIES	—	—	—	2	6	6	6	6	4	4	4	38
STIRRING SCIENCE STORIES	—	—	—	—	1	1	3	—	—	—	—	4

Number of Issues

Magazine	Number of Issues											
	Up to 35/6	36/7	37/8	38/9	39/40	40/1	41/2	42/3	43/4	44/5	45/6	Total
I SF—North American												
SUPER SCIENCE STORIES	—	—	—	—	1	6	4	4	1	—	—	16
THRILLING WONDER STORIES	78	4	6	6	8	12	6	6	5	4	4	139
UNCANNY STORIES	—	—	—	—	—	—	1	—	—	—	—	1
UNCANNY TALES (Canadian)	—	—	—	—	—	4	11	5	1	—	—	21
	257	24	24	35	68	102	100	88	54	37	37	826
SF—British												
FANTASY	—	—	—	2	1	—	—	—	—	—	—	3
TALES OF WONDER	—	—	2	4	4	3	2	1	—	—	—	16
YANKEE SF	—	—	—	—	—	1	1	1	—	—	—	3
	—	—	2	6	5	4	3	2	—	—	—	22
SF—Foreign												
CONQUETES (French)	—	—	—	—	2	—	—	—	—	—	—	2
JULES VERNE MAGASINET (Swed)	—	—	—	—	—	27	52	52	52	52	52	287
NARRACIONES TERRORIFICAS (Arg)	—	—	—	—	12	11	10	5	4	4	12	58
II Weird—North American												
DOC SAVAGE	37	12	12	12	12	12	12	12	12	12	12	157
HORROR STORIES	11	6	6	6	6	5	1	—	—	—	—	41
STRANGE STORIES	—	—	—	1	6	6	—	—	—	—	—	13
TERROR TALES	19	8	6	6	6	5	—	—	—	—	—	50
THRILLING MYSTERY	5	12	9	6	4	—	—	—	—	—	—	36
UNKNOWN (WORLDS)	—	—	—	1	12	10	6	6	4	—	—	39

WEIRD TALES	147	11	12	12	10	6	6	6	6	6	6	228
THE WITCH'S TALES	—	2	—	—	—	—	—	—	—	—	—	2
	219	51	45	44	56	44	25	24	22	18	18	566

Weird—British

FIRESIDE GHOST STORIES	—	—	1	—	—	—	—	—	—	—	—	1
GHOSTS AND GOBLINS...	—	—	—	1	—	—	—	—	—	—	—	1
OCCULT SHORTS	—	—	—	—	—	—	—	—	—	—	2	2
TALES OF GHOSTS & HAUNTED HOUSES	—	—	—	—	1	—	—	—	—	—	—	1
TALES OF TERROR	—	—	1	—	—	—	—	—	—	—	—	1
TALES OF THE UNCANNY	—	—	1	1	—	—	—	—	—	—	—	2
WEIRD SHORTS...	—	—	—	—	—	1	—	—	—	—	—	1
WEIRD STORIES MAGAZINE	—	—	—	—	—	—	1	—	—	—	—	1
YANKEE WEIRD SHORTS	—	—	—	—	—	1	—	2	—	1	—	3
	—	—	3	2	1	1	1	2	—	1	2	13
Grand Total	476	75	74	87	144	189	191	173	132	112	121	1774

Note: *The last two issues of *Future* were called *Science Fiction Stories*, but continued the volume numbering of *Future*.

The above should not be regarded as an exhaustive list, particularly as regards weird magazines, which are only listed for comparison purposes. In the North American sf magazines, *Fanciful Tales* and *Stardust* were both semi-professional publications. All these magazines, plus more are discussed in detail in the introduction.

(C) GLOSSARY OF MAGAZINE EDITORS

BROWNE, Howard Associate Editor *Amazing Stories*, Jan 43-Oct 47 (38)
Associate Editor *Fantastic Adventures*, Dec 42-Oct 47 (31)

BUCHANAN, Lamont Associate Editor *Weird Tales*, Nov 42-Sep 49 (42)

CAMPBELL, John Editor *Astounding Stories/SF*, Oct 37-Dec 71 (411)
Editor *Unknown (Worlds)*, Mar 39-Oct 43 (all 39)

CHADBURN, Tom Editor *Witch's Tales*, Nov-Dec 36 (both)

ERISMAN, Robert O. Editor *Marvel Science Stories*, Aug 38-Apr 41 (all 9)
Editor *Dynamic Science Stories*, Feb-Apr 39 (both)
Editor *Uncanny Stories*, Apr 41 (1)

FRIEND, Oscar J. Editor *Thrilling Wonder Stories*, Aug 41-Fal 44 (18)
Editor *Startling Stories*, Jul 41-Sum 44 (10)
Editor *Captain Future*, Fal 41-Spr 44 (10)

GILLINGS, Walter Editor *Tales of Wonder*, Sum 37-Spr 42 (16)

GNAEDINGER, Mary Editor *Famous Fantastic Mysteries*, Sep 39-Jun 53 (81)
Editor *Fantastic Novels*, Jul 40-Apr 41 (5)

HAMLING, William L. Editor *Stardust*, Mar 40-Nov 40 (5)

HORNIG, Charles D. Editor *Science Fiction*, Mar 39-Sep 41 (12)
Editor *Future Fiction*, Nov 39-Nov 40 (4)
Editor *Science Fiction Quarterly*, Sum 40-Win 41 (2)

LOWNDES, Robert A. W. Editor *Future (Science) Fiction,* Apr 41-Jul 43 (13)
Editor *Science Fiction Quarterly,* Spr 41-Spr 43 (8)

McILWRAITH, Dorothy Editor *Weird Tales,* May 40-Sep 54 (87)

MERWIN, Sam Editor *Startling Stories,* Fal 44-Sep 51 (39)
Editor *Thrilling Wonder Stories,* Win 45-Oct 51 (38)

NORTON, Alden H. Editor *Astonishing Stories,* Nov 41- Apr 43 (7)
Editor *Super Science Stories,* Nov 41- May 43 (7)
Editor-in-Chief *Famous Fantastic Mysteries & Fantastic Novels*

PALMER, Raymond A. Editor *Amazing Stories,* Jun 38- Dec 49 (117)
Editor *Fantastic Adventures,* May 39-Dec 49 (90)

PEACOCK, Wilbur Scott Editor *Planet Stories,* Fal 42-Fal 45 (13)

PERKINS, Henry Aveline Associate Editor *Weird Tales,* May 40-Sep 42 (15)

POHL, Frederik Editor *Astonishing Stories,* Feb 40- Sep 41 (9)
Associate Editor *Astonishing Stories,* Nov 41-Apr 43 (7)
Editor *Super Science Stories/Novels,* Mar 40-Aug 41 (9)
Associate Editor *Super Science Stories,* Nov 41-May 43 (7)

REISS, Malcolm Editor *Planet Stories,* Win 39-Sum 42 (11)

SLOANE, T. O'Conor Editor *Amazing Stories,* Nov 29-Apr 38 (85)

SPRIGG, T. Stanhope Editor *Fantasy* Jul 38-Jun 39 (3)

SWAN, Gerald G.	Publisher/Editor *Yankee SF*, 1940-41 (3) Publisher / Editor *Yankee Weird Shorts*, 1942 (3)
TARRANT, Catherine	Assistant Editor *Astounding SF*, Jan 42-Nov 43 (23)
TREMAINE, F. Orlin	Editor *Astounding Stories*, Oct 33-Sep 37 (48) Editorial Director *Astounding Stories/SF*, Oct 37-May 38 (8) Editor *Comet Stories*, Dec 40-Jul 41 (5)
WEISINGER, Mort	Editor *Thrilling Wonder Stories*, Aug 36-Jun 41 (38) Editor *Startling Stories*, Jan 39-May 41 (15) Editor *Strange Stories*, Feb 39-Jan 41 (13) Editor *Captain Future*, Win 40-Sum 41 (7)
WHITEHORN, Chester	Editor *Planet Stories*, Win 45-Sum 46 (3)
WOLLHEIM, Donald A.	Editor *Fanciful Tales*, Fal 36 (1) Editor *Stirring Science Stories*, Feb 41-Mar 42 (4) Editor *Cosmic Stories*, Mar 41-Jul 41 (3)
WRIGHT, Farnsworth	Editor *Weird Tales*, Nov 24-Mar 40 (179)

Note: Even though this volume deals solely with the period 1936–45, I have given the full dates where they overlap to avoid confusion. It is worth pointing out here that Reiss remained in overall charge of *Planet Stories* despite the ensuing legion of editors. In addition while the Norton/Pohl combine dealt with *Astonishing* and *Super Science*, Pohl left before the magazines were folded and Ejler Jakobssen helped with the clearing up. To add to the confusion the magazines' Statements of Ownership in their last issues give only publisher Henry Steeger as editor!

(D) NOTE ON KEY COVER ARTISTS

Obviously a magazine's cover must be eye-catching and attractive to warrant it attention on the book-stall, and all the more so with the boom after 1939. The following shows which artists did what work for the different publishing companies.

ALBING PUBLICATIONS	Hannes Bok	4	(57%)
(*Cosmic* and *Stirring*)	Leo Morey	2	(29%)
	Elliott Dold	1	
COLUMBIA	Frank R. Paul	17	(47%)
PUBLICATION	Hannes Bok	5	(14%)
(*Future, Science Fiction* and	John Forte	4	(11%)
Science Fiction Quarterly)	Milton Luros	4	(11%)
	J. W. Scott	3	(8%)
	Jack Binder	1	
	John Mussachia	1	
	Unknown	7	
FICTION HOUSE	Parkhurst	7	(27%)
(*Planet*)	A. Drake	5	(19%)
	Rozen	3	(12%)
	Leydenfrost	2	
	Gross	2	
	Virgil Finlay, Frank Paul, Hannes Bok, Murphy Anderson, Norman Saunders, Ingels, unknown	1 each	
H-K PUBLICATIONS	Leo Morey	3	(60%)
(*Comet*)	Frank Paul	2	(40%)
NEWNES	S. R. Drigin	3	(100%)
(*Fantasy*)			
POPULAR FICTION	Margaret Brundage	21	(66%)
(*Weird Tales*)	Virgil Finlay	7	(22%)
	J. Allan St. John	2	
	A. R. Tilburne	1	
	Ray Quigley	1	
POPULAR	Virgil Finlay	28	(37%)
PUBLICATIONS	Stephen Lawrence	12	(16%)
(*Astonishing, Super Science,*	Bob Sherry	5	(7%)

Famous Fantastic Mysteries and *Fantastic Novels*)	Frank R. Paul	4	(5%)
	J. Binder, L. Morey and G. Mayorga	3 each	
	Milton Luros	2	
	H. Wesso, H. Rogers	1 each	
	Unknown	8	(11%)
	No picture	5	(7%)
SHORT STORIES, INC. (*Weird Tales*)	Virgil Finlay	9	(19%)
	Margaret Brundage	8	(17%)
	A. R. Tilburne	8	(17%)
	Hannes Bok	7	(16%)
	Harold DeLay	4	(8%)
	Lee Brown Coye	3	
	P. Kuhlhoff, E. Wittmack and Ray Quigley	2 each	
	R. Bennett, J. Giunta, and M. Fox	1 each	
STANDARD (BEACON) MAGAZINES (*Thrilling Wonder, Startling, Strange* and *Captain Future*)	Earle K. Bergey	58	(45%)
	Howard V. Brown	25	(19%)
	Rudolph Belarski	16	(12%)
	Hans Wesso	2	
	Rosen, G. Mayorga	1 each	
	Unknown	26	(20%)
STREET & SMITH (*Astounding* and *Unknown*)	William Timmins	40	(25%)
	Hubert Rogers	33	(21%)
	Howard Brown	23	(14%)
	Hans Wesso	7	(4%)
	Graves Gladney	6	
	H. W. Scott	6	
	Charles Schneeman	4	
	Ed Cartier	4	
	Gilmore, M. Stein, M. Isip Thomson, J. Frew, Carlson, V. Finlay, A. von Munchhausen, F. Haucke,	2 each	
	Unknown	1	
	No cover	23	(14%)
TECK PUBLICATIONS (*Amazing*)	Leo Morey	13	(100%)

WESTERN PUBLICATIONS (*Marvel, Dynamic* and *Uncanny*)	Norman Saunders	3	(25%)
	J. W. Scott	3	(25%)
	Frank Paul	2	
	Hans Wesso	1	
	Unknown	3	(25%)

WORLD'S WORK (*Tales of Wonder*)	J. Nicolson	8	(50%)
	W. J. Roberts	6	(38%)
	Caney and Turner	1 each	

ZIFF–DAVIS (*Amazing* and *Fantastic Adventures*)	Robert Fuqua	31½	(25%)
	J. Allen St. John	21½	(17%)
	Harold W. McCauley	19	(15%)
	Robert Gibson Jones	17	(13%)
	Malcolm Smith	8	(6%)
	Rod Ruth	4	
	Leo Morey	3½	
	Stockton Mulford	3	
	Julian S. Krupa	2½	
	C. Hartman, J. Settles	2 each	
	W. Juhre, H. Hammond, L. R. Jones, Hadden, F. Paul, W. Parke, P. Lehman, R. Epperley and A. Kohn	1 each	

In addition the Ziff–Davis magazines featured back cover illustrations. In this period the artists were:

Frank R. Paul	55	(52%)
James B. Settles	23	(22%)
Julian S. Krupa	8	(8%)
Malcolm Smith	5	
H. W. McCauley	4	
Howard M. Duffin	3	
H. R. Hammond	2	
W. Juhre, S. Ryter, P. Maxwell, R. Fuqua, J. A. St John	1 each	

Quite a collection. And to save those among you who are wondering, from any unnecessary calculations, as far as front cover artists are concerned the most honoured are:

1	Earle K. Bergey	58
2	Howard V. Brown	48
3	Virgil Finlay	46
4	William Timmins	40
5	Hubert Rogers	33
6	Robert Fuqua	$31\frac{1}{2}$
7	Margaret Brundage	29
8	Frank R. Paul	27
9	Leo Morey	$24\frac{1}{2}$
10	J. Allen St John	$23\frac{1}{2}$

Notes: In many cases cover artists were not credited – sometimes a blessing! From the above it is clearly noticeable how many artists worked solely for one publisher, particularly Bergey, Timmins and Rogers.

Bibliography

Every effort has been made to consult original magazines and documents in the course of the compilation of this book, as well as the standard reference works such as *Who's Who* and *Contemporary Authors*. Over and above this the following have proved a valuable source of information and I hereby acknowledge their use and also recommend them for those readers interested in researching further.

BOOKS

Gruber, Frank. *The Pulp Jungle* (Sherbourne Press; Los Angeles, 1967)

Harbottle, Philip. *The Multi-Man* (published privately; Wallsend, 1968)

Moskowitz, Sam. *Explorers of the Infinite* (World Publishing Co; Cleveland, 1963)

Moskowitz, Sam. *The Immortal Storm* (Hyperion Press; Connecticut, 1974). Reprint of Atlanta 1954 edition

Moskowitz, Sam. *Seekers of Tomorrow* (World Publishing Co; Cleveland, 1966)

Rogers, Alva. *A Requiem for Astounding* (Advent Publishers Inc; Chicago, 1964). March 1973 edition consulted

Sprague de Camp, L. *Science Fiction Handbook* (Hermitage House; New York, 1953)

Tuck, Donald H. *The Handbook of Science Fiction and Fantasy* (published privately, 1958)

Warner, Harry Jr. *All Our Yesterdays* (Advent Publishers Inc; Chicago, 1969)

INDICES

Cockcroft, T. G. L. *Index to the Weird Fiction Magazines* (published privately; New Zealand, 1964)

Day, Brad M. *The Complete Checklist of Science Fiction Magazines* (Wehman Bros; New York, 1961)

Day, Donald B. *Index to the Science Fiction Magazines: 1926–1950* (Perri Press; Portland, 1952)

Evans, Bill and Bob Pavlat. *Fanzine Index* (Reprinted by H. P. Piser; New York, 1965)

MAGAZINE ARTICLES

By Walter Gillings:

'The Impatient Dreamers', a series of personal articles in *Vision of Tomorrow*, issues 1 to 11 (1969–1970)

By Sam Moskowitz:

'Lo! The Poor Forteans', *Amazing Stories* (June 1965)

'Virgil Finlay', *Worlds of Tomorrow* (November 1965)